KNOWLEDGE
POWER

iPOLITICS: Global Challenges in the Information Age

RENÉE MARLIN-BENNETT, SERIES EDITOR

KNOWLEDGE POWER

Intellectual Property, Information, and Privacy

RENÉE MARLIN-BENNETT

LYNNE
RIENNER
PUBLISHERS

BOULDER
LONDON

Published in the United States of America in 2004 by
Lynne Rienner Publishers, Inc.
1800 30th Street, Boulder, Colorado 80301
www.rienner.com

and in the United Kingdom by
Lynne Rienner Publishers, Inc.
3 Henrietta Street, Covent Garden, London WC2E 8LU

Library of Congress Cataloging-in-Publication Data
Marlin-Bennett, Renée, 1959–
   Knowledge power : intellectual property, information, and privacy /
Renée Marlin-Bennett.
     p.   cm. — (iPolitics)
   Includes bibliographical references and index.
   ISBN 1-58826-256-1 (hardcover : alk. paper) — ISBN 1-58826-281-2
(pbk. : alk. paper)
   1. Intellectual property. 2. Data protection—Law and legislation. 3. Globalization.
I. Title. II. Series.
K1401.M367 2004
346.04'8—dc22   2004001837

British Cataloguing in Publication Data
A Cataloguing in Publication record for this book
is available from the British Library.

Printed and bound in the United States of America

    The paper used in this publication meets the requirements
∞ of the American National Standard for Permanence of
    Paper for Printed Library Materials Z39.48-1992.

5 4 3 2 1

To
Charles L. Bennett,
my beloved friend

Contents

Acknowledgments

I hardly know how to begin these acknowledgments, because I am extremely grateful to so many people who have helped me in this project. Several graduate students have assisted me in the collection of sources and documentation and have given feedback on the prose. Although it is probably inevitable that I will leave out someone, I would still like to mention by name Madoka Morimoto, Hui (Samantha) Xiao, Jill Nebel, Nancy Bernhardt, Robyn Yaker, Rebecca DeWinter, and Charles Lor. Huong Nguyen deserves special mention for her penetrating questions and excellent service as a sounding board. Teaching classes on the political economy of intellectual property and information has been especially enlightening, and I would like to thank both the graduate and undergraduate students who enrolled in my seminars.

Early in my research, I benefited greatly from a sabbatical taken at the University of Maryland, under the auspices of the Harrison Program on the Future Global Agenda. Dennis Pirages and Virginia Haufler listened to inchoate thoughts and theories and gave useful criticism. At American University, my institutional home, I have been lucky to have many colleagues from the School of International Service and other units of the university who have given graciously of their time and expertise. Louis Goodman is an excellent critic who shows me the holes in my argument, recommends alternative theoretical and substantive approaches, and is always quick to point out when I have reinvented a wheel first discovered generations ago by sociologists. Nanette Levinson has helped me analyze the intellectual property implications of Internet governance. Shalini Venturelli,

Erran Carmel, and Walter Park filled in some of the gaps in my knowledge of their fields. Patrick Jackson and Tamar Gutner helped me refine theoretical points. I am also thankful to the legal scholars who provided minitutorials and recommended reading. In particular, Peter Jaszi has been unfailingly agreeable and instructive when I have called or e-mailed with questions. He has given very graciously of his time, above and beyond what cross-campus collegiality required. His colleague, Christine Haight Farley, tutored me in trademark law. Patricia Wand and Mary Alice Baish have been excellent sources of information on the practical effects of domestic and international policies. Many thanks also to Harry Hochheiser, who carefully read the entire manuscript and provided a thoughtful and constructive review. I also thank the anonymous reviewers, who provided detailed and helpful criticism of the manuscript. Their comments have made this a much better book, I believe. Lynne Rienner and her staff have been extremely supportive, and I appreciate their substantive and stylistic assistance. It is always a pleasure to work with them.

My debt to my family is great, indeed. My children, Andrew and Ethan, have endured years of my fixation with this book. I thank them for putting up with me and for being great kids. My husband, Chuck Bennett, provided encouragement, insightful suggestions, and reality checks. Chuck is a challenging interlocutor, keenly aware of the cultural values of the scientific community and exceptionally knowledgeable about science policy. He cares deeply about the free flow of scientific information as essential to the conduct of science. And he is an example of someone whose deeds match his words: as Principal Investigator of WMAP (the Wilkinson Microwave Anisotropy Probe), he has been responsible for making a large quantity of data freely available to the scientific community. I delight in his love and friendship, and I am deeply grateful to have him be mine. He is a most excellent husband and father, and I cannot possibly thank him enough.

KNOWLEDGE
POWER

1

Introduction:
Products of the Mind

To create something from nothing: in all the natural world, this is a uniquely human ability. Using our minds, we originate works of art, generate inventions, accumulate knowledge, and discover truths about the world we live in. What sets the Information Age apart from prior periods in history is the price tag we put on these intellectual creations. The "new" economy depends on buying and selling ideas and facts, intangible and ephemeral though they are. And here lie the policy conundrums that pique public interest and concern. What kinds of creative or innovative products become intellectual *property,* how encompassing should these rights be, and for how long should these rights last before the creation or innovation enters the public domain? When do compilations of *information* become proprietary, and what kinds of property rights are granted to owners of sets of facts? When the information compiled into a dataset is personal information, what rights do the persons whose information has been recorded have? Finally, how is the situation complicated by a globalized economy in which intellectual products flow more freely than ever before?

The triad of intellectual property, information, and privacy, three political-legal concepts, is linked by the connection to the mental efforts of human beings. *Intellectual property* refers to copyrights, patents, trademarks, and similar means of marking ideas as one's own. *Proprietary information* is exemplified by databases of information, generally owned by firms. *Privacy* pertains to the control that individuals have over "their" information.[1] The legal and social meanings of these concepts are contested. The laws of different countries do not necessarily coincide with each other, and the rules of the game have changed over time and across cultures. Laws regarding intellectual property, information, and privacy are often out of sync with people's expectations. Most important, though, is that intellectual property, information, and privacy are fundamental to power in the interconnected global political economy of the twenty-first century.

There are no "natural" rules for intellectual property and privacy. Who gets to make the rules of the game? The answer can be found in an ongoing political process, grounded in historical and cultural circumstances. The end result is the current convoluted and dynamic situation. For example:

- Scientific inventions are property, but basic scientific discoveries are not. (An x-ray machine could be patented, but the discovery of x-rays could not.)
- Folk knowledge is not property, but a drug formula developed, in part, on the basis of folk knowledge is.
- Some compilations of information are considered to be proprietary (e.g., a marketer's database). Others are owned by governments and are either held in secret (information linking name, address, social security number, and tax filing information) or made public (landownership records, public library catalog holdings). Yet other compilations of information, such as names and telephone numbers listed in a published directory or the facts in an encyclopedia, are considered unowned all together.
- Citizens of the European Union (EU) have much more control over what happens to the information that they disclose to firms than do citizens of the United States. But because Americans have traditionally restricted the government's ability to collect information, one could argue that in the United States government is more limited by law in what it can do with citizens' personal information than are firms. Of course, citizens of countries that do not protect personal freedoms may have no control whatsoever over their personal information.

Better and faster telecommunications technologies mean that we can send ideas almost anywhere on the planet, twenty-four hours a day, seven days a week. The words, images, music, and numbers—"content"—can be transmitted almost instantaneously via telephone, fax, and the Internet. These dramatic changes have led to a fundamental change in the nature of global markets. A generation ago, Rita Cruise O'Brien and G. K. Helliener presciently wrote: "There is every indication that the sharpest aspect of competition in the future may be based more on the use of specialized knowledge, information, and new technological capacity for its communication and use than on more traditional factors."[2]

Today, intellectual property and information have become increasingly valued assets themselves. In addition, unwanted flows of personal information are an invasion of people's privacy, which can threaten livelihoods, social relations, and physical security. The commercial and security value of content being sent hither and yon heightens the importance of rules and the political process of rule making.

Rules for protecting mental efforts as intellectual property or proprietary information (*information property*) involve balancing the interests of the creator/innovator/compiler versus the public at large. When people and firms can profit from their intellectual labors, they have an incentive to engage in such tasks. Intellectual property rights and newer rights that protect compilations of information make it possible to profit from creativity, inspiration, and the hours spent collecting data and putting it in a useable format. Society as a whole benefits from the added store of human knowledge, the increased productivity, and the additional opportunities for enjoyment of the arts that property rights provide.

Be that as it may, if these property rights are too extensive or strong, we end up endangering the right of the public to share freely in our cultural, scientific, and technological heritage. The oft-cited U.S. constitutional provision enabling the protection of intellectual products is found in Article 1, Section 8 (emphasis added): "The Congress shall have Power . . . *To promote the Progress of Science and useful Arts,* by securing for limited Times to Authors and Inventors the exclusive Right to their respective Writings and Discoveries."

Thus the public purpose of granting intellectual property rights, under the U.S. Constitution, is the promotion of the public good. Overly strong property rights choke off future progress. At what point do we cross the line, elevating the rights to property over responsibilities to contribute to the public good of promoting progress in science and art?

Threats to equity emerge as well. First, individuals and firms are more likely to gain property rights to intellectual products than are communities. The system of intellectual property and related law assumes an identifiable individual (person or firm) as the creator or inventor. The process of applying for and being awarded property rights does not work well when the intellectual product results from communal activity—say, the efforts of generations of village farmers breeding a better plant variety. Second, the process of getting property rights can be extremely expensive. Even more expensive is the cost of monitoring global markets for infringers and litigating to stop them. These obstacles to enjoying property rights in innovation, creativity, and information affect people living in the developing world most acutely. As a result, an *intellectual capital divide* separates rich and poor countries. People in poor countries can reduce this gap only if they have fair access to new knowledge and can themselves benefit from property rights, appropriately implemented and enforced. We need, I believe, to look at intellectual property and proprietary information from the perspective of the *global* public good.

Ownership and control of information are also relevant at the personal level. Individuals' power over their own lives depends on their ability to control the flow of information of concern to them. The opportunity for benefit or harm increases with the economic value of personal information. Databases allow marketers to compile personal information that helps them identify likely consumers of their goods and thus streamlines their advertising. This (arguably) provides consumers with more of the junk mail they want and less of what they don't want. Databases that allow researchers to identify genes associated with disease have obvious benefits. These are tools to help find cures, prevent illnesses, and improve quality of life. The downside is that losing control of personal information really bothers many of us, both as consumers and as citizens. We feel that our privacy is increasingly being invaded. We are even more insecure when personal information is used without our consent for purposes we know nothing about.

Current policy problems concerning intellectual property rights, proprietary information, and privacy point to the role that ownership and control play. *How do the ability to own intellectual property and information and the ability to control how information flows become a source of power?* This is the book's central question. But there are more questions: How does ownership or control of products of the mind translate into wealth or into political-military might? What role do markets play in creating opportunities for the ownership and control of information? What role do technological breakthroughs play in changing the social, economic, and political playing field? And perhaps most interesting, how did we as a global society get where we are today in terms of placing value on information, and where are we likely to be going?

The political, economic, and legal language surrounding these topics can be off-putting, and the rules can seem arcane and indecipherable. The subject matter becomes much clearer when viewed in the context of our everyday lives. In the section that follows I introduce three familiar examples of the concepts at hand: aspirin, sports statistics, and increased surveillance after the terrorist attacks of September 11, 2001.

■ Intellectual Property: Aspirin

Intellectual property represents the commodification of creativity or innovation. The most common forms of intellectual property are copyrights, patents, and trademarks, but several "related rights" fall into this category as well. Governments grant time-limited property rights in inventions and creative works to encourage people to spend time and other resources innovating and creating. (Trademarks are the exception to the time-limited rule.)

In the United States, *aspirin* is a generic term, but in Canada and several other countries, *Aspirin* spelled with an uppercase *A* is a trademarked brand name. In either case, we are talking about acetylsalicylic acid (ASA). The story of aspirin's development and marketing brings out the contingent quality of assigning (and revoking) property rights in creativity and innovation.

The latter part of the nineteenth century marked the beginning of pharmaceutical research, development, and marketing as an industry. It was during this time that several researchers successfully isolated forms of salicylic acid (derived from willow bark or leaves) for combating fever and pain. The most commercially successful of these efforts was the 1897 synthesis of ASA by Felix Hoffmann, a chemist working for the Farbenfabriken vorm. Friedr. Bayer & Co. (later known as the Bayer Corporation of Germany). The brand name Aspirin was trademarked in Germany in 1899.[3]

Bayer was unable to get a patent on the product in its home country. At that time, German authorities granted patents in the chemical industry only for new processes, and Bayer's representatives were unsuccessful in making a strong enough case that their process of producing acetylsalicylic acid was innovative. Nevertheless, ASA was an improvement over its closely related variants, such as salicylic acid and salicin, which had been well-known painkillers and fever relievers for hundreds of years. The older formulations caused stomach irritation and had an objectionable taste. Despite its failure to obtain a German patent, Bayer was able to convince examiners in the United States that its product was innovative enough to merit a patent.[4]

The disparity between patent decisions in Germany and the United States highlights the idea that intellectual property rights are not standardized; nor do they derive from natural law. Rather, governments determine what kinds of inventions they wish to recognize, reward, and encourage. At the time, Germany granted patents only to new chemical processes, not new products, whereas the United States granted patents to both. Thus the intellectual work instantiated in the product—the formula—was patentable in the United States but not in Germany.

Though Bayer was not wholly successful in obtaining patents on the product, aspirin, it was successful in getting rights to another type of intellectual property: a trademark. At the time aspirin was first synthesized, the majority of medicines were simply prepared by a druggist from basic products that were widely available and not produced exclusively by a single firm. The pharmaceutical industry was relatively uncommercialized even as late as the first half of the twentieth century, and brand-name drug formulations played only a minor role.[5] Most drugs were made from herbs and other vegetable products, and a patient on a typical visit to the pharmacist might come home with an essential oil, such as oil of clove for a toothache, or with an herb, such as gentian violet for thrush.[6] No company owned the rights to these products; knowledge of their usefulness was simply part of the communal store of available medical knowledge. In those days, pharmacists compounded prescriptions according to the doctor's orders, carefully weighing the required ingredients on a balance scale. The pharmacist would provide a specific commercial product only if the patient's physician specified a brand name.[7]

Bayer was able to use its trademark to full advantage by advertising to promote its brand name. Advertising linked to trademarked brand names more generally led to increased revenues. Writing in 1928, Dorothea Braithwaite noted the disparity in prices between trademarked products and what we now call *generic* products. Before World War I, bulk ASA sold in Britain for 2 shillings per pound. She continued:

> The price of Bayer's Aspirin was about [18 shillings per pound] (less various discounts). It is extremely improbable that the extra care with which Bayer's Aspirin was prepared entailed a difference in cost at all proportionate to the difference in price between the [brand name] article and the commodity sold in bulk.[8]

Despite its ability to parlay this brand recognition into significant profits, Bayer's rights remained contingent on the laws and policies of governments; and governments' willingness to award or maintain intellectual property rights depended, at least in part, on the political situation. In 1939, Britain passed the Trading with the Enemy Act, which allowed the Custodian of Enemy Property to take control of a trademark owned by enemy firms. U.S. law contains a similar provision, and it was this rule that allowed a U.S. company to take over the "Bayer" trademark for aspirin during World War I.[9] Today, the global pharmaceutical industry is acutely aware of the power wielded by governments over intellectual property rights. Bayer is the maker of Cipro, an antibiotic effective against anthrax. In October 2001, the company, under heavy pressure from the U.S. administration of President George W. Bush, agreed to cut the price of the drug in half for U.S. government purchases rather than face the possibility of having its patent revoked.[10]

Although many details about intellectual property remain contentious, the category itself is widely accepted. Few people question whether copyrights and patents ought to exist at all. Less firmly established in society is the next subject, the notion of information as property.

▪ Proprietary Information: Sports Reporting

Compilations of facts are increasingly recognized as proprietary information, or information property.

Until fairly recently, compilations of facts (telephone numbers in a telephone book[11] or facts in an encyclopedia) did not receive any special legal protection that altered their nature from public good to private property. Increasingly, however, property rights to data—to compilations of information—are being asserted and protected by legal means.

Information is most valuable when organized in a manner that allows us to make useful (and valuable) connections between facts, but just plain facts may also have value. Imagine sitting in a history class in which you had to deposit a quarter for each historical event you learn about. Imagine restrictions on whether you could subsequently tell friends about those historical events. What if Albert Einstein "owned" his most famous equation, $E=mc^2$? Would we need to pay royalties to his estate to study physics? Though such scenarios sound preposterous, a discernable trend exists toward granting property rights in information.

Some firms have even asserted that they own certain rights, but at least for now the courts have tempered such claims. In 1996, Motorola and STATS, a sports statistics company, operated a joint venture, SportsTrax, to market play-by-play descriptions and other statistics in almost real time via pager messages. The National Basketball Association (NBA) sued Motorola and STATS, claiming that the companies' joint venture infringed on copyright and (according to applicable state law) misappropriated commercial information. The NBA charged that the information about what went on at the game, at least as it was happening, belonged to the NBA.[12] Lower courts ruled in the NBA's favor; but in 1997 a U.S. circuit court of appeals ruled that since STATS reporters collected the information and the company formatted it for distribution, SportsTrax was not taking anything from the NBA. Because the STATS reporters use their own powers of observation to collect information, which is then translated into a new form for distribution, SportsTrax is selling an original product.[13]

But there may be other ways for sports leagues to own information about the events that happen during the play of the game. The National Football League (NFL) and Major League Baseball have adopted other strategies, which may be more resistant to legal challenges. The NFL has asserted that it has a copyright in play-by-play coverage (as opposed to the reporting of statistics and the outcomes of plays every few minutes). By controlling the contractual agreements connected to press credentials, the NFL has been able to maintain control over web-based dissemination of NFL information. To receive credentials, reporters are required to agree that they will not violate the NFL's rules on the dissemination of information. Only the NFL's officially sanctioned website is allowed to post play-by-play coverage of games.[14] Similarly, Major League Baseball has begun an effort to increase its visibility online and to control access to information.[15]

This approach is not just a North American phenomenon; its impact extends to sports around the globe. It can be seen, for example, in the International Cricket Council's U.S.$500 million in earnings from the sale of media, sponsorship, and Internet rights. Also in Britain, a suit was brought by the British Horseracing Board to prevent owners of online gambling sites from using the board's data.[16] Exclusive contracts can be costly to consumers: in 1992 satellite television broadcaster BskyB won exclusive rights to broadcast English soccer matches, despite the fact that soccer fans would consequently need to purchase satellite dishes to watch Premier League games.[17] Information-starved fans may need to wait for their information when information is intentionally delayed, as the International Olympic Committee (IOC) did when it protected NBC's earnings by restricting Internet access to the Sydney summer games. The IOC even set up a special taskforce to surf the Internet, looking for unauthorized postings.[18] It is not, however, only the giant media firms and the teams themselves who benefit from such arrangements. Sometimes, new media service providers are able to use their skills to greater advantage, securing lucrative contacts. Recently, the Real Madrid soccer club signed a contract with Let Me Know Technology, an Israeli company, giving Let Me Know, in collaboration with Telefonica SA, an exclusive contract to provide sports information to Real Madrid fans via cell phones.[19]

Even though the owners of teams are justifiably concerned with maximizing profits, restrictions on the rights of the individuals to report what they themselves have seen is troubling to journalists and others who are concerned with access to information. "From a journalistic standpoint," noted a managing editor of *Wall Street Journal Online,* "it's hard for journalists to allow people being covered to dictate coverage."[20] By creating property rights in facts, the ability of the public to access those facts is restricted. In a free and open society, there is a tension between respecting proprietary information (e.g., by restricting access to certain facts) and the public's need or desire for facts. Baseball stats do not qualify as essential information, but they contribute to the pleasure that many sports fans and fantasy leaguers have in life. Within our political, social, and economic system, people are able to place value on recreation and the pursuit of happiness as a legitimate goal.

An entire industry has grown up around the provision and dissemination of sports statistics and other information. Sports journalists and fantasy league managers will suffer if the team owners' right to control information is too strong. In 1996, against the backdrop of negotiations at the World Intellectual Property Organization on a database treaty, the then–president of STATS, Inc., wrote:

> The "raw material" for STATS' analyses are sports statistics—the at-bats, shooting percentages, times sacked, goals scored type of figures familiar to every sports fan who reads box scores. STATS regularly accesses and uses the body of sports statistics which are compiled by the major sports leagues or their outside "official statisticians." STATS also compiles its own body of statistical information through STATS reporters who attend games or who observe public sources such as television and radio broadcasts. Both current and historical sports statistics have been a traditional feature of sports reporting and analysis for decades and have uniformly been considered to be within the public domain. Without free access to this data, companies such as STATS could not provide sports fans with the creative analyses they desire.[21]

The question of who has what rights to sports information remains open. Is knowing what is happening as good as seeing it on TV or listening on the radio? The sports industry fears that companies providing sports information in real time will compete with TV and radio networks, which pay handsomely for exclusive media arrangements. The value of the intellectual property in the games broadcast on TV or radio is diminished by the availability of competing proprietary information. As the means of communicating the game's events multiply—websites, 800 numbers, personal data assistants (PDAs), pagers—sports fans enjoy multiple options for keeping track of plays and statistics while doing the other things they need to do, and firms have opportunities for earning profits. With property rights as yet unresolved, the tension between free versus restricted access remains.

■ From Intellectual Property to Proprietary Information

The evolution of property rights in products of the mind—from patents, copyrights, and trademarks to proprietary rights for information—is only part of a larger evolutionary process. New efforts to create property rights for information are the continuation of a trend that began in the earliest periods of human societies, with the development of rules governing property rights in tangible things.[22] Societies since time immemorial have placed rules on what can be owned, the conditions under which something is owned, as well as the rights the owner enjoys, and what obligations the owner bears.[23] Of course, all property rights are contingent on the historical and cultural context. By prescribing, proscribing, and permitting relations, actions, and outcomes, property rules reinforce the distribution of power and the values (both in the material and in the ethical sense) of society. As R. Kurt Burch notes, "Property rights . . . constitute systems of rule and domination."[24]

Property Rights

Property rights include:

- the right to own something—to have it in one's possession;
- the right to use something; and
- the right to alienate something—to be able to sell it or give it away.

In nineteenth-century England, philosopher John Stuart Mill referred to the right to use and alienate:

> The institution of property, when limited to its essential elements, consists in the recognition, in each person, of a right to the exclusive disposal of what he or she [has] produced by their own exertions, or received either by gift or by fair agreement, without force or fraud, from those who produced it.[25]

Societies develop laws to constrain and enable ownership, use, and alienation. One important set of rules specifies who can be an owner. In many legal systems across time and across cultures, women's rights to own property have been severely limited. In colonial America and continuing through the middle of the nineteenth century, a woman's husband gained all rights to her property when they married, unless a special contract—a *marriage settlement*—protected her rights.[26] In contrast, biblical evidence demonstrates that in ancient Israel both women and men owned property, including land.[27] A different legal relationship is exemplified by Roman law, in which the paterfamilias—the father of the family—was the actual owner of the entire extended family's wealth (i.e., property held by all the men and women of the family).[28] Laws today specify what can be owned, as well as the conditions for its use and alienation: people can own pets, but it is illegal to treat them inhumanely. People may own cigarettes, but they may not smoke them wherever they choose or sell them to children.

Laws concerning intellectual property and proprietary information create new categories of what can be owned, who can be owners, and the conditions for use and alienation. For example, patents and copyrights provide—for a limited time—property rights to the people who invent and create. Rules protecting databases provide property rights to those who collect and organize information. Intellectual property and proprietary information laws prevent others from taking, using, and alienating the rights holders' intangible product without authorization.

It is fair to say that the overall historical trend has been to increase the scope of property rights: more people can own, more things can be owned, and there are fewer restrictions on use and alienation.[29] Although there are many examples of property rights that have been abolished over the years,[30] in the case of products of the mind the expansion of property rights seems even more pronounced. The evolution of ownership of scientific discoveries is one example. Prior to the middle of the seventeenth century, many scientists kept their findings secret so that no one would misappropriate the new knowledge and claim undeserved credit.[31] The establishment of scientific journals such as *Philosophical Transactions* of the Royal Society of London (1665) provided scientists an opportunity to disseminate the results of their efforts with their names firmly attached to their discoveries; to this day scientists often stress the importance of shared information and openness. However, this norm of openness often conflicts with the material interests of those conducting or sponsoring the research. And this is where the process of commodification comes into play. When a scientific discovery may potentially lead directly to a patentable invention, scientists have an incentive to avoid disclosing what they have discovered until that knowledge is protected by a patent.[32]

Commodification

Rules that create property rights for these products of the mind commodify them. The awarding of a patent, copyright, or proprietary data right commodifies the invention, creative work, or data collection, and this legal sleight of hand changes the nature of the global marketplace. In the middle of the twentieth century, Karl Polanyi wrote of how new social rules allowing the commodification of land, labor, and money created the "great transformation" from feudal society into the modern market economy.[33] Today, we see how commodification of products of the mind has enabled another transformation, this time into the global Information Age economy. As with Polanyi's transformation, the transformation to the global Information Age has taken a long time but has accelerated with the advent of new technologies.

To be commodified, goods must be *scarce* and *excludable* (the classic definition of pure private goods), and in and of themselves products of the mind are neither. *Scarcity* refers to the finite resources necessary to produce the good or service, the consequence being that one person's consumption of the good diminishes the possibility of others' consumption; *excludability* refers to the ability to allow or disallow others from having access to it. Unlike tangible goods like turnips, ideas and facts do not fit neatly into such categories.[34]

Turnips are scarce because there is a practical and actual limit to the amount of turnips that the Earth can produce. In contrast, there is no limit to the carrying capacity for products of the mind. The fact that one person thought of an idea does not preclude another person from independently thinking of the same idea. Likewise, turnip ownership is excludable: the turnip seller can sell to one person but refuse to sell to another. But when a person disseminates an idea—sells an invention—there is no automatic means to exclude observers from taking the machine apart to see how it works and then building replicas.

Instead, property rights laws for intangible products of the mind create scarcity and excludability where neither existed before. By assigning exclusive, time-limited monopolies, these rules transform ideas and facts into private goods (which are scarce and excludable) or club goods (excludable but not scarce for members of the club). The resulting commodified products—intellectual property and proprietary information—exist because of these rules. The rights holders now have an incentive to create, innovate, and collect data because they are able to sell products knowing that the law prohibits others from imitating or copying their works. Under ideal circumstances, the bargain would provide a win-win solution: the rights holder makes money, and the public gains new creative, innovative, and informational resources.[35] Of course, finding the perfect balance is difficult.

Balancing the interests of multiple parties is also a challenge for privacy policy, the final component of the knowledge triad.

■ Privacy: Surveillance After September 11

Privacy can be conceptualized as an information space attached to an individual.[36] The content of this space is personal information. *Privacy rights* can be understood as rights to control the flow of information in and out of this private zone. Advances in information storage, retrieval, analysis, and transmission are heightening concerns about violations of privacy.

Citizens and consumers are sensitive to the control of personal information. The terrorist attacks of September 11, 2001, have had the collateral effect of changing how Americans value privacy. Since those events the United States has been engaged in a war on terror against a shadowy network of people whose physical locations remain uncertain. For Americans, our equanimity has been disturbed, and we have come to realize how closely linked we are to the rest of the world, for good or for ill. As a consequence, U.S. political culture has shifted toward a greater acceptance of technologies of surveillance, technologies that cannot help but invade privacy in ways that would not have been acceptable prior to the events of that day. Americans are waiting calmly and patiently in line at airports to have their shoes and other belongings examined for explosives and weapons and presenting picture ID multiple times as they make their way from the check-in counter to the departure gate. Tom Ridge, secretary for homeland security, has called upon people to get to know their neighbors and what they are doing, incorporating terrorism prevention into Neighborhood Watch programs.[37] The U.S. Bureau of Citizenship and Immigration Service's rules for student visas require universities and colleges to put much more effort into keeping tabs on students.

In May 2002, the U.S. Department of Justice issued new procedures for the FBI, which is now charged with fighting terrorism as its primary responsibility.[38] The new procedures allow the FBI more latitude in conducting surveillance, with fewer restrictions to protect the privacy rights of the potential subjects. Many people are concerned about the appropriate balance between what the state needs to know to protect the nation's security and what the individual has a right to maintain as private.[39]

The new guidelines are a major departure from the post-Hoover restrictions on federal law enforcement's ability to conduct surveillance. During the period J. Edgar Hoover ran the FBI (1924–1972),[40] the agency routinely conducted surveillance on U.S. citizens believed by the administration (or at least by Hoover) to be political foes. Influenced by Hoover's urging, the administration of President John F. Kennedy agreed to the surveillance of civil rights activist Martin Luther King Jr. The Secret Service was similarly involved in spying on Americans (particularly African Americans), and in 1972 *New York Times* columnist Jack Anderson provided the Congressional Black Caucus with a list of 5,500 African Americans on whom the Secret Service maintained dossiers. Included in this group was baseball star Jackie Robinson. The FBI, according to Anderson's investigative report, targeted moderate blacks simply because of their support for minority causes or their opposition to the Vietnam War. The FBI even conducted surveillance on Martin Luther King's wife.[41]

Public outcry over the Hoover-era activities resulted in new rules that limited law enforcement agencies' ability to collect information. Specifically, the new rules required FBI agents to obtain authorization from the Department of Justice before being allowed to intercept any verbal communication, unless they had the permission of all the parties to the communication.[42] This meant that undercover FBI agents could no longer routinely attend political rallies and other events to take notes on what was said or done by whom. The agents needed to convince the appropriate attorney within the Department of Justice that the monitoring of oral communications had a reasonable law enforcement purpose. These restrictions even carried over to investigations in which a civilian participant was willing to be wired with a recording device—so-called consensual monitoring. According to Attorney General John Ashcroft, who took office in 2001 under President Bush, "The number of requests for consensual monitoring that were not approved [in the years since the rule was implemented] had been negligible" because, he claimed, strict guidelines were adhered to.[43]

Nevertheless, perceived threats to security, whether from drug trafficking or politically motivated crimes, led to increased reliance on surveillance by law enforcement agencies during the conduct of their investigations, even before the terrorist attacks on September 11. Louis Freeh, director of the FBI during the administration of

President Bill Clinton, relaxed some of these privacy protections. In the wake of the Oklahoma City bombing, he encouraged increased powers for the FBI, including the use of surveillance to fight terrorism.[44] According to the *Washington Post,* the Clinton administration approved "sharply increased use of federal telephone wiretaps and other electronic surveillance."[45]

In the aftermath of September 11, Americans' sense of urgency for the fight against terror increased. This urgency, born of insecurity, produces pressure to allow the FBI and other law enforcement agencies to work more effectively and proactively by using information better. Attorney General Ashcroft's new rules for the FBI simplify the process for getting permission to collect information via consensual surveillance. Moreover, agents are now authorized to surf the Internet, collect information in public settings (including houses of worship), and purchase information from proprietary data warehouses to screen for potential security risks. The goal, of course, is to protect Americans by identifying terrorists and their plans before they have the opportunity to act. The side effect is that the FBI will end up collecting a lot of information about innocent people while trying to identify miscreants. These new procedures may enhance our security, but the new policies also raise important questions. For example, should the U.S. government be collecting information on people just because they voice opposition to the United States and its policies? The difference between defensible investigations and negative stereotyping based on religion and ethnicity has not yet been determined. Also, how will people even know that information is being collected about them? What kinds of redress are available to persons who are falsely branded as a suspect because of incorrect information?[46] When people lose control over who has access to information about them, their personal power has been diminished.

▪ The Privacy–Intellectual Property– Information Connection

Rules establishing, protecting, and eroding privacy have a close, policy-relevant connection to rules governing intellectual property and—even more so—to rules governing proprietary information. With the commodification of ideas and information, *personal information* has newfound economic value: others (especially firms and governments) can reap material benefits from having access to facts about individuals. It is a small step from creating and manipulating large databases to creating and manipulating large databases of information about individuals.

Personal information can be found in government as well as private databases. The state has a dual role, as the legitimate body for making, implementing, and enforcing rules and as a collector and owner of information. Yet access to data enables regulation and enforcement by private actors, as well. Sorted, cross-referenced data can tell a government if I am paying my taxes and whether I am spending more than one would expect given my income. Insurance companies might want to regulate my behavior by charging a penalty on my insurance if I smoke. The gathering of personal information makes it possible for government and private-sector actors to exercise such control. Likewise, governments and firms can also exercise control by preventing individuals from gaining access to information that they have an interest in obtaining.

In essence, privacy relates to the individual ability to control the flow of information across an imagined barrier that divides the private from the public.[47] Even though personal information has not been commodified in a way that gives a person ownership of information about himself, controlling the movement of personal information is critical to the meaning of privacy. Rules, again often in the form of laws, establish the conditions under which an individual can control that flow of personal information. If I cannot stop information about myself from being transmitted against my will, my privacy has been breached. Controlling personal information flows concerns not only unwanted disclosure but also other types of privacy breaches: when information is foisted upon me (e.g., as propaganda or as e-mail spam); when I am not allowed to put my personal information (e.g., political opinions) into the public; and when someone or some institution refuses to disclose information I want or should have (e.g., the failure of the tobacco industry to disclose information it possessed about the dangers of smoking). As we go through life and interact in society, we are constantly negotiating the location of the public-private boundary; and we are constantly trying to maintain control of the passage of information across that boundary.

■ Rule Making: Then, Now, and Tomorrow

The chapters that follow examine rules to regulate intellectual property, information, and privacy.[48] I have paid close attention to the origins of these rules because history suggests the future trajectory of policy. I also examine current issues, including the challenges of balancing the rights of the individual against the rights of the community. What are the social rules enabling commodification, redefining intangibles as property, establishing property rights, and limiting and expanding the individual's right to privacy? What can be owned, and how does the public welfare—particularly the global public welfare—figure into the mix?

▪ Notes

1. I give more detailed definitions later in this chapter.

2. Rita Cruise and G. K. Helleiner O'Brien, "The Political Economy of Information in a Changing International Economic Order," *International Organization* 34, no. 4 (1980): 445.

3. Anne A. J. Andermann, "Physicians, Fads, and Pharmaceuticals: A History of Aspirin," *McGill Journal of Medicine* 2 (1996). Also, for a complete overview, see Charles C. Mann and Mark L. Plummer, *The Aspirin Wars: Money, Medicine, and 100 Years of Rampant Competition*, 1st ed. (New York: Knopf, 1991). The history, as reported by the corporation itself, can be found in Bayer Group, *Company History* (August 2, 2001 [cited June 4, 2002]), available from www.bayer.com/en/unternehmen/historie/index.html.

4. See A. Samuel Oddi, "Un-Unified Economic Theories of Patents—the-Not-Quite-Holy-Grail," *Notre Dame Law Review* 71 (1996): 267. Britain also granted a patent, but it was subsequently ruled invalid.

5. See Robert P. Fischelis, "What Is a Patent or Proprietary Medicine," *Scientific Monthly* 46, no. 1 (1938).

6. Thrush is a yeast infection of the mouth, not uncommon in children.

7. I am thankful for the reminiscences of my father (of blessed memory), who earned his pharmacy degree in 1938.

8. Dorothea Braithwaite, "The Economic Effects of Advertisement," *Economic Journal* 38, no. 149 (1928): 30.

9. Bayer Group, *About Bayer: History* (January 15, 2003 [cited August 28, 2003]) available from www.bayer.com/en/bayer/history/ug_1925.php; "Bayer Takes Sterling North American Business," *OTC Business News*, September 15 1994; Allen Z. Hertz, "Proceedings of the Canada–United States Law Institute Conference, NAFTA Revisited; Shaping the Trident: Intellectual Property under NAFTA, Investment Protection Agreements and the World Trade Organization," *Canada–United States Law Journal* 23 (1997).

10. "Drug Patents," *Financial Times*, October 29, 2001.

11. *Feist Publications, Inc. v. Rural Telephone Service Company*, 499 U.S. 340 (1991).

12. SportsTrax was not paying the NBA for media credentials, but other, similar services were. See Paul Enright, "Sportstrax: They Love This

Game! A Comment on the *NBA v. Motorola,*" *Seton Hall Journal of Sport Law* 7 (1997).

13. Maria D'Amico, *Sports Statistics on the Net, Online FAQ* (April 1997 [cited March 12, 2002]), available from www.madcapps.com/writings/faqsports.htm. D'Amico is an attorney specializing in intellectual property.

14. Kevin Featherly, "NFL, Other Leagues, Sell Exclusive Online Rights," *Editor and Publisher* 132, no. 44 (1999). Website owners try to get around the NFL's restrictions by posting descriptions that fall just shy of play-by-play. For example, PioneerPlanet's *Vikings Now* site "does not recount every single play. But it doesn't miss much. During the October 17 [1999] contest between Minnesota and the Detroit Lions, [the sites' reporters] posted messages to users a total of 50 times during the course of the game." See also Cicely K. Dyson, "Online Journalists Have Major-League Issues over Sports Credentials," *Asne Reporter 2001* (April 6, 2001 [cited March 14, 2002]), available from www.asne.org/2001reporter/friday/sports6.html.

15. "Major League Baseball Adds MLB Radio to Official Website Line Up," press release, July 7, 2000 [cited March 13, 2002], available from cbs.sportsline.com/u/baseball/mlbcom/pressrelease/mlbradio_070700.htm [note: link is no longer available].

16. The law invoked by the plaintiffs in this case was the new EU Database Directive, which I discuss in Chapter 10. Tony Samuel, "Sports Rights Are Valuable Too," *Managing Intellectual Property,* May 2001.

17. Joe Arace and Mark Hayes, "World League," *USA Today,* May 27, 1992.

18. Ariana Eunjung Cha, "Olympic Fans Face Online Hurdles: IOC Limits Airing of Sydney Games on Web," *Washington Post,* August 13, 2000.

19. Gregg Gardner, "Silicon Wadi," *Jerusalem Post,* January 24, 2002.

20. Rich Jaroslovsky, quoted in Dyson, "Online Journalists Have Major-League Issues over Sports Credentials."

21. John Dewan, *Comments [of the President of Stats, Inc.] on the WIPO Database Treaty and Sports Statistics; Letter to the US Commissioner of Patents and Trademarks* (November 22, 1996 [cited March 12, 2002]), available from www.public-domain.org/database/stats.html.

22. Brander Matthews, "The Evolution of Copyright," *Political Science Quarterly* 5, no. 4 (1890).

23. In this analysis, I am strongly influenced by Nicholas Greenwood Onuf, *World of Our Making: Rules and Rule in Social Theory and International Relations* (Columbia: University of South Carolina Press, 1989). Onuf, drawing on the work of John Searle and Max Black, provides a typology of social rules, depending on their purpose. *Instruction rules* identify social relations and define what objects are or are not; *directive rules* articulate orders or requests; and *commitment rules* specify promises that one party makes to another. What can be owned and who can own it can be understood as instruction rules, which identify what something is. In this book, I detail historical moments when instruction rules emerge. When, for example, did a sound recording become something ownable under the law?

The focus is on when and why something becomes property and when and why that property is commodified. Looking at commodification—the ability to buy and sell kinds of property—shifts the attention to directive and commissive rules. What are the limits of the sound recording owner's rights? How will governments promise to enforce those rights? What does the rights holder have to do to uphold the bargain? My discussion of rules is also influenced by Anthony Giddens, who divides rules into two types, those that relate to the constitution of means (rules about *relations*), and those that are normative (rules about *actions* and *outcomes*). Anthony Giddens, *The Constitution of Society* (Berkeley: University of California Press, 1984). See also Sue E. S. Crawford and Elinor Ostrom, "A Grammar of Institutions," *American Political Science Review* 89, no. 3 (1995); Howard Margolis, "Equilibrium Norms," *Ethics* 100, no. 4 (1990); and a review essay by Gregory A. Raymond, "Problems and Prospects in the Study of International Norms," *Mershon International Studies Review* 41, no. 2 (1997).

24. R. Kurt Burch, *"Property" and the Making of the International System* (Boulder, CO: Lynne Rienner, 1998), 154.

25. John S. Mill, *Principles of Political Economy with Some of Their Applications to Social Philosophy,* edited and with an introduction by W. J. Ashley, based on 7th ed. (London: Longmans, Green, 1909 [1870]).

26. Marylynn Salmon, "Women and Property in South Carolina: The Evidence from Marriage Settlements, 1730 to 1830," *William and Mary Quarterly* [3rd ser.] 39, no. 4 (1982).

27. See Joshua 15:17-19, for example.

28. Charles Donahue Jr., "Symposium: Relationships among Roman Law, Common Law, and Modern Civil Law: Ius Commune, Canon Law, and Common Law in England," *Tulane Law Review* 66 (1992).

29. For a discussion of this topic, see Suzanne Holland, "Contested Commodities at Both Ends of Life: Buying and Selling Gametes, Embryos, and Body Tissues," *Kennedy Institute of Ethics Journal* 11, no. 3 (2001); Christopher May, *A Global Political Economy of Intellectual Property Rights: The New Enclosures?* Routledge/RIPE Studies in Global Political Economy (London and New York: Routledge, 2000); and Edward A. Comor, "Governance and the 'Commoditization' of Information," *Global Governance* 4 (1998).

30. For example, the delegitimization of the institution of slavery eliminated the "right" of people to own human beings. See Ethan A. Nadelmann, "Global Prohibition Regimes: The Evolution of Norms in International Society," *International Organization* 44, no. 4 (1990). This is not to say that slavery no longer exists, because there is much evidence that it does. However, the predominant global norm no longer considers anyone to have a property right in another human being.

31. National Academy of Engineering, National Academy of Sciences, Institute of Medicine, Committee on Science, Engineering, and Public Policy, Panel on Scientific Responsibility and the Conduct of Research, *On Being a Scientist: Responsible Conduct in Research* (Washington, DC: National Academy Press, 1995).

32. National Academy of Engineering, National Academy of Sciences, Institute of Medicine, Committee on Science, Engineering, and Public Policy, Panel on Scientific Responsibility and the Conduct of Research, *Responsible Science: Ensuring the Integrity of the Research Process* (Washington, DC: National Academy Press, 1992).

33. Karl Polanyi wrote the seminal work that revealed how what becomes commodified is contingent on historical circumstances. Karl Polanyi, *The Great Transformation,* 1st Beacon paperback ed. (Boston: Beacon, 1957).

34. The commodification of services works in a similar fashion, though it is a bit more complicated because a service does not have the discrete characteristic of taking up a fixed amount of physical space, of having edges and borders. Nevertheless, the purveyor of a service controls the provision of that service. The service is provided only where and when the service provider is willing to work. The worker providing a service can easily stop the flow of the service by simply not providing it.

Commodification and the creation of markets for a good or service also requires the agreement in at least some part of society that it is legitimate for the good or service to be bought and sold. These markets may be legal or illegal (e.g., the market for heroin). A black market is no less a market for being illegal. An introduction to public and private goods can be found in Paul A. Samuelson and Peter Temin, *Economics,* 10th ed. (New York: McGraw-Hill, 1976). See also Elinor Ostrom, *Governing the Commons: The Evolution of Institutions for Collective Action.* Political Economy of Institutions and Decisions (Cambridge, UK, and New York: Cambridge University Press, 1990), which discusses common pool resources.

35. A caveat to this admittedly simplified discussion: in some circumstances, governments (and others) choose to provide products of the mind as public goods. By law, the U.S. government does not have copyright in its publications. Therefore, neither the government nor the workers writing at their federal jobs have a copyright in any thing they write for their jobs. Government scientists who publish articles in scientific journals, for example, cannot sign over their copyright to the journal because they do not have one to begin with. The situation for patents is different, however. The government does own patents.

36. Chapter 8 provides a more complete discussion.

37. White House, "Strengthening Homeland Security since 9/11," press release, April 11, 2002 [cited June 4, 2002], available from www.whitehouse. gov/homeland/six_month_update.html.

38. Federal Bureau of Investigation. "Facts and Figures 2003" [cited February 9, 2004], available from www.fbi.gov/priorities/priorities.htm.

39. And, in light of revelations about the failure of law enforcement agencies to use the intelligence reports that they received about the terrorists prior to the acts of September 11, whether the state has the ability to make sense of the information that it does gather.

40. Federal Bureau of Investigation, *History of the Federal Bureau of Investigation* [cited June 7, 2002], available from www.fbi.gov/libref/historic/

history/text.htm. At the time Hoover took the helm, the agency was named the Bureau of Investigation.

41. "Anderson Alleges Surveillance of Many Blacks," *New York Times,* June 28, 1972.

42. John Ashcroft, U.S. Attorney General, "Memorandum for the Heads and Inspectors General of Executive Departments and Agencies, on 'Procedures of Lawful, Warrantless Monitoring of Verbal Communication'" (May 30, 2002 [cited June 3, 2002]), available from www.usdoj.gov/olp/lawful.pdf.

43. Ibid.

44. Helen Dewar and Kevin Merida, "FBI Chief Urges Broader Federal Reach," *Washington Post,* April 28, 1995.

45. Jim McGee, "Wiretapping Rises Sharply Under Clinton: Drug War Budget Increased Lead to Continuing Growth of High-Tech Surveillance," *Washington Post,* July 7, 1996.

46. It is not unusual to find incorrect information or information taken out of context in databanks. According to the Electronic Privacy Information Center,

in January 2002, a New York jury awarded $450,000 in damages to an individual who lost a job opportunity because his profile [in a commercial database] contained a false criminal conviction.

Electronic Privacy Information Center, Privacy and Electronic Records (June 1, 2002 [cited June 1, 2002]), available from www.epic.org/privacy/publicrecordsa. The source cites Obabueki v. IBM, 145 F. Supp. 2d 371 (2002).

47. Perhaps the most famous definition of privacy, the right to be left alone, was first outlined by Samuel Warren and Louis D. Brandeis, "The Right to Privacy," *Harvard Law Review* 4 (1890). My more expansive definition of privacy, as introduced below and elaborated in Chapter 8, encompasses this definition and the more recent definition of privacy as autonomy, which arises from *Griswold v. Connecticut,* 381 U.S. 479 (1965).

48. In essence, these rules comprise overlapping international regimes. Among the most widely referenced works on regimes are Oran Young, *Resource Regimes: Natural Resources and Social Institutions* (Berkeley: University of California Press, 1982); Stephen D. Krasner, *International Regimes,* Cornell Studies in Political Economy (Ithaca, NY: Cornell University Press, 1983); Robert O. Keohane, *After Hegemony: Cooperation and Discord in the World Political Economy* (Princeton, NJ: Princeton University Press, 1984); Fredrich Kratochwil and John G. Ruggie, "International Organization: A State of the Art on an Art of the State," *International Organization* 40, no. 4 (1986); and Volker Rittberger, ed., with Peter Mayer, *Regime Theory and International Relations* (Oxford, UK: Clarendon, 1993). I detail a dialectical approach to international regimes in Renée Marlin-Bennett, *Food Fights: International Regimes and the Politics of Agricultural Trade Disputes* (Langhorne, PA: Gordon and Breach, 1993).

2

Intellectual Property

s I noted in the Introduction, the social rules for intellectual
property are more formalized than those for proprietary information and privacy. In this chapter, I examine intellectual
property in more depth. How did innovation and creativity become
intellectual property, initially in the West and then around the globe?
What are the different kinds of intellectual property as constituted
under current laws? How have different cultures defined knowledge
and other products of the mind?

■ From Privileges to Rights:
Commodifying Intellectual Property

The origins of intellectual property can be traced to the system of
granting privileges in medieval Europe. Western culture did not
always treat the products of intellectual effort like commodities. In
the medieval European knowledge regime, the Roman Catholic
Church enjoyed great power with respect to knowledge, playing a
pivotal role in determining what could be known and who could
make use of knowledge. Most of the books being produced were
religious texts, which required the imprimatur of ecclesiastical
authority, and most were produced and copied by monks. Books of
secular knowledge were often produced by scholars at universities,
but even those works would not escape oversight, since the Church
governed the universities. The power of the Church allowed it to
assign value to certain texts, which were then copied, disseminated,

and preserved. Although independent scribes did exist, they produced fewer books compared to the system of monasteries and universities.

Control of ideas also resulted from the organization of craftsmen into guilds. The guild masters determined which ideas would be used to produce the guild's products, and guildsmen were required to keep the production techniques secret. Knowledge was passed from craftsman to apprentice, and it was not shared with nonmembers. In the heyday of the guilds, opportunities for nonmember innovators were limited, especially within towns. Today we would describe the processes and tools that comprised the guilds' secret knowledge as *club goods.* By maintaining the secret and controlling production and pricing, guilds were able to make ideas excludable, available only to members of the club-guild. The overarching legal structure in the towns supported such exclusivity. Even if a nonguild interloper managed to find out the secret or independently invent a better process, he might be prohibited from profiting because the authorities (i.e., guild masters, local noblemen, or Church authorities) controlled how new practical knowledge could be put to use.

Guild control was part of a larger economy in which an individual had to seek permission from church or state authorities to enter an occupation. The privilege to engage in a certain trade—to sell wine in a town, to publish prayer books, or any other—was granted at the discretion of those who held power. Real property (meaning land, as opposed to personal property) in the feudal system was held by privilege, not by right. Church authorities and secular rulers bestowed privileges on chosen people, who were then beholden to their benefactors. Those already in power thereby gained even more power, including control over the dissemination of products of the mind. Moreover, authorities did not necessarily award the privilege to use a particular innovation or to produce a particular creative work to the original innovator or creator. The connection between intellectual effort and monetary reward (gained through monopoly privileges) had not been made.

Johannes Gutenberg's movable-type printing press, invented around 1450, created many opportunities to break the control over knowledge held by the guilds and the Church.[1] By the 1500s, printing had become a commercial enterprise, and the publishing industry was emerging. The demand for books increased as literacy rates rose, and more writings in the vernacular opened a market for creative works to be read by wealthy and literate people who were not associated with monasteries or universities. The guild system began to erode as those who had been excluded from craft secrets sought knowledge in other ways.

More importantly, prior to the fourteenth century, rulers commonly awarded favored individuals exclusive rights to exercise a trade, to sell a product, or to use a process. But from the fourteenth century onward authorities began to associate privileges with inventing something new or with importing inventions from abroad. People began to earn privileges by being creative and by contributing to society's productivity—a shift from the earlier custom of privileges for the favored few. Making the connection between invention and reward, according to Edith Tilton Penrose, was the pathbreaking legal innovation of the Italian *letters patent.*[2]

The patent in its current form developed out of this "systematic use of monopoly privileges" to encourage invention.[3] The granting of the privilege to inventors became so routine that people began to view it as a right. In the fifteenth century, the Republic of Venice "generally promised privileges of ten years to inventors of new arts and machines."[4] Similarly, in sixteenth-century England, Queen Elizabeth I's government developed a system of royal privileges that protected domestic industries that imported new technologies. The system gave a monopoly of limited duration that would compensate the new technology's importer for the cost of transplanting the technology, learning to use it, and making it profitable. These privileges were gradually transformed into rights. One of the earliest forms of patent rights, the English Statute of Monopolies (1623), limited the term of patents to fourteen years.

Copyright evolved from book privileges. In the early part of the eighteenth century, the London Company of Stationers (a publishing company) lobbied for the passage of a law that would ensure its ability to purchase and publish works. The resulting law, the Statute of Anne (1709), is generally credited as the first modern copyright law. Prior to this, authors could not make money from their works because as soon as they were printed they could be copied. To earn a living, authors depended on the generosity of an aristocratic or ecclesiastical patron. The establishment of copyright allowed authors to become independent economic actors who could contract with publishers.[5]

Thus the period from the fourteenth to the seventeenth centuries saw the metamorphosis of the monopoly granted for producing an invention or creative work from a privilege into a time-limited property right. Moreover, the establishment of these property rights made possible the commodification of intellectual property. Authors could sell the right to copy their works to a publisher, who could in turn sell books to consumers without worrying that another publisher would come along and simply reprint the works. Inventors could sell inventions without fear of being undersold by a copycat manufacturer. While in earlier times the Church and other authorities sought to limit the kinds of creative works or innovations being produced, the creation of patent rights and copyrights encouraged creativity and innovation. The legal structure of rules supporting intellectual property rights served to institutionalize this shift.

▪ International Trade and Intellectual Property

An obvious reason for state support of innovation was that it would allow a country to be more productive and therefore wealthier and more powerful militarily than other countries. For this reason, the initial laws regarding intellectual property protected the patents and copyrights of a state's own citizens but allowed or even encouraged the violation of patents or copyrights held by citizens of other countries. This was a way for states to maximize the amount of new information, technology, learning, and creativity that came within their borders. For example, during the early period of U.S. history (until 1891) Americans were notorious for copying books printed in Great Britain without providing any compensation to the hapless author.[6]

Encouragement of such piracy was economically rational because the United States was a net consumer of information and technology. In Europe, however, the development levels of the various states were more evenly matched. Opportunities for trade could be eroded through piracy of intellectual property, as innovators did not want to see sales undercut by imported versions of patented products. Eventually, trade problems led to bilateral agreements between states to protect the copyrights and patents of their respective citizens.

The planned International Exhibition of Inventions in Vienna in 1873 was the impetus for the creation of a more fully international patent treaty. Potential exhibitors quickly realized that international patent protection was essential for preventing theft of the innovations that were planned for display. Ad hoc arrangements protected intellectual property at the exhibition, but interest in a more formal treaty continued. Ten years later, fourteen countries signed the Paris Convention for the Protection of Industrial Property. This was soon followed, in 1886, with the Berne Convention for the Protection of Literary and Artistic Works.[7] Both conventions have been renegotiated several times; their provisions, along with subsequent treaties, form an international regime for protecting intellectual property.

The first formal institutions of the regime were the secretariats of the Paris Union and the Berne Union, both of which were housed in a bureau of the Swiss government. In 1893, the Swiss combined the secretariats into a single office, the International Bureaux for the Protection of Intellectual Property (BIRPI, its French acronym), for administrative reasons.[8] The World Intellectual Property Organization (WIPO), founded as an independent international organization in 1970, was created when the administrative requirements of the regime outgrew the resources of BIRPI. In 1976, WIPO became a specialized agency of the United Nations. (The treaties and WIPO are discussed in greater detail in Chapter 3.)

■ Types of Intellectual Property

From the Paris Convention and Berne Convention, along with subsequent international treaties, we derive the definitions of different kinds of intellectual property. From the earliest negotiations, intellectual property was divided into two categories: industrial property and artistic property. *Industrial property* includes patents, trademarks, industrial designs, and similar forms. *Artistic property* refers to copyright and related rights. The distinction is important because the purpose for protecting industrial property is to increase or improve society's productivity, whereas the purpose for protecting artistic property is to encourage the ennoblement of humanity through creative endeavors. Though these two aims have become increasingly difficult to separate as productive processes have evolved in the Information Age, the basic differences can still be outlined.

Industrial Property

Patents. Patents confer property rights on processes or inventions that are new, useful, and nonobvious. Patent rights—a time-limited monopoly granted to the inventors—reward them for their efforts and

provide incentives to be innovative. Society's interest in technological progress is satisfied in three ways. First, the inventors themselves
are willing to invest time, money, and energy in research and development assured that they will be the sole provider of the invention or
process for a set number of years, thereby garnering all the profits
derived from it. Second, potential inventors can learn from the work
that was done by the patent holder because the requirement for
obtaining a patent requires disclosure of the engineering model (or
equivalent). Third, consumers (including firms, of course) have a
new gizmo or process that will make life easier, more efficient, more
varied, or otherwise better.

No one else can produce the invention or use the process without
a license from the patent holder during the term of the patent. Even
the innocent inventor who independently invented substantially the
same idea (a common occurrence) would not be allowed to compete
until the patent expired. The social bargain is that inventors disclose
how the invention works in exchange for government protection of
the monopoly while the government agrees to grant the monopoly in
exchange for new knowledge.

Patents require a government decision that says, in effect, "this
invention is worth rewarding the inventor for." The inventor must
first submit an application, which must then be reviewed. As it has
evolved in the United States, the patenting process can be difficult
and costly for the inventor. Governments must also make major
expenditures to provide a patent office for processing applications.

Here is the procedure in the United States. Typically, an inventor will go to a patent attorney (or to the in-house counsel of a firm)
with an invention. Then the lawyer (or a patent agent acting for the
lawyer) conducts a search to determine whether there are preexisting
patents on the invention and to check whether it is really novel or
simply "prior art." Assuming that there are no prior patents and that
the invention does not constitute prior art, the attorney files a patent
application on the inventor's behalf.

A patent application consists of a description of the invention
and its utility and a statement of the claims the inventor is making
about what is new and different. The inventor must also pay a fee to
have the application considered.[9] At this point, when the application
has been filed and the fee transmitted, the invention receives some
protection—the patent is *pending,* and other inventors know that it
has been filed.

In the United States, the first to invent a new process or device receives the patent; but in most of the rest of the world the rule is first to file. The distinction is important because people working independently often arrive at essentially the same invention at about the same time. Under the U.S. first-to-invent rule, the inventor who can provide evidence of having invented first (e.g., dated lab notebooks) receives the patent. Under the first-to-file rule, the inventor who is able to get the legal wheels turning first receives the patent. In theory, the first-to-file system provides more privileges to the inventor who has more resources to begin with. The company with more resources, for example, might already have an attorney on retainer. In practice, though, an inventor working for a firm with significant resources generally has an advantage even under the first-to-invent rule, simply because highly innovative sectors tend to be characterized by aggressive patent-filing strategies.[10] The major benefit of a first-to-file rule is that it keeps down some costs for the government, which must foot the bill for examining competing patent applications and determining whether the claims are valid.

In the next step a patent examiner examines the application, conducts her own search for prior art, and decides whether the invention is worthy of a patent. Is it novel? Is it useful? Is it something that a person skilled or knowledgeable in that particular area would not already know how to do? To make this determination, the patent examiner must have a sophisticated understanding of technology and engineering. For example, a patent examiner in the field of biotechnology must have the competence to determine whether other scientists in the field would find a particular process or device novel. Because of the expertise such judgments require, the patent office must attract and retain examiners who might otherwise find lucrative positions in industry or academia. This is a continuing challenge for patent offices.

If granted the patent, the inventor has a monopoly on the invention, generally for 20 years from the date of filing for the patent.[11] However, the patent will cost: patent issue fees, any required renewal fees, and the cost of defending the patent. It is up to the patent holder to monitor global markets for infringements and to seek redress through litigation. In general, government agencies do not police patent rights. Enforcement is often a civil matter (in the United States at least), and it is up to patent holders to defend their own rights. Defending a patent can be expensive. And some countries require that patent holders work the patent, that is, use the process or produce the device. Rules for working the patent vary. Some countries require that the patent holder actually use the process or manufacture the device in the country. Under other countries' laws, exporting to the country suffices. The costs of defending the patent and of working it must be weighed against potential revenue derived from it.

Inventors who decide that the patent system has too many drawbacks have two options. First, they can choose to make the invention public by disseminating information without seeking a patent (e.g., publication in a professional journal). In this way inventors can prevent someone else from patenting their inventions. When it is publicly disclosed, the invention enters the public domain and becomes a public good and prior art. Initially, inventors have the advantage over potential competitors: inventors already know how to make the product or use the process. Of course, this advantage evaporates as competitors become efficient at producing or using the invention. Still, in fast moving fields, the early bird gets the worm: the best opportunity for making profits might come immediately after introduction. The second option is to keep the invention a secret.

Trade secrets. Trade secrets are, in some ways, the opposite of patents. "A trade secret is information of any sort that is valuable to its owner, that is not generally known, and that has been kept secret by the owner."[12] Inventors choosing to keep their inventions secret opt for the protection of laws that prohibit a person from the misuse of proprietary information. In other words, trade secret laws protect against stealing or otherwise misappropriating know-how. As long as the secret stays secret, and as long as no one else independently figures it out, the holder of a trade secret has an advantage over potential competitors. If someone hacks into a computer system and steals the secret, or if a disgruntled employee spills the beans, trade secret law can be invoked to punish the thief. However, once the secret is out, it is out. Although laws protecting trade secrets do so in perpetuity as long as the secret remains secret, once the secret is disclosed anyone can produce the invention or use the process.

Perhaps the most famous trade secret is the formula for Coca-Cola. By virtue of its tight security policies, the Coca-Cola company has been able to maintain the secrecy of its product's formulation since 1886. Had the company sought a patent, its rights to the formula would have expired by 1906. The company reportedly goes to extreme measures to protect its secret formula for Coke. The actual recipe is kept in a bank vault in Atlanta, and corporate rules require a resolution of the board of directors to open the vault. Only those very few people who oversee the mixing of Coke syrup are allowed to know the formula, and they are not allowed to fly on the same airplane.[13]

Certain inventions are more easily kept secret than others. If it is relatively easy to reverse engineer a product to find out how it works and how it was made, trade secret law will not be much help. Similarly, consider the situation if a trade secret is a special way of doing something—a process—that makes manufacturing something easier. It will be difficult to make sure that former employees do not use their knowledge of the process when they begin work elsewhere. If one company decides to recruit the ten best technologists at a competing firm by offering higher salaries, is that evidence of intent to steal trade secrets?[14] Companies increasingly seek to protect their trade secrets through nondisclosure contracts or noncompete agreements between employer and employee. The problem is that overprotection of trade secrets may prevent a former employee from making a living. Such agreements are especially egregious when the employee in question is a low-level worker who really is not contributing or taking away much intellectual capital. In December 2000, *U.S. News & World Report* reported on this practice, citing the experiences of a laser eye surgery technician in Maryland, Frappuccino makers at Starbucks, and body-piercers in California.[15]

Trademarks and service marks. Patents and laws protecting trade secrets are designed to reward the inventor for inventiveness. A second form of industrial property targets the relationship between producer and consumer. Trademarks, service marks, industrial designs, and geographic designations are used to protect a producer's or service provider's reputation and to provide reliable information to consumers about who has produced the goods or who is providing the service.

Trademarks and service marks are names and graphic symbols that represent a brand or a company name. Firms gain by being able to create a recognizable brand to attract consumer loyalty. At the same time, the public gains by being able to identify whose product or service they are using. In some cases, the trademark confers status or cachet to a product. Other watches may keep time just as well and look just as nice as a Rolex, but a Rolex watch—just by its name—

carries prestige. Moreover, Rolex's manufacturer has a reputation to protect. Watch buyers know that when they buy a Rolex, the company will stand behind its product. Purchasers of counterfeit Rolex watches—which look just as good but whose manufacturer illegally copied the design and insignia—would have no guarantee of quality. Rolex Watch U.S.A. is concerned about counterfeiting because of the problem of dilution: the value of the trademark decreases if it becomes associated with schlock products manufactured by counterfeiters.[16]

In some cases, it is not only the reputation of the company that suffers, because passing off fake products as the real thing can be deadly. In August 2001, CBS News reported that "counterfeit Gentamicin [an antibiotic] was blamed in at least 66 deaths and hundreds of severe reactions."[17] Thailand, a country plagued by fake pharmaceuticals, has a special unit in its Food and Drug Administration dedicated to detecting and eliminating counterfeit drugs.[18] The World Health Organization has also made this issue a priority.[19] Baby formula has also been counterfeited. In 1995, the U.S. Food and Drug Administration discovered that counterfeit packages of a popular baby formula Similac were appearing on store shelves. According to reports, the similarity between the genuine and the counterfeit products was astounding.[20] Although no deaths are known to have occurred in this case, counterfeits pose serious risks. Formula counterfeiters, like drug counterfeiters, have no interest in making sure that their product is safe.

Trademarks and service marks, unlike patents and copyrights, are not time-limited. As long as a company continues to use the mark, defend it against dilution, and renew the registration when necessary, the company retains exclusive rights to the mark.[21] Sometimes companies have to work hard to keep brand names from becoming a part of the general lexicon, an outcome that would threaten their retention of the trademark. The Xerox Corporation, for example, has been diligent in running advertisements reminding people that Xerox is not a verb: one should *photocopy* a page, not "Xerox" it. Johnson & Johnson faces a similar problem with its BAND-AID® brand. On the one hand, the company tries to emphasize its trademark rights, referring to "BAND-AID® brand adhesive bandages"; on the other it is difficult to control the evolution of language. Indeed, the company's efforts may be nothing more than "BAND-AID®" solutions.

Other important limitations on trademarks and service marks are geographic location and purpose. Acme Plumbing and Acme Printing can coexist in the same city as long as the contexts make it clear that they are different. Similarly, Acme Plumbing in the United States and Acme Plumbing in the United Kingdom may be two completely separate firms. There would be no trademark infringement, because a trademark valid in one country may not necessarily be valid in another. In some cases in the United States, marks are valid only within a single state. Acme Plumbing in California and Acme Plumbing in Louisiana can conceivably coexist without any risk of confusion.

The globalization of trade in products and services has changed this to some extent. The restaurateur who opens a fast-food burger joint anywhere in the world and calls it McDonald's has a trademark problem, even if the proprietor's name is Joe McDonald. The mark owned by McDonald's has become famous around the world for a particular commercial activity, and *McDonald's* is no longer available anywhere for use by fast-food restaurants not part of the famous chain. But McDonald's Plumbing is still available. The problem arises in the borderless world of cyberspace. McDonald's Plumbing might want to use McDonalds.com for its website, but that is already owned by the restaurant corporation. Even if the plumber got there first, the McDonald's company has rights as the holder of a famous mark. Because commerce can now often ignore national boundaries, marks are becoming less tied to specific locations and types of businesses. In short, trademarks and service marks are becoming increasingly strong forms of intellectual property as a direct consequence of globalized markets and the Internet.

Industrial designs. Industrial designs, also known as *design patents*, are the aesthetic design features in a product that make it recognizable and attractive. An industrial design, unlike a patented invention, does not have any functional purpose. As the ornamental component of a product, the design must not be hidden from view. Like utility patents, industrial designs have limited terms, fourteen years in the United States and generally between fifteen and twenty-five years in other countries. Industrial designs are similar to trade and service marks because they give a product its recognizable "look." The difference is that an industrial design must be ornamental, but it need not be distinctive. Counterfeiting industrial designs goes hand-in-glove with counterfeiting trademarks. The counterfeited Similac was packaged in containers that looked very much like the genuine products.

Geographic indication. A geographic indication (or geographic designation) specifies where a particular product comes from. Among the more famous examples are Parmigiano-Reggiano cheese, which comes only from the Parma and Regio Emilia regions of Italy, and Scotch Whiskey, which comes from Scotland. Unlike rights to trademarks and industrial designs, which protect an individual producer or service provider, geographic indications protect a group of producers. In the case of Parmigiano-Reggiano cheese, the Voluntary Consortium for the Safeguard of Grana Reggiano was founded in 1928 to guarantee the quality of cheese produced in the region. Cheese meeting the consortium's qualifications is marked with the year and the wording "C.G.T. Parmigiano-Reggiano."[22]

Most uses of geographic indications are for agricultural products. Advocates of rules protecting geographic indications as intellectual property contend that the soil, vegetation, air, light, microclimate, and other factors of an area create a unique product. Anyone from outside who duplicates the product and passes it off as coming from that area dilutes the value of the product because, so the reasoning goes, the unauthorized product cannot possibly possess the same attributes and qualities. This form of protection raises questions about the balance between encouraging production and encouraging competition, as well as the extent to which luxury goods in the developed world (especially wines and spirits) are more likely to receive protection than staple products of the developing world (e.g., basmati rice).

Inventions versus discoveries. Industrial property, it is argued, promotes the public good by encouraging people to be creative and innovative. When individuals and firms know they can receive a return through patents and other protections, they will be more willing to invest time and resources. Yet not every new idea or bit of knowledge qualifies as intellectual property per se. Most notably, scientific discoveries are excluded from protection. How does one distinguish between an invention (which is patentable) and a discovery (which is not)? The question of when new knowledge becomes property is complex.

The standard distinction is that scientific discoveries reveal truths about nature and how it works; inventions use principles of nature and technology for new devices or processes that are novel, useful, and nonobvious. For example, a researcher who figures out some aspect of the human immune system has made a scientific discovery. Someone else could use that new knowledge to create a new drug. That second person would have created a patentable invention.

Literary Property

However, the scientist who makes a discovery is not without any intellectual property rights. When she writes up her discovery for publication in a scholarly journal, she has a copyright in the written words.[23] Law rewards her creativity by limiting others' ability to copy that. Rules for literary property—which includes copyright and *neighboring rights*—share the same social goal of encouraging creative activity. The difference between literary property and industrial property is that the latter must fulfill the criteria of novelty, nonobviousness, and utility. Literary property, by contrast, must meet a relatively loose standard of *originality* and *creative expressiveness*.

Copyright. Copyright (or author's rights) is the right to determine who can copy a literary or artistic work. It protects the fixed expression of the work: the unique way in which the ideas are expressed is copyrighted, not the ideas themselves.[24] *Fixed* means written down or recorded in some other way: writing down the poem, painting the work on canvas, and so on. If I imagine a poem but never write it down or record it, I have no copyright in it. If I stand on the street corner and recite it, I still do not own it as intellectual property.[25] But if I write it down, it immediately becomes fixed; it is now my property. Registering the copyright with the appropriate governmental authorities is generally not necessary, but in many countries doing so makes it easier to prevail in a suit against an infringer.

It is important to remember that copyright protects the exact form of the fixed expression, not the ideas captured by the expression. Thus the ideas conveyed in our scientist's scientific paper on the immune system are not copyrighted. Rather, the words and figures she used to express those ideas are the protected property. Here is the distinction between copyright infringement and plagiarism: *copyright infringement* is a crime in which an individual copies the expression of ideas without permission; *plagiarism* is a violation of ethical behavior in which someone's ideas are used without giving the originator credit. People who take chunks of text written by others and represent it as their own are infringing the copyright *and* plagiarizing.

Under the Berne Convention, a copyright lasts from the time that the work is fixed to at least fifty years after the author's death. In the United States, changes in copyright law have led to a complex system of variable copyright terms. The Sonny Bono Copyright Term Extension Act, signed into law in 1998, extends copyright for 70 years after the author's death for works created after January 1, 1978, with other provisions for works created and published at other times, to extend the number of years a work is protected. After the term of a copyright has expired, the work enters the public domain, that is, anyone is free to copy it. (Note that the rules on plagiarism still apply.) As with a patent, the copyright holder is responsible for monitoring unauthorized copies and undertaking legal action to remove them from circulation.

Thus copyright provides expansive protections for the creators of literary and artistic works. In that way, it encourages people to invest time and effort in creative activities—a benefit for society as a whole. However, copyright, if used too expansively, limits the creative activities of those who do not yet hold copyrights. Overly strong copyright protections prevent people from building on past creations. Imagine how difficult it would be if students could not use direct quotes in any term paper. What if they were not allowed to make photocopies of sources, or even to copy them by hand?

Under current rules, an individual charged with infringement can claim *fair use* as a legal defense. Fair use, as currently defined, allows one to copy a small portion of a work for education, criticism, or parody. Under current U.S. law there is no right to fair use per se; it is merely a legal defense to a claim of copyright infringement. In other words, unauthorized copying for educational and critical purposes is still infringement, but the law does not allow the copyright holder to obtain money damages if the infringer can demonstrate fair use. Thus the question remains: Should fair use be guaranteed in law as a right?

Neighboring rights. In addition to copyright, creative works are sometimes protected by *neighboring rights:* performances by performing artists (musicians, actors, dancers, etc.), sound recordings (phonograms), and broadcasts are examples. Laws protecting performances make it illegal for concert-goers to record the music. Similarly, laws protecting rights to sound recordings make it illegal to copy a CD or DVD or to make a copy and redistribute programs that are broadcast. That means, of course, that commonplace practices may indeed be illegal. For example, consider *platform shifting*. If I purchase a musical CD, I may want to burn a second copy on a CD-RW to play in my car. Some who advocate strong intellectual property protection want to eliminate such copying, even though the harm that I may have caused is minimal (I am not, after all, selling the copies I make). Nevertheless, proponents of strong intellectual property protection would argue that all copying is illegal and should stop. Are such practices equivalent to stealing? I think not: I purchased the CD, the recording has not been bootlegged, and the record company and artist received their royalties. It seems to me that purchasing the CD ought to give me the right to use it however I wish as long as my use of the copy is for personal purposes.

But making multiple copies of a CD to then sell, or to distribute for free via the Internet and peer-to-peer connections, does cross an ethical boundary, though the extent to which unauthorized infringement is wrong would vary according to the circumstances. Neighboring rights also come into play with the widespread copying and sale of bootleg recordings of performances. One widely cited study reports an explosion of online pirating of motion pictures with the May 2002 releases of *Spider Man* and *Star Wars Episode II: Attack of the Clones*. This report estimates that 2–3 million computer users downloaded copies of either film.[26]

Moral rights. A major difference between continental and Anglo-American rights to literary property is the concept of moral rights. Rules for moral rights grant creators an expansive right to determine how creations and inventions are used. The subject of moral rights comes up mostly with reference to copyright and neighboring rights, but it might be applied to industrial property as well. If I paint a picture of my mother, and Joe purchases the copyright so that he can sell multiple copies of it, does Joe have the right to reproduce Mom's visage with a mustache superimposed on her face? Can Joe market my portrait of Mom as a dartboard? Once I sold the painting, should I, the artist, have any say? Such moral rights raise the question of what exactly consumers are buying when they purchase forms of intellectual property. Does a work of creativity or innovation have some sort of spirit that the creator or innovator forever has a right to, or is the piece of intellectual property fully commodified, all aspects of it subject to sale? To date, international harmonization on moral

rights has not been achieved, and it continues to be a subject of discussion in international forums.

Plant Breeders' Rights

A more recently commodified form of intellectual property is plant
breeders' rights. Plant breeding has occurred, in all likelihood, since
the beginning of human agriculture. Farmers traditionally saved
seeds from the best, most vigorous crops to plant the next year. Many
people in the developed and developing worlds continue this practice. Many, if not most, farmers depend on saved seeds.

History is full of stories of how plant breeding, saving seeds, and
exchanging seeds serves the common good. Thomas Jefferson is
widely quoted as having said that the "greatest service which can be
rendered any country is to add an useful plant to its culture." Across
the United States, the system of land grant colleges was established
in part to conduct research and produce new varieties of plants and to
breed better livestock for the benefit of farmers. Beginning in the
1960s and 1970s, new public domain plant varieties were developed
by international research centers. The improved rice varieties that were
the foundation of the Green Revolution, for example, were bred in the
mid-1960s at the International Rice Research Institute (IRRI) funded
by the Ford and Rockefeller Foundations.[27] Funding for IRRI's continuing research into creating improved varieties of rice that allow for
sustainable use of natural resources now comes from a combination of
governmental, intergovernmental, and foundation sources.

Despite the continuing efforts by IRRI and other international
research institutes, as well as those of national agricultural research
centers, support for large-scale public research into new plant varieties has dropped. National public expenditures on research and
development (R&D) have slowed, and official development assistance for agriculture dropped precipitously—by 50 percent—between
1987 and 1997. By contrast, *private* investment in agricultural research
and development has increased. Rough estimates cited in a report published by the United Nations Food and Agriculture Organization
demonstrate a shift to private-sector funding of agricultural R&D
(including research into new plant varieties, machinery, methods of
cultivation, and fertilizer, pesticide, and other inputs) in the United
States. In 1960 private-sector agricultural R&D expenditures came
to U.S.$177 million. By 1992, the amount had jumped to U.S.$3.3

billion. To put it differently, by 1992 private sector expenditures on R&D for agriculture in the United States were 27 percent greater than public-sector expenditures. This trend is consistent with those in other industrialized countries; such privatization has resulted in a similar trend in developing countries.[28] We have also seen an increase in public-private partnerships in agricultural R&D. In these mixed approaches and in privatized R&D, intellectual property rights provide incentives to private companies.

The big difference between plant breeders' rights and other intellectual property forms is that the subject of the intellectual property—the plant—is sometimes capable of reproducing. The ease with which some improved plant varieties can spread highlights the problem of excludability and the difficulty of constructing a rule for making genetic information into a private good when the good itself—a potato, let's say—pays no mind to human rules. The question is and will continue to be: What is the right balance between the public's right to information on improved plant strains versus the private actor's right to profit from its expenditures and efforts?[29]

■ Intellectual Property in Other Cultures

These definitions of intellectual property forms and rights have now spread around the world through international agreements and commercial relations. Nevertheless, these are fundamentally Western rules, emerging from medieval Europe and, later, from Industrial Age Europe and North America. Some of the current tensions in international debates about intellectual property, however, arise from contending sets of beliefs about owning creativity and innovation. Many suggest that there is tension between Asian culture and intellectual property. According to the Asian tradition, a person's attitude should be one of humility and attention to the accumulated wisdom of the past. William Alford explains that the Chinese culture understands the past as a shared reservoir. Advances in knowledge belong to society as a whole, not to the individual. Confucius even reinforced this concept of learning and creativity as part of a communal process: "I am a transmitter, rather than an original thinker. I trust and enjoy the teachings of the ancients."[30] Alford points to the history of government control over information production and dissemination as evidence of a social purpose, not an individual purpose, for creativity. In ancient China, when the government granted an exclusive license to someone to produce a calendar or some other written work, the purpose was not to reward that person's ingenuity. Rather, as was the case with Church control over publications during medieval times, the purpose was to preserve the orthodoxy of expression: unofficial publications might be wrong or cut against the authorities' intent, which could be damaging to the public.[31]

Alford argues that this approach to the communal source and social purpose of creativity and innovation coincided with Marxist approaches, which made it much easier for the government of the People's Republic of China (PRC) to oppose Western-style intellectual property rights as antisocialist. The difficulties that the PRC has experienced in adopting and enforcing intellectual property laws—a condition of membership in the World Trade Organization (WTO)—stemmed from this contradiction between Chinese socialist and Western capitalist values. The state's ambivalence toward intellectual property rights, combined with dominant cultural norms, he argues, has meant continuing infringement despite the laws on the books.[32]

Other cultures have articulated rules that govern products of the mind. In Jewish law,[33] for example, the production of knowledge is simultaneously individual (a specific person is credited for a particular insight and for intellectual effort), communal (prior teachers are recognized, as is the social setting in which ideas are produced), and divine (God is the ultimate source of wisdom).[34] The laws protecting what could be considered intellectual property arise primarily not from property rights as understood in Western law but rather from rules protecting the right of the individual to earn a living. For example, under Jewish law rabbinic authorities can provide an author or publisher with a temporary monopoly (an agreement, *haskamah*) that prevents somebody else from coming along and republishing a work. The purpose is to protect the reasonable earnings of the recipient of the *haskamah*. However, because promoting learning by making scholarly works widely available is also a public good, the *haskamah* is of limited duration and often of limited geographic reach.[35]

Western, Chinese, and Jewish laws share a formal character: each of these bodies of law has been codified and written down, which allows easy access to rules and the rationales underlying them. Rules protecting and supporting intellectual efforts and the production of knowledge in indigenous cultures provide a contrast. Even though indigenous cultures have rich stores of creative and innovative goods, the way in which such societies value products of the mind is often overlooked because the rules are not written down. Many indigenous cultures place great value on sharing knowledge rather than owning it. The wealth and aspirations of the individual are secondary to the needs of the community. Valuable knowledge is understood in a much broader sense, encompassing wisdom and know-how, as well as technical expertise.[36]

For organizations tasked with making the global economy work better, the fact that indigenous knowledge cannot be easily commodified is a problem.[37] Siddhartha Prakash, for example, notes the "dilemma" of identifying novelty and nonobviousness for inventions in indigenous cultures because

> in most traditional communities, knowledge is acquired over time and passed on from one generation to the next. Through this process it keeps evolving and changing in character. Therefore it is difficult to establish when such knowledge was actually discovered and when it entered into the public domain.[38]

Even though Prakash clearly makes the case for expanding protection of intellectual property to indigenous knowledge for the benefit of indigenous people, this statement assumes that commodification is normal and normative. This highlights yet another tension: Does it make sense to protect indigenous knowledge by reframing it to fit into intellectual property categories, or is such an approach inherently self-contradictory?

▪ What the Past Tells Us

The history of intellectual property sheds light on the complex and often contradictory policies in place today. The history of the development of rules protecting intellectual property rights explains a good deal about the tension between compensating creativity and increasing the store of creativity and innovation that is available to the public at large. Because the acceptance of property rights for products of the mind is so widely accepted in Western political economy, the need for strong protections might seem self-evident. Yet when we look more closely at property rights from the historical and comparative perspectives, we see that the rights, their purposes, and their breadth are not natural phenomena. Rather, they are socially constructed rules that have developed over time. Technological innovations and spontaneous new ideas continue to challenge the categories, labels, and rights that apply.

■ Notes

1. A press with movable type had been invented in 1041–1049 in China, but because of different historical and cultural circumstances the Chinese press did not commodify the written word. See Ithiel de Sola Pool, *Technologies of Freedom* (Cambridge, MA: Harvard University Press, 1983), p. 12.

2. Edith Tilton Penrose, *The Economics of the International Patent System* (Baltimore: Johns Hopkins University Press, 1951), p. 2 (citation omitted).

3. Ibid.

4. Ibid.

5. Sam Ricketson, *The Berne Convention for the Protection of Literary and Artistic Works: 1886–1986* (London: Centre for Commercial Law Studies, Kluwer, 1987), p. 4. Throughout the case study, I rely heavily on Ricketson's detailed history of international discussions and negotiations surrounding copyright protection.

6. Benjamin Kaplan and Ralph S. Browne Jr., *Cases on Copyright, Unfair Competition, and Other Topics Bearing on the Protection of Literary, Musical, and Artistic Works,* 3rd ed. (Mineoloa, NY: Foundation, 1978), pp. 703–715.

7. World Intellectual Property Organization (WIPO), *General Information* (June 2001 [cited January 25, 2003]); available from www.wipo.int/about-wipo/en/gib.htm. Interest in formalizing these treaties came from the epistemic communities of inventors and writers and publishers. For example, The International Literary and Artistic Association prepared a draft convention that resulted from a conference of authors, scholars, publishers, and others with private economic interests in the protection of copyright. The acceptance of the role played by authors as legitimate resulted in the inclusion of prominent authors and scholars in the official delegations of many countries to the diplomatic conferences. Ricketson, *The Berne Convention for the Protection of Literary and Artistic Works,* pp. 48–80. See Peter Haas, "Introduction: Epistemic Communities and International Policy Coordination," *International Organization* 46, no. 1 (1992), p. 18, for a discussion of differences between epistemic communities, interest groups, and other collectivities.

8. Ricketson, *The Berne Convention for the Protection of Literary and Artistic Works,* pp. 696–97.

9. In fiscal year 2003, planned basic fees for filing start at $380 for a small entity, with multiple claims adding costs. See United States Patent and Trademark Office, Revision of Patent and Trademark Fees for Fiscal Year

2003; Notice of Proposed Rulemaking, 37 *CFR* Parts 1 and 2, May 7, 2002, *Federal Register 67,* No. 88 30634-37.

10. Strategic patenting in the e-commerce sector has created an "avalanche of patenting of software and method-of-doing-business in the USA". Josephine Chinying Lang, "Management of Intellectual Property Rights: Strategic Patenting," *Journal of Intellectual Capital* 2, no. 1 (2001).

11. WIPO *General Information.* Also, see United States Patent and Trademark Office, *Nature of Patents and Patent Rights* [cited August 21, 2003], available from www.uspto.gov/web/offices/pac/doc/general/nature.htm.

12. Dianne Brinson and Mark F. Radcliffe, *An Intellectual Property Law Primer for Multimedia and Web Developers* (1998 [cited July 10, 2002]), available from www.laderapress.com/lib/laderapress/primer.html.

13. Keith Orum, "Trade Secrets Made Simple," *Beverage World,* October 1995.

14. See the conflicts between software companies Avant! and Cadence, both in Santa Clara, California, and between Mentor Graphics Corporation (Wilsonville, Oregon) and Verplex Systems Inc. (Milpitas, California), also software firms. Richard Goering and Brian Fuller, "Criminal Probe, Civil Suit Hit High-Flying IC-CAD Vendor—Police Raid Stuns Avant," *Electronic Engineering Times*, December 11, 1995; and Richard Goering, "Mentor Sues EDA Startup Verplex," *Electronic Engineering Times,* May 29, 2000.

15. Kim Clark, "Noncompete Contracts: Be Loyal or See You in Court, Employers Warn Workers," *US News & World Report,* December 18, 2000.

16. An indicator of this company's concern can be seen on its website. Upon loading the page, the first thing the viewer sees is box containing a statement of the company's intellectual property rights in trademarks, service marks, designs, etc. Rolex Corporation, *Official Rolex Website* [cited August 21, 2003], available from www.rolex.com.

17. CBS News, "Faking It: Counterfeit Drugs Are Hitting the Market; Drug Companies Are Posting Warnings on the Web Sites; Potentially Deadly Fakes Have Turned up in at Least Seven States," (August 1, 2001 [cited September 4, 2001]); available from www.cbsnews.com/now/story/0,1597,304497-412,00.shtml.

18. For the Thai government's response to counterfeit drugs, see Thailand Food and Drug Administration, *English Information* [cited August 21, 2003], available from www.fda.moph.go.th/enginfo.htm.

19. World Health Organization, Counterfeit Drugs—Guidelines for the Development of Methods to Combat Counterfeit Drugs, Essential Drug and Medicine Policy, WHO/EDM/QSM/99.1, 1999, [cited July 11, 2002], available from www.who.int/medicines/library/qsm/who-edm-qsm-99-1/who-edm-qsm-99-1.htm.

20. U.S. Food and Drug Administration, "FDA Alert: Counterfeit-Labeled Similac," *FDA Fact Sheet* (April 5, 1995 [cited July 11, 2002]); available from vm.cfsan.fda.gov/~lrd/tpsimila.html.

21. In some cases, registering the mark is not necessary; simply using something as one's trademark is sufficient. However, the rights accorded a registered mark are more certain.

22. Consorzio del Formaggio Parmigiano-Reggiano, website [cited August 21, 2003], available from www2.parmigiano-reggiano.it/database/parmigianoreggiano/parmigianoreggiano2.nsf/home/$First?OpenDocument.

23. The major exception is an employee of the U.S. government whose scientific research is part of her job. Since the work is being produced as work-for-hire (what she was hired to do), the U.S. government owns it, and the U.S. government does not copyright its written products.

24 . For historical treatments of the development of copyright in law, see Martha Woodmansee and Peter Jaszi, eds., *The Construction of Authorship: Textual Appropriation in Law and Literature* (Durham, NC, and London: Duke University Press, 1994).

25. I probably would have a performance right in my recitation of the poem, so I would be able to prevent you from taping me without my permission.

26. Andrew C. Frank, *The Copyright Crusade II* (Viant Corporation Media and Entertainment, May 21, 2002 [cited July 16, 2002]), available from www.viant.com/pages2/pages/frame_thought_copyright_2.html.

27. IRRI is now one of the sixteen research institutes that comprise the Consultative Group on International Agricultural Research. International Rice Research Institute, website [cited August 21, 2003], available from www.irri.org; and Consultative Group on International Agriculture Research, website, August 14, 2003 [cited August 21, 2003], available from www. cgiar.org.

28. Randy A Hautea, "Agronomic Research and Plant Improvement Programmes in Asia and the Pacific: Overview of Roles, Objectives and Activities" (Manila, Philippines: United Nations Food and Agriculture Organization, July 14, 1999).

29. Margreet H. van den Berg, *The Agricultural Knowledge Infrastructure: Public or Private? An Exploratory Study About Evolving Public and Private Goods and Roles* (Food and Agriculture Organization, Sustainable Development Department, September 9, 2001 [cited August 21, 2003]), available from www.fao.org/sd/2001/KN1103a_en.htm.

30. William P. Alford, *To Steal a Book Is an Elegant Offense: Intellectual Property Law in Chinese Civilization* (Stanford, CA: Stanford University Press, 1995), p. 25, quoting the slightly different translation of Book 7, Chapter 1 of the Analects of Confucius. This translation is from Confucius, *The Analects* (2003 [cited August 21, 2003]), available from www.hm.tyg.jp/~acmuller/contao/analects.htm.

31. Alford, *To Steal a Book Is an Elegant Offense.*

32. Ibid., pp. 56–94.

33. It is important to differentiate between religious Jewish law that relates to intellectual property and Israeli law, which has its origins in the British laws of Mandatory Palestine.

34. For this reason, the traditional blessing to be recited upon seeing a person of great learning (religious or secular) is: Blessed are You, Lord our God, who gives a portion of His wisdom to humans. The connection to the divine also explains why the literal meaning of the Hebrew term for intellectual property would be "spiritual acquisition" (*kinyan ruchani*).

35. Although some refer to this right as a property right, the right to a livelihood seems distinct from a modern Western right to property. A discussion of the right to a livelihood and its connection to copyright can be found in Meir Tamari, *With All Your Possessions: Jewish Ethics and Economic Life* (New York: Free Press, 1987), pp. 106–110. Ironically, the prohibition against taking away someone's livelihood has also been used by some rabbinic authorities to prohibit the use of an innovation—a matzah-making machine—on the grounds that it would take away the jobs of the poor people who were employed in the baking of matzah (Tamari, *With All Your Possessions,* p. 109). On copyright and Jewish law, see also Samuel J. Petuchowski, "Toward a Conceptual Basis for the Protection of Literary Product in a Post-Printing Era: Precedents in Jewish Law," *University of Baltimore Intellectual Property Law Journal* 3 (1994); and Israel Schneider, "Jewish Law and Copyright," *Journal of Halacha and Contemporary Society* 21 [cited February 19, 2004], available from www.jlaw.com/Articles/copyright1.html.

36. Raymond Obomsawin, "Indigenous Knowledge and Sustainable Development," *Development Express* [Canadian International Development Agency—Policy Branch] 3 (2000–2001).

37. Graham Dutfield, "The Public and Private Domains: Intellectual Property Rights in Traditional Knowledge," *Science Communication* 21, no. 3 (2000).

38. Siddhartha Prakash, "Indigenous Knowledge and Intellectual Property Rights," in *IK Notes,* No. 19 (2000).

3

The Global Governance
of Intellectual Property

One important conclusion from the previous chapter is that intellectual property has become normal, a generally uncontested feature of modern life. This is especially so in the member countries of the Organization for Economic Cooperation and Development (OECD), which have a longer tradition of free-market economies. The demands of the global marketplace, along with the pressures exerted by OECD countries on the rest of the world, have thus led to a more general global acceptance of intellectual property. The network of international treaties, as well as domestic laws, create an international regime for protecting intellectual property rights, and it seems that every new innovation begets a new treaty.[1] International organizations—the World Intellectual Property Organization (WIPO), the International Union for the Protection of Varieties of Plants (UPOV, after the French acronym), and the World Trade Organization (WTO)—provide institutional homes for these regimes by encouraging compliance with the regime rules and providing some means for settling disputes between countries on issues related to intellectual property. These organizations are simultaneously part of the structure in which the international intellectual property regime exists and agents within the global political economy working to promote the regime. What do these organizations do, and how do they promote the intellectual property regime? What are the rules, codified in treaties, that make up the substance of the regime?

47

■ The World Intellectual Property Organization

The World Intellectual Property Organization has its origins in the Swiss bureaux that administered the first intellectual property treaties. Today, as an international organization attached to the United Nations, it is tasked with encouraging states to adopt and enforce laws protecting intellectual property. Embedded in the mandate of the organization is the assumption that

> international protection acts as a spur to human creativity, pushing forward the boundaries of science and technology and enriching the world of literature and the arts. By providing a stable environment for the marketing of intellectual property products, it also oils the wheels of international trade.[2]

Thus the purpose of global coordination of intellectual property rights is instrumental; it is meant to fulfill the social and economic purposes of encouraging creativity and innovation that will, in theory, enable more commerce. This line of argument emerges directly from nineteenth-century concerns about the connection between the theft of intellectual property and international trade. In today's global economy, the necessity of international coordination is even more pressing because of advances in communications and increases in international exchange.

WIPO's tasks include working to

- harmonize intellectual property legislation and procedures; provide services for international applications for industrial property rights;
- exchange intellectual property information;
- provide legal and technical assistance to developing and other countries;
- facilitate the resolution of private intellectual property disputes; and
- marshal information technology as a tool for storing, accessing, and using valuable intellectual property information.[3]

WIPO serves as the home institution for several treaties on intellectual property. One of the most important functions of the WIPO secretariat is to provide expert guidance for drafting new treaties or for revising existing ones. Having input in the drafting process means it has an important voice in the future direction of intellectual property protection. However, WIPO is not charged with determining the right balance among competing interests. Thus establishing intellectual property rights strong enough to motivate creators and innovators without negatively effecting the public good is not among its objectives.

WIPO facilitates the simultaneous application for rights in multiple countries and serves as a depository for marks and designs. In this way, the organization provides some of the services that have traditionally been under the control of national governments. By disseminating information about intellectual property law and by training officials of developing countries in how to administer intellectual property rules, WIPO extends its vision of intellectual protection beyond the OECD countries and their traditionally strong intellectual property regimes. Since 1995, WIPO's role has shifted to assisting the World Trade Organization with the implementation of the Trade Related Aspects of Intellectual Property (TRIPS) provisions of the General Agreement on Tariffs and Trade (GATT).

In recent years, WIPO has moved into more direct contact with private actors—firms, for the most part—in addition to states. WIPO's Arbitration and Mediation Center specializes in cross-border intellectual property disputes and helps private parties resolve their differences. WIPO's experts arbitrate many of the Internet domain name disputes under the Uniform Domain Name Dispute Resolution Policy (UDRP).

WIPO's role may expand if more kinds of communal goods are assigned to the category of property. Exploratory studies by WIPO have begun to examine the relationship between intellectual property and genetic resources, traditional knowledge, and folklore. The difficulty with assigning intellectual property rights to such products is that the identity of the rights holder is unclear. Current intellectual property rules assume that a person (whether a human being or a corporation) is the owner of intellectual property by virtue of being *the* creator/innovator. In the case of genetic resources, traditional knowledge, and folklore, however, it is often impossible to identify creators or innovators. If ownership is ascribed to a community or a tribe, the problem of determining who qualifies as a member remains. Also unresolved is the question of whether national governments have any rights. Appropriate protection for these kinds of communal products of the mind has yet to be sorted out.

Traditionally, intellectual property treaties under WIPO were divided into industrial property treaties and literary property treaties.

Advances in technology have blurred the boundaries between copy-righted literary property versus patented industrial property. Accordingly, WIPO sorts its twenty-two intellectual property treaties into three categories: *intellectual property protection treaties, global protection system treaties,* and *classification treaties.*[4] Below, I discuss each category; within the categories, I have ordered the treaties chronologically.

Intellectual Property Protection Treaties

Two late-nineteenth-century treaties mark the beginning of international coordination of intellectual property rules: the Paris Convention for the Protection of Industrial Property (1883), and the Berne Convention for the Protection of Literary and Artistic Works (1886). Other intellectual property treaties supplement these two.

The Paris Convention. An international exposition of inventions held in Vienna in 1873 was the impetus for this major international agreement. As noted in Chapter 2, the potential exhibitors refused to attend without the guarantee that no one would be able to steal their ideas, inventions, trademarks, or industrial designs. At the time, Austria enacted a special law for the duration of the exhibition. In addition, an international congress on patent reform was convened. Individuals with an interest in promoting international protection of patent rights attended the congress, and they followed up with another in Paris in 1878. The participants at the 1878 congress prevailed upon the French government to invite other countries to a diplomatic conference, which eventually met in 1883. The end result was the first version of multilateral patent protection, the Paris Convention of 1883, which created the Paris Union for the Protection of Industrial Property, meaning inventions, trademarks, and industrial designs.[5] As with most international agreements, the Paris Convention saw many revisions;[6] member countries are bound by the latest version to which they have acceded (most countries are party to the Stockholm Act of 1967).

Rights are protected according to rules determining national treatment and priority. *National treatment* requires governments to grant foreign individuals and firms the same rights to protection of industrial property as those enjoyed by its own citizens. From the first iteration of the Paris Convention, the rule of national treatment has prevailed over the alternatively proposed rule of reciprocity. (According to the rule of reciprocity, if State B grants more favorable intellectual property protection than State A, then State A would have to provide more favorable intellectual property protection to a national of State B than to its own citizens.[7])

The *right of priority* affects the determination of the filing date. If a patent holder in one member country files for protection within the allowed time window, the date of filing (which is critical for claims under a first-to-file system) corresponds to the date the patent holder applied in the initial country. The right of priority does not, however, force countries to accept the claims and award a patent.

Despite the way in which these rules help countries coordinate patenting, the Paris Union also stipulates the *independence of patents,* meaning that each member country determines whether an invention is or is not granted a patent. Each country's grant of a patent is made independently of decisions made by other countries. Expiration, denial, or revocation of a patent in one member country has no effect on the patent's validity in other countries.

Though patents can serve to reward and encourage innovation, they are also subject to abuse and can even stifle innovative efforts and competition. Consider the problem of a patent an inventor obtains for an invention that she chooses not to bring to market but instead allows to hide below the surface of the industry's attention. If she later uses this so-called "submarine patent" as a legal weapon against a subsequent inventor of a similar product, she can torpedo his attempts to acquire a patent or sue for infringement.

To prevent such negative outcomes, some countries implement requirements for *working the patent.* Under the Paris Convention, states are allowed to stipulate that failure to work the patent—either by producing in the country or by importing into the country—will result in compulsory licensing. Put simply, the patent holder is forced to license the technology to a firm willing to produce or to otherwise fulfill the conditions of working the patent. However, the use of compulsory licensing to protect the public interest is not unlimited. Patent holders have at least four years from the date of filing their application (or three years from the date of receiving the patent) to gear up; they must (1) produce the product in the country, or (2) import the product into that country from another Paris Union member state. An extension must be granted if obstacles prevented the patent holder from working the patent sooner. Furthermore, if the patent holder is forced to agree to a compulsory license, the license must be nonexclusive, that is, the patent holder must be allowed to license the invention to more than one firm.

The Paris Convention also allows for compulsory licensing in the public interest under limited conditions. The United States used this rule in the wake of the domestic anthrax attacks following September 11 when it threatened to require Bayer Pharmaceuticals to license Cipro, an antibiotic known to be effective against anthrax, to other pharmaceutical manufacturers if Bayer did not reduce the price of its product.

Trademarks also fall under the jurisdiction of the Paris Convention. Some trademark provisions parallel those for patents. For example, countries are allowed, under limits, to require that trademarks actually be used. The convention requires that governments permit trademark holders adequate time to introduce their trademark into the country and take into consideration any mitigating factors that would slow down that process. As with patents, the convention requires a grace period for fees, protection of trademarks shown at international exhibitions, and the independence of marks.

Trademarks, again like patents, are independent, and one country's decision whether to grant trademark protection does not necessarily affect another. There is a slight difference, however. Among the countries of the Paris Union, after the initial registration of the patent in the country of origin, other countries can only choose to register the patent—or not—"as is." In other words, they cannot decide that one component of the mark is protected while another is not.[8]

The Paris Convention also contains a special provision protecting well-known trademarks. Let's say that Company A owns a well-known mark registered in the country where it is headquartered (Country A). Company B in Country B wants to register the same mark or one easily confused with that of Company A. Even though Company A has not registered its mark in Country B, Company A has the right to block registration of the conflicting trademark. If Country B has gone ahead and registered Company's B's trademark and Company A finds out about it after the fact, Company A can have Company B's trademark cancelled. (Under the Paris Convention, countries can specify that companies have a limited number of years—at least five—to contest conflicting trademarks. Trademarks registered in bad faith may be contested at any time.)

Industrial designs under the Paris Convention must be protected, but each country is free to implement protection as it chooses. In the United States, the U.S. Patent and Trademark Office (PTO) issues *design patents* for industrial designs, as well as *utility patents* for inventions.

Among the other rules of the Paris Convention are provisions protecting service marks and collective marks that distinguish groups of products (e.g., a mark held by the Better Business Bureau that companies are authorized to display if they meet certain criteria). Trade names, whether or not they are protected by a registered trademark, must also receive protection; such protection must not be dependent on having registered the name. This treaty protects the official symbols of governments and international organizations, as well as geographic indications (which are also covered in other treaties). Member countries must provide protection against unfair competition as well. The other provisions of the Paris Convention address the technical details of administering the convention and organizing and managing the Paris Union.

The Berne Convention. The Berne Convention for the Protection of Literary and Artistic Works of 1886 was launched in the same political, social, and economic setting as the Paris Convention. Prior to the Berne Convention, the international coordination of copyright was accomplished through bilateral treaties.[9] In the absence of such treaties, governments might not allow foreigners to apply for copyrights and might not honor copyrights awarded to foreigners by other countries. Pirating copyrighted works was a real problem during the nineteenth century as it eroded the earning power of many authors who received no remuneration from the sale of unauthorized copies of their original works.[10] Even authors who were protected by copyrights suffered because their publications were then in competition with cheap copies of famous authors' works. Nevertheless, such reciprocal treaties were confusing and hard to implement.

Author Victor Hugo led an effort by authors and publishers, organized as the International Literary Association, to convince governments that it was time for an international conference on copyright. The organization convinced the president of the Swiss Federal Council to invite other countries to a diplomatic conference in Berne, which was held September 8–19, 1884. This marked the first time that governmental representatives worked on a draft agreement. After further negotiations during the next two years, the Berne Convention was finally signed on September 9, 1886, by Belgium, France, Germany, Great Britain, Haiti, Italy, Liberia, Spain, Switzerland, and Tunis. The United States was not among the signatories.[11] Indeed, the United States did not join the Berne Union until 1989.[12]

The Berne Convention has seen several revisions (again, member states are bound by the most recent version that the country has ratified). Unlike some other treaties, earlier versions of the Berne Convention remained open for ratification even after another revision had been completed. Of the 149 parties to the convention, thirteen adhere to prior versions.[13]

The Berne Convention obligates countries to protect the rights of authors and artists who have produced any original work "in the literary, scientific, or artistic domains, whatever may be the mode or form of its expression."[14] Members of the Berne Union must adhere to the rules of national treatment, automatic protection, and independence of protection. As in the case of the Paris Convention, the Berne Convention's rule on *national treatment* (not reciprocity) requires governments to protect nonnationals and nationals alike. The requirement of *automatic protection* means that states cannot require artists and authors to go through an application or registration process in order to obtain the copyright. Unlike patents and trademarks, however, copyright is not subjected to an examination process. *Independence of protection* comes into play because governments may have different criteria for what can and cannot be copyrighted. For example, a folkloric work might be copyrightable in one country but not in another. Under the rules for independence of protection and national treatment, member states must treat all works equally regardless of their country of origin.

The Berne Convention also establishes categories of works that governments must protect, and it specifies the categories for which governments have discretion. Moreover, the convention specifies the minimum standards of protection: copyright must include the exclusive right to translation; to reproduce the work in any format, including a sound recording; to broadcast the work by loudspeaker, by radio or television, or by any other technology; to recite the work in public; to alter the work; and to make the work into a movie.

The Berne Convention protects the economic rights and the moral rights of the author/artist. *Moral rights* refer to the unalienable right of the author to be recognized as the author and to prevent the work from being distorted or mutilated in any way. Since the author's reputation rests on the integrity of the work, protecting moral rights satisfies the intangible, emotional connection between the author and the work, as well as the legitimate material interests every author has in protecting her reputation.[15]

The Berne Convention generally requires that copyrights last at least for the life of the author plus fifty years, though different rules may apply to some categories of works (e.g., movies and photographs). Limitations of copyright protection include the acceptance of fair use and the right of governments to require compulsory licensing for broadcasting a work or recording music. The 1971 Appendix to the Paris Act of the Berne Convention limits the rights of copyright holders by providing special rights to developing countries in the interest of encouraging the spread of knowledge. Developing countries may force compulsory licensing of a translation of a protected work if, after the specified period, the work has not been translated into the language of the country. Alternatively, the developing country may choose to reserve the right to limit the term of copyright with respect to translation to ten years. Developing countries may also have special rights to reproduce a work if it is not made available in the country at the usual price charged for such works.

Other WIPO intellectual property protection treaties. The other treaties falling into the WIPO's category of intellectual property protection include:

- Madrid Agreement for the Repression of False or Deceptive Indication of Source on Goods (1891);[16]
- Rome Convention for the Protection of Performers, Producers of Phonograms [recordings], and Broadcasting Organizations (1961);[17]
- Phonograms Convention (1971);
- Satellites Convention (1971);
- Convention Relating to the Distribution of Program-Carrying Signals Transmitted by Satellite (1974);
- Nairobi Treaty on the Protection of the Olympic Symbol (1981);[18]
- Trademark Law Treaty (1994);[19]
- WIPO Copyright Treaty (1996);
- WIPO Performances and Phonograms Treaty (1996); and
- Patent Law Treaty (2000).[20]

Several of these agreements fill in the gaps in intellectual property protection arising from the social effects of technology. The advent of technologies that record performances or broadcasts led to the Rome Convention, which clarifies that broadcasts of performances, either live or recorded, are also to be protected. (In other words, the rule defines broadcasts as property.) Similarly, the introduction of satellites and their use for transmitting encoded signals spurred the drafting of two other conventions.

More recently, the WIPO Copyright Treaty and the WIPO Performances and Phonograms Treaty, both signed in 1996, address the challenges posed by the Internet and related digital technologies. Building on the provisions of the Berne Convention and the Rome Convention, these treaties revisit the protection of copyright in light of technological advances. They clarify that reproducing a work in digital form and storing it on a hard drive or other form of computer memory is, indeed, reproduction. Originally, the WIPO Copyright Treaty stipulated that even temporary copies of a work (such as those automatically performed on a computer network) would have been considered a violation of copyright. Such an expansive view of copying would have placed severe limits on the development of the Internet for commerce and communications, as even browsing could be considered a violation of copyright.[21] At the urging of network and Internet site operators and other interest groups such as the Digital Future Coalition, this provision was demoted to a declaration rather than a binding rule.[22] Also, though the treaties contain provisions prohibiting users from circumventing technological measures put in place to prevent illicit copying, member states are free to craft legislation toward that end as they choose.[23]

Global Protection System Treaties

Five WIPO treaties fall into the category of global protection system treaties. WIPO provides an administrative function for the signatories to these treaties by serving as the office where individual applications and filings can be made.[24]

- Madrid Agreement Concerning the International Registration of Marks and the Protocol Relating to the Madrid Agreement (1891 and 1989, respectively);[25]
- Hague Agreement on the International Deposit of Industrial Design (1925 and 1999);[26]

- Lisbon Agreement for the protection of Appellations of Origin and their International Registration (1958);[27]
- Patent Cooperation Treaty (1970);[28] and
- Budapest Treaty on the International Recognition of the Deposit of Microorganisms for the Purposes of Patent Protection (1977).[29]

These are prosaic, administrative treaties. Nevertheless, they are important for considering how a web of interconnected treaties constitutes a system of global governance for intellectual property. These treaties incorporate rules detailing how the patent and trademark process is to be conducted. In doing so, power relations are often reinforced, with some countries or firms gaining more than others from routinized practices. Consider, for instance, two examples.

First, the Budapest Treaty is an example of how technological and scientific change drive changes in the domestic and global governance of intellectual property, with global regulation generally following domestic. Early inventors and their governments, therefore, have the first-comer advantage in establishing global rules. In 1955, a bacterium, *Streptomyces sparsogenes var. sparsogenes,* was used in a new process for producing antibiotic compounds. In order to make proper disclosure of the invention and receive a U.S. patent for the process, the applicants deposited a sample of the bacteria with the Department of Agriculture.[30] Special arrangements had to be made to keep the information secret until the patent was granted.

With advances in bioengineering and decisions in the United States and other countries to allow the patenting of specially bred or genetically altered microorganisms, cases such as this have come up with increasing frequency. A routinized and coordinated way of handling deposits of microorganisms was needed because of the practical difficulties that would be associated with making deposits of microorganisms in every country in which an inventor applied for patent protection. To this end, the Budapest Treaty allows the deposit of a microorganism with one of the approved depository authorities to suffice for meeting all requirements for patent applications in any Paris Union member country. The two depositories in the United States hold more than 50 percent of the world's deposits, as of the end of 1999.[31]

Second, the Lisbon Agreement highlights the importance of locality within a globalized market. With the Lisbon Agreement, consumers the world over can be confident that the bordeaux wine they were drinking was, in fact, from vineyards in the region of Bordeaux, France. The treaty allows producers who are nationals of or domiciled in signatory countries to apply for international registration and protection of appellations of origin, as long as the country of origin has granted such protection. Geographic indications are eligible for protection if the product gains its special character because of the human and natural characteristics of the place where it is produced.[32]

Although traditionally it has been producers in advanced countries who have made claims of intellectual property rights in geographic indications, there may be radical uses for the Lisbon Agreement and associated treaties. Instead of reinforcing existing power hierarchies (in which the advantages are skewed toward the haves rather than the have-nots), these treaties might be employed to extend intellectual property rights to communities who share traditional knowledge. An indigenous group may be able to take advantage of the provisions protecting geographic indications to prevent others from commercializing traditional knowledge without the community's consent.[33] Geographic indications, unlike patents, do not require novelty or the identification of an inventor. All that is required is a valid claim that the uniqueness of the local conditions imbues the product with special characteristics.

Classification Treaties

The final set of treaties administered by WIPO are even more focused on administrative details than the global protection system treaties. These agreements address the question of how to classify different intellectual property products so that examining authorities can locate prior art or prior registrations. These treaties specify classes and provide a list of each possible element and the class to which it is assigned.

- Nice Agreement Concerning the International Classification of Goods and Services for the Purposes of the Registration of Marks (1957);[34]
- Locarno Agreement Establishing an International Classification for Industrial Designs (1968);[35]
- Strasbourg Agreement Concerning the International Patent Classification (1971);[36] and
- Vienna Agreement Establishing an International Classification of the Figurative Elements of Marks (1973).[37]

Considering WIPO Treaties

WIPO and WIPO treaties, especially the Paris Convention and Berne Convention, have been important to the creation of a system of global governance for intellectual property despite the inherent weaknesses of the organization. WIPO, the treaties it administers, and its other operations are important because they institutionalize rules representing the interests of the dominant parties in the global trading system. These interests are also institutionalized by the system for protection of intellectual property rights in plants that, though not under the aegis of WIPO, is administered by WIPO.

■ The International Union for the Protection of New Varieties of Plants

The International Union for the Protection of New Varieties of Plants is closely associated with WIPO. The two organizations share a building and a chief executive (the director-general of WIPO is also the secretary-general of UPOV), and UPOV receives support services from the WIPO secretariat. UPOV administers the International Convention for the Protection of New Varieties of Plants (1961),[38] which sets out the intellectual property rights of breeders in the new varieties of plants they breed. UPOV's importance resides primarily in its relationship to the TRIPS Agreement (Trade Related Aspects of Intellectual Property; see below), which requires UPOV-based intellectual property protection standards for plant varieties.

Under UPOV, to receive protection, new plant varieties must be:

• distinct from existing, commonly known varieties;
• sufficiently uniform;
• stable; and
• new in the sense that they must not have been commercialized prior to certain dates established by reference to the date of the application for protection.[39]

Governments are required to put a system into place for evaluating claims of plant breeders' rights and assigning protection qualifying new plant varieties. As with the Paris and Berne Conventions, the UPOV Convention also requires national treatment and assigns a right of priority (the date of filing for protection in the first country is used as the date of filing in subsequent applications in other countries).

Three compulsory exceptions limit the protections. The UPOV Convention allows use of otherwise protected plant material for private, noncommercial purposes, for experimental purposes, and for breeding or exploiting other varieties.[40] However, the most recent revision of the agreement (1991) strengthened intellectual property rights, extending the scope of protection by requiring that the creation, use, or selling of any kind of propagating material (e.g., seeds, cuttings, etc.) requires permission from the breeder. Even though the UPOV Convention allows states to decide whether to continue allowing framers the privilege of saving seeds for planting in the next season, the wording of the text and the formal recommendation associated with it clearly prefers a strong breeder's right to the farmer's privilege. Moreover, the discussions around the 1991 revision concluded that "the breeder's right extends to harvested material of the protected variety and even to products produced by processing the harvested material" if the products were produced by using unauthorized propagation of the protected variety.[41]

The 1991 revisions also limit the extent to which people can use protected material for the breeding or exploiting of other varieties by carving out protection for *essentially derived varieties*. Under prior versions of the convention, a farmer or breeder who purchased protected varieties had a right to use that variety to create a new variety. Although that remains the case, the new variety must be substantially different from the protected variety. The 1991 text's reference to essentially derived varieties draws the scope of acceptable efforts much more narrowly. According to UPOV documents, the prohibition against essentially derived varieties is necessary to prevent someone from receiving protection for a minor variation of a plant variety. In describing the need for this rule, a UPOV document states:

> Under the 1978 Act, any protected variety may be freely used as a source of initial variation to develop further varieties and any such variety may itself be protected and exploited without any obligation on the part of its breeder and users towards the breeder of the variety which was used as a source of initial variation. These rules have with certain exceptions worked well in practice and have been reaffirmed in the 1991 Act. However, the rules did not prevent a person finding a mutation within a plant variety (such mutations are quite frequent in some species) or select some other minor variant from within a variety, from claiming protection for the mutant or variant with no authorization from or recognition of the contribution to the final result of the original breeder. The lack of recognition

of the contribution of the original breeder in such circumstances was generally considered to be unfair. Modern biotechnology has greatly increased the likelihood of such unfairness; it may take 15 years to develop a new variety but a mere three months to modify it by adding a gene in the laboratory.[42]

As with many other conventions, some states have not signed and ratified newer versions of the UPOV Convention. States that have ratified the 1978 UPOV Convention but not the 1991 revision are only bound by the 1978 rules. Nevertheless, the 1991 revisions have led to controversy over the appropriate balance of the intellectual property rights of plant breeders and the farmers' traditional practice of saving seeds. The concern is particularly acute in WTO member countries, which are now obligated to join UPOV or to create their own form of plant variety protection.[43]

▪ The World Trade Organization

The World Trade Organization is the other major international organization that deals directly with intellectual property. Indeed, the WTO, which has the ability to enforce rules by authorizing trade sanctions against violators, is much more powerful than the WIPO. However, intellectual property concerns are only a recent addition to global negotiations on trade. Not until 1986, with the beginning of the Uruguay Round trade negotiations of the GATT, was intellectual property on the agenda.[44] The OECD countries insisted that intellectual property be included in the Uruguay Round because they understood the rising value of their trade in intellectual property products such as pharmaceuticals and movies. The intellectual property–rich countries saw a need for making protection of intellectual property rights stronger and more universal. The signing of the 1994 GATT revision at Marrakesh led to the Agreement on the Trade Related Aspects of Intellectual Property, as well as the creation of the WTO (as of January 1995), along with improved market access for goods and services.[45]

TRIPS, WIPO Treaties, and UPOV

TRIPS plays an exceptionally important role in constituting the current international regime for intellectual property because of the

WTO's global coverage. The separate WIPO treaties, in the absence of TRIPS, obligated only those countries that had ratified the treaties. For other countries, the treaties were only soft law—that is, strongly recommended rules rather than binding rules. By incorporating key rules from the WIPO treaties and UPOV, TRIPS extends the reach of the intellectual property protection rules to all WTO member states. Moreover, by bundling intellectual property rules into the new GATT, member states could take advantage of the WTO's dispute resolution mechanism, which allows retaliation (e.g., countervailing tariffs) against countries found to be in violation of treaty rules. Because of the expense and technical difficulties associated with establishing a working system for protecting intellectual property rights, developing countries were allowed a grace period for implementing the new rules (five years for developing countries, eleven for the least developed countries; developing countries may take up to ten years to implement protection for previously unprotected products).

In all, TRIPS covers copyright and related rights, registered marks, geographical indications (including appellations of origin), industrial designs, patents (including the protection of new varieties of plants), integrated circuit layouts, trade secrets, and test data. To enforce these rules, TRIPS requires states to use WTO procedures to settle international disputes on intellectual property issues. In these procedures, a panel of experts (generally economists) examines a complaint to see if a government's policies violate the rules of the WTO. If the complaint is determined to be valid, the offending country must change its policies. If the offending country does not comply, then the WTO can authorize the plaintiff country to impose trade sanctions to counterbalance the effects of the offending policies.

Some TRIPS rules reinforce protections conferred by WIPO treaties and then blend them with WTO rules. TRIPS requires that each member state of the WTO have minimum standards in place for the protection for intellectual property. Countries must abide by national treatment rules, as well as most-favored-nation (MFN) rules (a WTO rule that forbids an importing country from discriminating between importing countries for the purpose of trade policy). States are prohibited from using procedural difficulties in obtaining intellectual property protection as a form of nontariff barrier to trade. Although technology transfer is identified as a fundamental GATT rule, arguably on par with national treatment and MFN treatment, no specific provision in TRIPS enforces technology transfer. Instead,

TRIPS supporters assume that technology transfer is a natural consequence of intellectual property rights protection.

Other TRIPS Rules

Other TRIPS rules expand intellectual property rights beyond what is covered in the WIPO treaties and UPOV.

Trade secrets and test data. Trade secrets and test data are not protected under any of the WIPO treaties, except indirectly under the Paris Convention's prohibition of unfair competition. Countries wishing to be members of the WTO must agree to all these provisions.

Biological products. Although TRIPS does not require states to patent animals, it does require protection for microorganisms and plant varieties. Governments must make microorganisms eligible for patent protection. New plant varieties must be eligible for protection that is at least as strong as the provisions of the UPOV Convention.

Geographical indications. TRIPS increases the strength of the protections of geographic indications established through the Madrid and Lisbon Agreements by adding special provisions for wine and spirits. Many have noted that wine and spirits are produced in the advanced industrialized countries (e.g., Scotch Whiskey), whereas the kinds of products produced in developing countries (e.g., basmati rice) do not have special protection.

Integrated circuit designs. The 1989 WIPO Treaty on Intellectual Property in Respect of Integrated Circuits (the Washington Treaty) essentially became a part of the TRIPS provisions even though it never went into effect under the auspices of WIPO. These provisions solve a problem presented by integrated circuit designs (also called mask works). An *integrated circuit design* is essentially a template that is used to etch the desired pattern into a silicon wafer, an essential step in the fabrication of a semiconductor chip. Small alterations in the template can create important changes in the quality and function of the resulting chip. So what is an integrated circuit when considered from an intellectual property perspective? Neither copyright protection nor patent protection seems to apply because an integrated circuit design falls somewhere between an invention and an artistic work. Despite the value of these designs within the computer industry, finding the appropriate legal formulation proved difficult. The Washington Treaty was to provide sui generis (unique) protection for this new form of intellectual property. Though the Washington Treaty never went into effect as a freestanding treaty, its provisions were copied into TRIPS and strengthened. For example, TRIPS requires that all WTO members protect integrated circuit designs for at least ten years.

Criminal penalties. Member states must enforce intellectual property rights through civil and administrative procedures and remedies, as well as criminal procedures in the case of intentional violations. In other words, violation of intellectual property rights must be ensconced in the law as a criminal as well as a civil offense.

TRIPS serves the interests of the United States and other advanced industrialized countries, but is stronger, harmonized protection of intellectual property a good thing? Is it more efficient or better for social welfare? Although better intellectual property protection would help sellers of intellectual property–laden goods and services in developed countries, it would, many argue, have devastating effects on the developing world.[46] Intellectual property protection puts an unacceptable price tag on the transfer of technology, which would result in making it harder for disadvantaged countries to develop. Moreover, countries had differing ethical standards on what ought to be protected. India, for example, did not allow product patents for pharmaceuticals, foods, or agrochemicals because such patents would deny people access to what they needed for food and health.[47] For all the increased efficiency promised by TRIPS, changes that can lead to increased standards of living for many, the net effects on developing and least developed countries are not as clear.

■ Is the Global Governance of Intellectual Property Working?

WIPO, UPOV, WTO, and their associated treaties provide a sturdy legal framework for the global intellectual property regime. Though specific rules continue to be contested, it appears that the trend is to strengthen intellectual property rights, perhaps at the expense of public access to new knowledge. Supporters of strong intellectual property rights, however, claim that the social benefit from incentives to innovate is much greater than any loss due to increased commodification of knowledge as property. As Chapter 4 illustrates, these two opposing contentions play important roles in several current global debates on intellectual property policy.

■ Notes

1. References to the literature on international regimes are provided in chapter 1, note 47.

2. World Intellectual Property Organization (WIPO), *General Information* (June 2001 [cited January 25, 2003]); available from www.wipo.int/about-wipo/en/gib.htm.

3. Ibid.

4. Information on the WIPO treaties comes from World Intellectual Property Organization, *WIPO Intellectual Property Handbook: Policy, Law and Use,* Pub. 489 (E) (Geneva, Switzerland, 2001), unless I provide a citation of an alternate source. Most of the information can be found in chapter 5 of the *Handbook.* I give page citations only where I quote material or paraphrase closely. Text of the WIPO-administered treaties can be found by following the links at World Intellectual Property Organization, *Treaty and Contracting Parties* [cited July 31, 2002], available from www.wipo.int/treaties/index.html.

5. The original members of the Paris Union were Belgium, Brazil, El Salvador, France, Guatemala, Italy, the Netherlands, Portugal, Serbia, Spain, Switzerland, Great Britain, Tunisia, and Ecuador. The United States became a member in 1887. B. Zorina Khan, "Intellectual Property and Economic Development: Lessons from American and European History," Study Paper 1a, Commission on Intellectual Property Rights [cited July 26, 2002], available from www.iprcommission.org/documents/Khan_study.pdf.

6. The Paris Convention was revised in 1900 (Brussels—this version is no longer in force), 1911 (Washington—also no longer in force), 1925 (the Hague), 1930 (Rome), 1958 (Lisbon), and 1967 (Stockholm).

7. On the tension between reciprocity and other fundamental rules in the related regime of international trade, see Carolyn Rhodes, "Reciprocity in Trade: The Utility of a Bargaining Strategy," *International Organization* 43, no. 2 (1989).

8. This is referred to as the *telle quelle* principle, from the French "as is." The convention does specify exceptions to the *telle quelle* principle, however. WIPO, *WIPO Intellectual Property Handbook.*

9. Brander Matthews, "The Evolution of Copyright," *Political Science Quarterly* 5, no. 4 (1890).

10. Max M Kampelman, "The United States and International Copyright," *American Journal of International Law* 41, no. 2 (1947): 413. Kampelman notes, for example, that Harriet Beecher Stowe is reported to have earned no

money at all on the more than half-million copies of *Uncle Tom's Cabin* that were sold in the first year of its publication.

11. Ibid.

12. WIPO, "Parties to the Berne Convention for the Protection of Literary and Artistic Works: Berne Convention for the Protection of Literary and Artistic Works," April 2002 [cited July 30, 2002], available from www.wipo.org/treaties/documents/english/word/e-berne.doc.

13. Ibid.

14. WIPO, *WIPO Intellectual Property Handbook.*

15. The inclusion of moral rights in the convention marks the acceptance of continental intellectual property rules over the Anglo-American approach, which did not consider moral rights.

16. The Madrid Agreement, revised in 1911, 1925, 1934, and 1958, requires signatory countries to protect the interests of consumers by requiring that markings on goods clearly indicate their place of origin.

17. Some countries, notably those following the continental tradition of intellectual property law, do not consider performances, whether recorded or broadcast, subject to copyright protection as such. The Rome Convention provides the protection by establishing protection floors: a twenty-year protection period from the time of the performance or its fixing in a phonogram; guarantees that performers cannot be forced to broadcast a live performance, to record a performance, or to allow copies of an unapproved recording of the performance to be made; and determination by producers of phonograms about whether the phonogram can be copied. Article 12 of the convention requires that the person replaying the recording to the public pay an "equitable" fee, though states may put restrictions on this. WIPO, *WIPO Intellectual Property Handbook.* The United States is not a signatory to this convention; instead, it includes rights to recordings of performances under the umbrella of copyright law. Subcommittee on Commerce House Committee on Energy and Commerce, Consumer Protection, and Competitiveness. Response to Questions Posed by Cardiss Collins, Chairwoman, Prepared by Harry F. Manbeck Jr., Assistant Secretary and Commissioner of Patents and Trademarks, 102d Cong., 2d sess., August 4 1992. House Report 102-780 Part 1.

18. The 1981 Nairobi Treaty on the Protection of the Olympic Symbol is unusual because it is an entire treaty that protects what is essentially a single mark. Neither the United Kingdom nor the United States are signatories to this treaty, but both have laws in place protecting the Olympic symbol: the Olympic Symbol, Etc., Act of 1995 and the Amateur Sports Act of 1978, respectively. Edward Bragiel, "Protection Only Goes So Far for Olympic Symbols," *The Times* (London), September 19, 2000; and David Usborne, "Olympics Crackdown on Sponsorship Parasites," *The Independent* (London), March 26, 1995.

19. The Trademark Law Treaty of 1994, which entered into force in 1996, serves primarily to harmonize international registration of trademarks. The treaty standardizes the term of the trademark protection as ten years, with the first renewal term also lasting ten years, and provides model trademark

registration forms that are accepted in national and international trademark offices. "Treaty to Simplify Process," *Business Law Europe*, December 6, 1994.

20. Like the Trademark Law Treaty, the Patent Law Treaty would simplify the application process for patents. Among the innovations this treaty will introduce if it enters into force are standardized forms, possible electronic filing, removal of requirements that a local agent be employed to apply or to pay fees in person, creation of procedures for reinstatement of trademark protection, and streamlined procedures making application in foreign countries easier and less costly. Jenna Greene, "Treaty Helps Harmonize Patent Rules," *Legal Times*, May 29, 2000.

21. Frances Williams, "Welcome for Updated Rules on Copyright: Publishers and Software Groups Greet New Laws for Digital Age," *Financial Times*, December 23, 1996.

22. There had also been an attempt to formulate a treaty on property rights in the information contained in databases. The initial attempt failed in the face of opposition from groups fearing that the provisions of the treaty would provide too much protection and would unfairly limit the public's access to information.

23. "Intellectual Property: EU Backing Two International Treaties," *European Report*, December 24, 1996; "Bruce Lehman on New Intellectual Property Treaties," *M2 Presswire*, April 7, 1997; and Peter Jaszi, "Oral Testimony of Peter Jaszi on Behalf of the Digital Future Coalition before the Senate Foreign Relations Committee" (September 10, 1998 [cited August 18, 2003]), available from www.dfc.org/dfc1/Archives/wipo/pjorltst.html.

24. Information for this section comes from World Intellectual Property Organization, "Protecting Your Trademark Abroad: Twenty Questions About the Madrid Protocol," (2001 [cited August 2, 2002]), available from www. wipo.int/madrid/en/index.html.

25. The 1891 Madrid Agreement Concerning the International Registration of Marks was concluded in conjunction with the Madrid Agreement for the Repression of False or Deceptive Indication of Source on Goods (noted above). Almost a century later, in 1989, the Protocol Relating to the Madrid Agreement of 1891 was created to facilitate the international registration of trade and service marks. This global system reduces costs and streamlines procedures for trademark registration applicants who seek protection in multiple countries.

26. The agreement was revised in 1925 and again in 1934, with supplementary agreements signed in 1961, 1967, and 1975, and an amendment in 1979. The 1925 agreement was the first to create a central depository for the world that would allow owners of industrial designs to protect those designs in all the signatory states with a single application, which is now filed at the WIPO International Bureau. A new act was adopted in 1999 and awaits ratification. World Intellectual Property Organization, "What Are the Advantages of Protecting Industrial Designs Under the Hague Agreement?" [cited August 21, 2003]; available from www.wipo.org/hague/en/advant.htm.

27. This agreement, first signed in 1958, revised in 1967, and amended in 1979, complements the Madrid Agreement of 1891. Producers who are

nationals of or domiciled in signatory countries can apply for international registration and protection of appellations of origin, as long as the country of origin has granted protection. Geographic indications are eligible for protection if the product is made special by the human and natural characteristics of the place where it is produced.

28. The Patent Cooperation Treaty simplifies the process of applying for a patent in multiple countries. The treaty designates the patent offices of Australia, Austria, China, Japan, the Republic of Korea, the Russian Federation, Spain, Sweden, the United States, and the European Union as international searching authorities. An inventor in one of the 115 countries that have ratified this treaty can use the services of one of these patent offices to conduct the required search for prior art (patents and other technical information that have already been released).

29. The 1977 Budapest Treaty on the International Recognition of the Deposit of Microorganisms for the Purposes of Patent Protection established thirty-one approved depository authorities in North America, Europe, and Asia.

30. *Application of Argoudelis* before the Court of Customs and Patent Appeals, 434 F.2d 1390 (1970), cited in U.S. General Accounting Office, "Intellectual Property: Deposits of Biological Materials in Support of Certain Patent Applications," GAO\-01-49, October 2000 [cited August 20, 2003], available from www.gao.gov/new.items/d0149.pdf.

31. Ibid.

32. The TRIPS Agreement contains a specific provision on food geographic indications that is not as restrictive as the Lisbon Agreement. TRIPS provides protection to geographic indications when "a given quality, reputation or other characteristic of the good is essentially attributable to its geographic indication." TRIPS Agreement, quoted in Judson O. Berkey, "Implications of the WTO Protections for Food Geographic Indications" *ASIL Insights* (April 2002 [cited November 23, 2003]), available from www.asil.org/insights/insigh43.htm.

33. David Downes, "How Intellectual Property Could Be a Tool to Protect Traditional Knowledge," *Columbia Journal of Environmental Law* 25: 253ff.

34. The Nice Agreement was revised in 1967 and 1977 and amended in 1979. It deals with the registration of marks by dividing all possibilities up into thirty-four classes of goods and eight classes of services.

35. The Locarno Agreement, which was amended in 1979, deals with the registration of industrial designs. The more than 6,000 goods listed under this agreement are divided into thirty-one classes and 211 subclasses.

36. The Strasbourg Agreement Concerning the International Patent Classification (1971), which as amended 1979, was modeled on the 1954 European Convention on the International Classification of Patents for Invention under the auspices of the Council of Europe.

37. The Vienna Agreement, which supplements the Nice Agreement on mark registration, deserves special mention. The treaty specifies an international classification system that divides images into four main categories: (1) celestial bodies, natural phenomena, and geographical maps; (2) human

beings; (3) animals; and (4) supernatural, fabulous, fantastic, or unidentifiable beings. Within Category 4, we can find the following among the many subcategories: (4.1) winged or horned personages; (4.2) beings partly human and partly animal; and (4.3) fabulous animals. Category 4.3, in turn, includes: (4.3.1) winged lions, griffons; (4.3.2) dragons; (4.3.5) winged horses (Pegasus). World Intellectual Property Organization, *International Classification of the Figurative Elements of Marks Under the Vienna Agreement*, 4th ed., January 1, 1998 [cited August 21, 2003], available from www.wipo.int/classifications/fulltext/vienna/enmain0.htm.

38. UPOV was revised in 1972, 1978, and 1991.

39. Information on UPOV in this section comes from WIPO, *WIPO Intellectual Property;* and UPOV (L'Union Internationale pour la Protection des Obtentions Vegetales), *International Union for the Protection of New Varieties of Plants: What It Is, What It Does,* No. 437(E), August 2003 [cited August 21, 2003], available from www.upov.org/en/about/pdf/pub437.pdf; and other documents available on the UPOV website. See also Stanley Burgiel, "Negotiating the Trade-Environment Frontier: Biosafety and Intellectual Property Rights in International Policy-Making" (doctoral diss., American University, 2002).

40. UPOV, *The UPOV System of Plant Variety Protection* [cited August 21, 2003], available from www.upov.org/en/about/upov_system.htm.

41. WIPO, *WIPO Intellectual Property Handbook.*

42. UPOV, *International Union for the Protection of New Varieties of Plants.*

43. Genetic Resources Action International (GRAIN), "Sprouting Up: UPOV Continues to Influence," *Seedling,* July 2002 [cited November 23, 2003], available from www.grain.org/seedling/seed-02-07-5-en.cfm. GRAIN "is an international non-governmental organization which promotes the sustainable management and use of agricultural biodiversity based on people's control over genetic resources and local knowledge."

44. For a history of the TRIPS negotiations, see Michael P. Ryan, *Knowledge Diplomacy: Global Competition and the Politics of Intellectual Property* (Washington, DC: Brookings Institution, 1998); Susan K. Sell, *Power and Ideas: North-South Politics of Intellectual Property and Antitrust* (Albany: State University of New York Press, 1998); Susan K. Sell and Christopher May, "Moments in Law: Contestation and Settlement in the History of Intellectual Property," *Review of International Political Economy* 8, no. 3 (2001).

45. Information from this section comes from documents and information presented at the World Trade Organization website [cited August 21, 2003], available from www.wto.int. See especially, World Trade Organization, *Trading into the Future* (2nd ed.) (March 2001 [cited August 4, 2002]), available from www.wto.org/english/res_e/doload_e/tif.pdf.

46. Oxfam, for example, has taken a very strong stand against TRIPS and the WTO. See also Dave Timms, "Double-Dealing in Doha," *The Ecologist* 32, no. 1 (2002); Rashid Kaukab, *TRIPS, TRIMS, Agriculture, and Services: A Southern Perspective,* speech presented at the Wilton Park Conference

"Multilateral Trade Negotiations: The Way Forward" (June 28–July 2, 1999 [cited August 18, 2003]); available from www2.cid.harvard.edu/cidtrade/Issues/wps.pdf; and T. N. Srinivasan, *The TRIPS Agreement: A Comment Inspired by Frederick Abbott's Presentation* (November 29, 2000 [cited August 5, 2002]), available from www.econ.yale.edu/~srinivas/TRIPS.pdf.

47. In compliance with TRIPS, India now allows product as well as process patents on foods, pharmaceuticals, and agrochemicals. Previously, only process patents were granted. See information posted by an Indian consumer advocacy organization, Centre for International Trade Consumer Unity and Trust Society (CUTS), Economics, and the Environment, website [cited August 5, 2002], available from www.cuts-india.org/CITEE.htm.

4

Global Intellectual Property Policy Conundrums

T here is actually much agreement on a global scale regarding intellectual property rights. Fake baby formula in counterfeit packaging, for example, is rather universally considered to be a bad thing. Few people would want copyrights to last in perpetuity, and not even the strongest proponents of protection are trying to track down Shakespeare's heirs so that they can receive royalties. Yet many disagreements remain concerning the effects of intellectual property rights protection. Advocates of strong intellectual property rights believe that protection causes creativity and innovation; others are not so certain. Opponents of strong intellectual property rights point to the inherent individualism underlying the assignment of rights and the way intellectual property rules ignore the prior intellectual contributions that make no invention or creation truly novel.

In the absence of consensus about the fairness and usefulness of intellectual property protection, whether providing intellectual property protection benefits society sufficiently becomes an even thornier issue. The four global policy examples here—pharmaceutical patents, genetic material, digitized works, and domain names—are characterized by disagreement over the proper balance of public versus private good—and how to achieve it.

■ Global Protection of Pharmaceutical Patents

Pharmaceutical research involves universities, governments, and the private sector. The initiative of pharmaceutical companies to develop new drugs and bring them to market is an essential characteristic of the sector today, and these companies have been marvelously successful in bringing out drugs that offer hope for previously incurable or untreatable illnesses. Nevertheless, we must ask whether the current situation is good enough. Have we achieved the right balance between public good and private good? What are the effects of patents on decisions about research directions? Do patents' effects on drug costs outweigh the benefits derived from patents?

Under the international regime for intellectual property, TRIPS requires all member states of the World Trade Organization to protect intellectual property rights, including patent rights for pharmaceuticals. The difficulties that this rule has presented for many countries are substantial, and the WTO has responded to demands for loosening the requirements. The TRIPS council has recently decided to allow the least developed countries to delay implementation of patent protection until 2016, and the Doha Declaration on the TRIPS Agreement and Public Health affirms that states may grant compulsory licenses in public health crises.[1] Nevertheless, pharmaceutical companies have been particularly vocal about getting their governments (primarily the United States and the European Union) to make sure that their intellectual property rights are supported around the world, especially because many countries, including some advanced industrialized countries, have been loath to grant full patent rights to pharmaceuticals.[2]

It is undeniably true that investing in research and development for new drugs is a risky business. Only five promising compounds out of 5,000–10,000 ever reach the clinical trial stage.[3] Of those that do make it through the clinical trials, only a few will be very profitable. Of these, however, some will become extremely popular and will be extremely profitable for pharmaceutical companies. Most of a company's profits on a new drug will accrue during the period when the drug is protected by patent. The Pharmaceutical Research and Manufacturers' Association notes that only three in ten drugs that reach the market achieve enough sales to recoup the average R&D costs.[4] After that period is over, generic drug manufacturers can use the public information about the chemical composition of the drug and, using standard manufacturing techniques, produce competing products. Companies must make strategic choices about which drugs to develop and how to price them.

Deciding Research Directions: Effects of Patents

Anyone interested in developing new products or processes must first decide what to work on. Investors are willing to invest in a particular R&D venture when they believe the result will be profitable. *Profitable* does not necessarily mean "of great social value." Society gains something from the introduction of metallic gel pens adored by children; but had the R&D for metallic gel pens not worked out, society's loss would have been rather minimal. Other areas of research have more enduring effects on our lives.

Here's a thought experiment. Imagine a world in which there is only one pharmaceutical company, and it has limited funds for the research and development of new drugs. Assume that it has only enough funds to work on one problem. Marketers for the firm see a great potential demand for an antihistamine that the patient would have to take only once at the beginning of the hay fever season. Even if this drug was very expensive, the market researchers find, people of sufficient means would be willing to pay for the convenience of a single-pill cure for springtime allergies. Alternatively, the company could invest its R&D money in developing new treatments for tuberculosis. The projected income from tuberculosis sales would be lower than the antihistamine sales, but tuberculosis is a more serious problem than hay fever—at least from a global perspective. Unless national government or international organization funding for tuberculosis treatments provides the R&D resources that the firm has little incentive to provide, the global social good loses out to the firm's interest in pursuing profits. The firm's interest is reasonable because it has a responsibility to make a profit. That is why the shareholders have invested in the firm: to see a return in their investment.

It makes financial sense for pharmaceutical companies to work on developing drugs that would be in demand by many potential consumers with the money to buy them. Put bluntly, there is a financial incentive for firms to invest in developing drugs for conditions that afflict lots of rich people: high blood pressure, heart disease, even some cancer treatments. Drugs and vaccines for illnesses of the developing world, like malaria and tuberculosis, do not have the same profit potential because the prospective users do not have the resources to purchase treatment.[5] Because pharmaceutical companies need to recoup R&D costs within the period of patent protection, drugs for the well-to-do with common ailments will be the most attractive research projects.[6]

Several observers have suggested that the increasing reliance on private R&D for pharmaceutical development results in skewing research priorities away from the most socially pressing problems to the most potentially profitable. This danger is exacerbated by the increased reliance on private R&D. Between 1986 and 1995, the share of total health R&D spending in the United States by private industry rose from 42 percent to 53 percent.[7] The growing connection between academic research and private industry, a result of public funding cutbacks in the 1970s and 1980s[8] and the U.S. Bayh-Dole Act of 1980, further encourages market-worthy drug development over socially important drug development. The Bayh-Dole Act was created to encourage the commercialization of government-funded research. Before this law was put in place, "Ownership rights to inventions resulting from federally funded research vested with the government. However, the government had no means to manufacture or commercialize inventions and many good ideas and products were left undeveloped."[9] Under the act, universities and firms can receive patents for inventions developed with government funds, although the government does retain a right to license the invention. One consequence of the act was that the interest of universities became more closely aligned with the interests of profit-seeking firms.[10]

In addition, there is an incentive to create incrementally better drugs rather than totally new drugs, because an incremental improvement will allow the drug company to gain a new patent. An easily developed change that allows more convenient dosing—say, one dose per day instead of every four hours—does not require the same kind of research investment that a completely new therapy requires. The pharmaceutical company, however, will still be able to benefit because a substantial number of consumers are willing to pay more for convenience. It would be strategically rational for the company to introduce such an innovation to the market just as the patent for the older formulation was set to expire.

Another similar effect can be seen when other companies use the results of the research—the new knowledge disclosed in the patent— to invent a similar product to compete with the original. One can reasonably ask whether it is socially optimal to commit R&D dollars to easy-to-develop copycat products that are similar but not identical to existing treatments for a single condition.[11] A study of the market share of top-selling ulcer drugs from 1985 to 1988 reveals "a tendency for newer, more expensive drugs to be more popular."[12] The issue is one of balance. Although it is certainly good to have choices of therapeutic agents, patent policies can influence the direction that research and development are likely to take.[13]

What Happens When Those Who Need the Drugs Can't Afford Them?

The high price of pharmaceuticals, which is driven in large measure by companies' patent rights, leaves global society with a problem regarding access to medication. The roughly $12,000-per-year cocktail of drugs taken by AIDS patients who can afford it is not a cure, but it does keep them healthier longer. Is it in the global public interest to provide low-cost drugs in countries that cannot afford patented products? Is it an ethical responsibility?

If the answer to both these questions is yes, then several policies could reduce the costs of AIDS medications. Countries could simply ignore the requirements of TRIPS and contract with generic drug makers to produce drugs at lower cost. In 2001, an Indian company, Cipla, announced it was prepared to sell the cocktail of three anti-HIV drugs for $600 per year. Merck and Co., the owner of a patent on two such drugs, responded with an offer to cut the price for Crixivan to $600 and for Storcrin to $500 per year to developing countries as long as the governments of those countries pledge not to reexport the drugs. Other pharmaceutical companies followed suit: Bristol-Meyers Squibb and GlaxoSmithKline both set out conditions for reduced prices.[14]

In order to work, such differential pricing schemes must fulfill two requirements: companies must be willing to sell lower-priced drugs in developing countries, and consumers in high-income countries must be willing to accept the idea that they are paying more for the same medications. Even with differential pricing, however, many people in developing countries will still not be able to afford necessary medications. "International funding [will be] required for ensuring effective access to essential medications in poor countries and the most appropriate mechanisms for the mobilization and distribution of such funds."[15]

There are several other options. Wealthy governments could purchase the drugs, perhaps under the aegis of the World Health Organization, and donate them to public health officials in target countries. Alternatively, grants could be provided by rich countries to offset costs. The Doha Declaration on the TRIPS Agreement and Public Health could be strengthened to facilitate compulsory licensing for pharmaceuticals at prices the market can bear in developing countries. Commitments to buy large quantities of low-profit products like vaccines, either by rich countries (which could then donate the vaccines to poorer countries), or by buyers' clubs made up of poorer countries, could provide enough incentive for companies to offer the product at a lower cost. Yet another alternative would be to offer companies a significant monetary prize (in lieu of a patent) for developing a useful essential medicine.[16]

Finally, the public can reassert its interest in funding the development of new pharmaceutical products, and states can undo provisions that hand over intellectual property to private firms. This could be done on a national or international scale. An international project would look like the international research institutes of the Consultative Group on International Agricultural Research (CGIAR), which have a track record of developing important new plant varieties and placing them in the public domain.[17]

Relying on patents and private research to produce new therapeutic agents will give us results that reward firms for innovating. But the direction of research and the kind of innovation that results may not be the best, most socially desirable outcome. Citizens must ask whether they want the incentives inherent in the patent system to drive research on this very important issue. Since patents represent the balance between public interest and private incentive, it is up to the public to decide whether the right balance has been achieved.

▪ Intellectual Property Rights on Life

The biotechnology revolution has produced marvelous new developments, not only in medicine but also in agriculture and other sectors. From insulin produced by using recombinant DNA, to bioprospecting for new therapeutic agents in developing countries, to unraveling the human genome, exciting avenues of commercial development are opening. Unlike inanimate objects, however, living things (or components of living things) are not simply manufactured. They grow and change. The creative process of invention is mixed with the random process of biological reproduction and the mystical or religious sense of the mystery of life. Intellectual property protection for biotechnology raises important questions about the nature of invention, discoveries, property, and the global public good.

The Convention on Biodiversity and TRIPS

The Convention on Biodiversity (CBD) and GATT's TRIPS provisions both aim to improve the human condition. They obligate signatory countries to take certain actions for the global public good. However, these agreements are, some have argued, incompatible.[18] Most notably, TRIPS and the CBD conflict over whether states must provide intellectual property protection to developers of new plant varieties. Article 27.3(b) of TRIPS requires states to enact patent or sui generis protection for new plant varieties. The CBD, in contrast, specifies that states have sovereign authority to prohibit the export of their biological resources.

Fundamentally, the CBD and TRIPS have divergent views of biological resources as potential forms of intellectual property. According to the text of the CBD, its

> objectives . . . are the conservation of biological diversity, the sustainable use of components and the fair and equitable sharing of the benefits arising out of the utilization of genetic resources, including by appropriate access to genetic resources and by appropriate transfer of relevant technologies, taking into account all rights over those resources and to technologies, and by appropriate funding.[19]

The CBD's emphasis on sharing and access to resources and technologies reflects the concern for local communities in the developing world, which remains the repository for most of the world's biodiversity. The signatories to the CBD, which went into effect in 1993, intend to end what can be seen as the predatory practices of exploiting biological resources from the developing world for the benefit of the developed world. The goal is not commercialization of useful new products but rather the preservation of biodiversity in the world's remaining wildernesses and the creation of a sustainable system of using those resources.

The CBD affirms the importance of local communities and traditional practices for understanding the benefits of various biological resources. Under the convention, when firms develop new products from resources available only in developing countries, local communities and the government have inherent rights to the biological resource and to the traditional knowledge that went into discovering it. To offer one example, representatives of a firm might talk to local residents and find out that a particular plant is good for curing some ailment. Researchers take samples of the plant and isolate the curative compound. The firm then commercializes the compound, originally derived from the plant, as a medication, which has potential benefits for many people. Under the CBD, the government of the country where the plant was found has the right to determine the conditions under which the plant can be used. The local community has a right to their traditional knowledge, and both the government and the local community have a right to the plant itself. Under these rules, the firm does not have the right to commercialize the product derived from this plant without the appropriate permissions and compensation.[20]

This approach is very different from TRIPS. TRIPS assumes that the value in a product comes not from the origins of its components but rather from the innovation involved in creating the product. Just as an individual can purchase a gadget while the inventor retains the intellectual property, protected by a patent, a new plant can be purchased while the plant breeder retains the intellectual property embedded in the creation of the new variety. In the example above, as long as the local people talked with the representatives of the firm willingly (with or without compensation), and as long as no researchers trespassed on private or state-owned property when they collected the plant (i.e., they didn't steal the plant), then nothing would be owed to the country of origin. The creative work that has value as intellectual property happens in the laboratory, when the key compound is isolated, its principles determined, its safety tested, and so on. Critics of the CBD approach who support strong intellectual property rights argue that there is no reason to attach some sort of communal ownership to a biological resource just because it is found in a developing country. If a company obtains a sample of a plant legally, then the company owns that particular sample of biological material and is free to use it to innovate. And, this line of argument continues, the firm that invests in research and successfully commercializes a new product deserves patent protection as a reward for contributing to progress in science and as an incentive for future research.

The United States did not ratify the Convention on Biodiversity, primarily because of what the United States characterized as weak protection of intellectual property rights. The U.S. pharmaceutical and chemical industries actively lobbied against the agreement and were influential in Congress's decision. The U.S. government has preferred the TRIPS view of innovation and intellectual property and has rejected the idea that biological resources are somehow distinct from other raw materials in the creation of new products.

The Neem Tree and Basmati Rice

The differences between TRIPS and the CBD can be seen in two intellectual property disputes involving the biological resources of India and U.S. companies.

Neem. The neem tree is native to South Asia. Products from the tree have been used traditionally by Indians for a variety of purposes: fuel and timber, toothbrushes, spermicide, medicine, and pesticide. To make the pesticide, Indian farmers soak neem seeds in water or alcohol overnight and then apply the brew to their crops. The mixture does not keep, so farmers need to make up a fresh batch whenever they want to apply pesticide. Benefits of the neem pesticide for Indian farmers include its low toxicity and its low cost as an input.

Though some in the West had apparently been aware of the usefulness of neem as a pesticide, it was not until 1985 that the product was used in the United States, first as a pesticide for timber developed by Robert Larson. In 1988, Larson sold his patent for the extraction process used in the production of the pesticide to the W. R. Grace Corporation. In 1992, W. R. Grace was awarded a patent by the U.S. PTO for the process of creating a stabilized version of azadirachtin, the active pesticidal chemical in the neem extract, as well as for the product of the stabilized form of azadirachtin.[21] In 1993, W. R. Grace entered into a partnership with PJ Margo Private Limited, an Indian firm, to sell neem-based products in India. In 1994, Grace received permission from the U.S. Environmental Protection Agency to market the product it developed, Neemix, for application to food crops.[22]

Activists inside and outside India cried foul. Some, including biotech gadfly Jeremy Rifkin, have argued in a challenge to the patent that there is nothing novel about W. R. Grace's invention. After all, Indian farmers have been using the emulsion from the neem tree for centuries, and some even developed a storage-stable version. The European Patent Office, the central patent office for the countries of the European Union, has rescinded W. R. Grace's patent to products from the neem tree on the grounds that they were not novel. In the United States, the legal battle continues.

The question is: Do W. R. Grace and similar companies have a right to patents based on traditional knowledge in India? Some have argued that the patents granted demonstrate the disregard of traditional knowledge under the TRIPS-based regime. Another argument is that W. R. Grace's patent represents one more example of biopiracy—the exploitation of developing countries and the extraction of their biological resources in violation of the CBD. As Emily Marden points out, "The neem dispute is at root an argument over whether patents on life, of living extracts should exist at all."[23] The idea that making some modification to a product of nature should be rewarded with a patent stands in sharp contrast to the philosophical position that defines nature and natural resources as communal goods, not private or club goods.

Basmati. The idea that the community possesses biological resources is also at the root of Indian displeasure over a Texas company's development, patenting, and marketing of American basmati rice. In India, as in Japan, rice plays an important role in culture, and the commercialization of basmati rice by a U.S. firm constitutes the misappropriation of India's heritage, according to opponents. Basmati rice, the highly aromatic long-grained rice typically used in Indian cuisine, has traditionally been grown in northwestern India and Pakistan, though its cultivation is hampered by its tall, flimsy habit and its low yields. During the Green Revolution in the 1960s, more vigorous rice varieties were developed by the International Rice Research Institute, which was established to create new plant varieties for the global public domain. More recently, researchers from RiceTec were able to create a variety that incorporates some of these advances, along with the embedded knowledge of generations of Indian and Pakistani farmers.[24] The RiceTec researchers were able to breed a basmati-like rice that could be grown in the climate and soil of the United States, that was sturdy, and that was as prolific as the pusa basmati developed in India. RiceTec received a U.S. patent in 1997. Since then, its patent has been under attack by activists and by the governments of India and Pakistan. The Indian government requested that the U.S. PTO revoke the patent, but in an attempt to ward off the revocation, RiceTec rescinded some its claims so that the patent is now more narrowly drawn.[25]

Some activists claim this is a case of biopiracy in which a U.S. company ripped off genetic material from India to produce rice that would compete directly with Indian exports. RiceTec apparently does not intend to compensate Indian or Pakistani farmers for having cultivated the basmati rice strain that is the foundation of the new variety. According to this view, RiceTec has simply stolen the rightful property of Indians and Pakistanis, property that should be protected by the sovereign authority of their governments.[26]

Others, such as M. S. Swaminathan, a leading rice researcher, see a more central problem. Though he regrets the commercialization of plant breeding, he takes changes in the agricultural environment as a given. Indeed, he patents his work to defend it from misappropriation by others. Instead, he views the problem as one of geographic appellation. "Basmati" should refer only to the original rice that is grown in India and Pakistan. Varieties that have been crossbred with other varieties like pusa basmati should not be referred to as basmati. Nor should varieties that are grown outside the region in which basmati is traditionally cultivated be called basmati. ("Pusa basmati," not "basmati," is the proper name for the variety he developed.) He does not object to RiceTec's use of Texmati or Kasmati, its brand names, but he does object to the use of American basmati. RiceTec's products are not basmati, in his view, and American basmati is an oxymoron.[27]

It is notable that the geographic indications for wine and spirits—e.g., Scotch Whiskey—add a special provision preventing any non-Scottish whiskey producer to use *Scotch* in the product name in any way. Even the term *Scotch-like Whiskey* is prohibited, even though there is little chance that someone would confuse it with the real thing. This protection does not carry over into other products, even though many are produced by developing countries.

From RiceTec's perspective, and those of other supporters of intellectual property rights on plant varieties, there is nothing wrong with the term *American basmati,* especially since the government of India has not taken any steps to protect *basmati* as a geographic appellation. Moreover, supporters of strong intellectual property rights argue that the U.S. patent is not on the rice grown by Indians and Pakistanis but rather on a unique hybrid variety.[28] From this perspective, RiceTec's patent is reasonable, especially since the United States has a long history of providing patent protection to hybrid varieties.

The cases of neem and basmati reveal serious concerns, even though Indian farmers are not currently suffering demonstrable negative effects from U.S. patent policies. Will commercialization of neem by W. R. Grace and other companies lead to a lack of neem seeds for Indian firms? Will the seed become too expensive for neem producers? Will RiceTec's commercialization of American basmati drive Indian rice exports from the United States and other markets? Will innovative Indian companies be able to penetrate world markets if the traditional knowledge of India's communities has been patented by outsiders? Will India be forced under TRIPS rules to respect the neem and Texmati patents and, if so, will Indian farmers see traditional products, as well as innovations, blocked by foreign companies? Finally, how will traditional farmers who initially developed the process for extracting the active ingredient from the neem tree and who initially bred basmati rice be compensated?[29]

Patents and the Human Genome

Advances in genetics and microbiology have led to astounding discoveries. The 2001 announcement of the sequencing of the human genome sparked widespread interest in the potential to use gene-based science to cure or at least screen for all sorts of diseases. At the same time, though, people debate whether genes, parts of genes, or processes to isolate and analyze genes ought to be ownable. Should the genetic makeup of human beings be property?

According to the biotechnology industry, patents for genes are perfectly legal and potentially very good for society, because the patents will spur further research. An industry publication notes:

• Isolated and purified genes are patentable inventions if they meet the PTO's standard criteria, including being novel, well-described, and useful.
• Gene-based patents have helped to secure the biotechnology and pharmaceutical industry's interests in the development of gene-based therapeutics. For example, the gene encoding erythropoietin was cloned in 1985, which lead to the production of recombinant EPO, patented by Amgen in 1987. The protein expressed by this gene is used in the treatment of anemia arising from several disease conditions.[30]

Moreover, industry representatives emphasize that a patent on genes does not mean that any individual's genetic information is up for grabs. "Instead, patents are granted on 'isolated' genes and gene products where the gene or gene product has real world applicability. That is, the patents cover genes and gene products that could be obtained from any person, for example from a blood sample."[31] Since "every gene (including complementary DNA, or cDNA forms) is a molecule that can be defined as a specific chemical structure,"[32] patents are not granted on Joe's gene but rather on an isolated chemical structure. A biotechnology industry publication asserts: "DNA as an isolated molecule does not exist within living cells. It is always associated with various other molecules such as proteins, sugars, and fats. . . . [I]solated nucleic acids do not exist in nature."[33]

In theory, the potential patent holder should be able to state what the gene does since utility has always been a requirement for receiving a patent. Some critics of patents for genetic material argue that the U.S. PTO has relaxed this requirement and allows firms to claim patent rights on DNA sequences (parts of genes) that have been characterized but perhaps not fully understood.[34] Once a gene or a DNA sequence has been identified and characterized, the biotechnology company that isolated it can figure out how to make use of it. No other company can use that particular patented gene without a license from the patent holder.

Proponents of patent rights for genetic material argue that such protection is exactly what is needed to convince firms to get involved in the risky business of trying to isolate DNA sequences that will have some therapeutic value. Proponents also argue that competition among biotech firms for patents will lead to the most progress, most quickly. They further claim that the private sector initiative to decode the human genome actually increased public access to genetic information. Because of competition from the private sector, the government-funded Human Genome Project raced ahead to determine the chemical structure of genes and DNA sequences so that the new knowledge could be placed safely in the public domain before firms had an opportunity to patent it.

In contrast, opponents of gene-based patents argue that the human genome should not be ownable. The reasons they offer fall into two categories. First, identifying genes means making a *discovery,* not an *invention.* The chemical structure of genes and DNA sequences is a part of nature; specifying the structure amounts to a discovery of a fundamental fact of nature. The difference is crucial, because discoveries are not patentable; only inventions are. Discoveries may end up having commercially useful consequences, but the discovery itself is not property. For example, Marie and Pierre Curie discovered radium, but they did not own the rights to either the element, its radioactive property, or the process of isolating it.[35] Inventions, such as therapeutic or diagnostic agents that are used in nuclear medicine, depended on the knowledge that came from the discoveries and could not have been invented without the initial discovery of radium and radiation. These subsequent inventions could be patented, but the scientific discovery could not be. Opponents of patenting human genes or components argue that the discovery of a gene should not be confused with the creation of a medication or medical test based on that gene. Moreover, once a gene is discovered, competition to see who can create a useful therapeutic agent that *is* patentable would serve the public good. Providing a patent to the discoverer for the discovery, however, shuts down competition over creating a useful new product.

The second objection to patents for genes stems from the fundamental notion that human genes belong to all humanity. If I own a book that I have not read, I still own the book, despite not knowing its contents. In a sense, each human being has a book that she has not read: the book of genes (though some would argue that God is the sole author). For a firm to say that it owns a particular gene because it has specified its structure and figured out the protein it expresses is a misappropriation of something owned by all of humanity jointly.[36]

The issue of patents for human genes and DNA sequences (as well as for other animal life) has not been fully resolved globally, though the United States continues to push hard for acceptance of these patents. Though TRIPS requires protection for new plant varieties and microorganisms, it does not require states to provide patents for discoveries or inventions involving animals (including humans). Rapid advances in unraveling the human genome and in the entire field of biotechnology will continue to keep this issue and related ones on the agenda.

■ Intellectual Property in the Digital Age

Computer technologies raises several different intellectual property dilemmas. As for copyright, the ability to copy and paste with a click of the mouse decreases the cost of reproducing copyrighted material. The ability to use the Internet to distribute material decreases the cost

of disseminating pirated material. The issue of trademark, complicated by the global reach of the Internet, comes into play when we
consider domain names.

Copyrights and Copywrongs

It is now established that saving a document or graphic in digital
form, whether on a hard drive, diskette, CD, DVD, tape, or some
other format, means that the author has produced a *fixed work* and
therefore has a copyright in that which has been created and fixed.
Copying material that is copyrighted is illegal, but it is also easy.

Policy responses include domestic and international legal mechanisms, as well as technical means. In the United States, the Digital
Millennium Copyright Act (DMCA) provides broad protections. The
most recent WIPO treaties on copyright, the WIPO Copyright Treaty
and the WIPO Performances and Phonogram Treaty (see Chapter 3),
address the problem of international protection of copyright since the
advent of digital technologies and the Internet. The success of these
legal means depends on the willingness of governments to enforce
the treaty and relevant domestic laws while maintaining a balance
between public good and private interests.

Has the balance tipped? Proponents of strong copyright protection laud the DMCA, but lament the difficulties of enforcing it.
Though infringement is a crime under the DMCA, the onus is still on
the rights holder to watch out for violations. The police do not routinely patrol the Internet for copyright violations. Instead, copyright
holders might hire the services of a company like Cyveillance, a firm
that scours the Internet for infringing usage of its clients' intellectual
property.[37]

Some rights holders spend a lot of resources protecting their
copyrights (as well as trademarks and service marks). The Church of
Scientology has been successful in using copyright laws to prevent
critics of the religion from posting secret church texts online.[38] The
infringer can also be an admirer: author Ann McCaffrey's lawyer has
sent a cease-and-desist letter to a fan who had the temerity to create
and post online artwork based on McCaffrey's *Dragonriders of Pern*
series.[39] Paramount Pictures, owned by Viacom, has taken action
against fans who created websites celebrating *Star Trek*.[40] Napster,
which popularized online file-swapping as a means to copy music
and video recordings, was driven out of business after it was held

responsible for the unauthorized copying of MP3 files.[41] Peer-to-peer file exchanges, in which files are exchanged directly without resorting to copying the files on a central server, are the next target of the media industry.[42]

The position of proponents of strong digital copyright protection seems clear: if a person or company creates a work, whether text, graphic, audio, or video, whether in tangible form or digitized, that person or company owns a copyright, can protect the property, and can determine how it is used. But there are concerns that the rights being conferred in a digital environment go beyond what has traditionally been granted, especially in the print medium. How so? First, the DMCA prohibits the circumvention of technological means to prevent copying. Physical books do not come copy-protected. If I want to copy a few pages, I plop the book on the photocopier and copy away. I am limited in what I can legitimately copy only by the strength of my claim to fair use and by the quality of the photocopy machine. If I want to incorporate some music or a film scene into my class lecture, I have no problem because the law allows for educational fair use of copyrighted material. I simply bring in the CD or video and play it to the class. However, the situation is different if I want to incorporate a music or film clip into a PowerPoint® presentation for class. Prior to the DMCA's implementation, making a copy from the CD I purchased legally and putting the copy into another platform—the PowerPoint® presentation—for use in an educational setting would have been an obvious instance of fair use. Now, however, the music and motion picture industries are using copy protection to prevent such duplication. The DMCA makes any attempt to circumvent copy protection a criminal offense, even if the ultimate goal is considered fair use.[43]

It may well be that many violations of the DMCA do, in fact, involve criminal intent. Nevertheless, there are many legitimate reasons for wanting to circumvent copy protection. Consumers may want backup copies. Software developers may be writing add-in programs that enhance the usability of a copyrighted program (they may need to circumvent the copy protection to ensure interoperability). Anti-virus software developers will need to make copies of other programs in order to make sure their product successfully identifies viruses. Someone might simply want to copy a program just to figure out how it works, learning for the sake of learning. Another legitimate reason to circumvent copy protection is to make sure that a system is secure. Or an individual with a scientific interest in the mathematics of encryption might want to determine how difficult it would be for a criminal to crack a system. Yet all these sensible reasons for circumventing copyprotection are illegal under the DMCA.

In addition, there is the question of *contributory infringement.* The DMCA imposes penalties on those who aid the infringer's ability to infringe. For example, an Internet service provider (ISP) may be held accountable for the infringing activity of its customers. For many college students, the university is their ISP. At the height of industry activity against Napster, many universities felt compelled to block access to MP3 sites from their computer networks because of the risk of being held liable as contributory infringers. Often, an ISP will err on the side of caution and not bother to determine whether or not a customer is in the right. The administrator will simply order that the allegedly offending material be removed, on penalty of having the service revoked.

One way for firms to limit consumers' right to use a work is to license rather than sell it. Even though we speak colloquially of buying software, we almost always pay for a license; we do not actually purchase a copy. When a user installs software on her computer, she is asked to agree to certain provisions of a contract that limits what she can do with the program she purchased. By clicking "I Agree," she binds herself to the terms of the contract. Of course, if she doesn't like the terms, she *could* try to return the software and get her money back, but how many people would go to that trouble? Users thus accept the contract's terms because it is more convenient than trying to figure out the other options. Such a contract might prevent the user from selling the software (or transferring the license) once she no longer needs it.

The contrast between buying a copy of a book and paying for a license to use software is stark. The *right of first sale* gives consumers the right to do whatever they want with a physical book: resell it, burn it, give it away, whatever. Consumers can read the words on the page without using them up or infringing on the copyright. They cannot make copies; nor can they make derivative works. But once done with the book, they can pass it on to someone else to enjoy the content. With the restrictive copyright contract, consumers' rights can be much more limited.

The contract system has set up barriers to the creation of a used software market. Although many software companies specify that the consumer can transfer the license for the software under fairly easy conditions, other licenses can carry tougher rules. It is important to remember that the reason for this licensing system is that the publisher is the owner of the copyright to the software. The property right in the computer code that makes up the program gives the publisher the right to determine the conditions under which consumers will have access to copies. As consumers, we agree to the terms of the contracts, so we are making informed decisions, but since we do not really have many alternatives (one cannot obtain a license to use WordPerfect without agreeing to the contract), the choices are limited. Again, society must balance the benefits and costs of strong intellectual property protection.

Trademarks and Domain Names

The global nature of the Internet has challenged the international coordination of trademark rules and has led to some interesting innovations in policymaking. The rapid rise in popularity of the Internet and the World Wide Web means that domain names (e.g., the "acme" in "acme.com") suddenly became global billboards. There can be only one "acme.com," and every company named Acme could realistically have an interest in the name. The problem is that traditionally marks have been applied only in a limited geographical region and for a limited purpose. So, the service mark of United Van Lines, a moving company, and United Airlines are not in conflict because consumers will not confuse a moving van with a 747. Given the inverted tree structure of the Internet's domain name system, however, there can only be one united.com.

So how does this work? The Internet has a root directory that branches into generic top-level domains (gTLDs) and country code top-level domains (ccTLDs). The gTLDs include the familiar extensions like .gov, .mil, .edu, .com, .org, and .net as well as the newer .info, .biz, and the like. Though .gov and .mil are gTLDs, they are controlled by the U.S. government and refer to U.S. civilian and military Internet addresses. Earlier in the development of the Internet, the idea had been that .edu, .com, .org, and .net TLDs would indicate the function of the domain name holder. An institution having the .edu TLD could be assumed to be an institution of higher learning that offered at least bachelor's or higher degrees (in other words, colleges and universities above the level of community college). The .com TLDs were commercial (for-profit) ventures, and the .org TLDs were to be nonprofit organizations. Originally, the .net TLD was expected to be restricted to network administration addresses. Those restrictions were never legally required, and the requirements for name registration in the various gTLDs (with the exception of those controlled by the U.S. government) have become looser. Many firms and organizations register names in more than one TLD (e.g., acme.net and acme.com) to make sure that competitors, opponents, and unrelated ventures with the same corporate name are not able to grab the name in cyberspace.

Which firm or organization gets united.com? What about peta.org? Should that go to People for the Ethical Treatment of Animals (an animal rights group) or to Michael T. Doughney, a PETA critic who registered peta.org for his group People Eating Tasty Animals?[44] Does Doughney's right to free speech trump PETA's trademark in its acronym, or vice versa? One way of dealing with this question is to let the courts decide, but because of the global nature of the Internet the plaintiff and the defendant may be located in different countries. When a court in one country makes a decision, there is no guarantee that its decision will be enforced in another. Also the number of disputes that arise over domain names could overwhelm the capacity of the courts, and litigation can be very expensive.

By the late 1990s, the problem of trademark infringement or dilution from the assignment of domain names was a significant impediment to the development of electronic commerce, especially in regard to gTLDs. To spur e-commerce and encourage self-regulation of cyberspace, the U.S. administration of President Bill Clinton essentially privatized policymaking regarding domain names. In 1998 the U.S. government mandated the creation of the Internet Corporation for Assigned Names and Numbers (ICANN), a nonprofit organization incorporated in California charged with administering the domain-name system for the global public good. ICANN establishes and implements policies, procedures, and standards. It regulates and enforces property rights in domain names through the rules of the ICANN-sponsored Uniform Dispute Resolution Procedure (UDRP), an arbitration system that determines who has the rights to a particular domain name. The UDRP, some have argued, favors the interests of the holders of trademarks over others in ways that greatly strengthen the global reach of trademark rights.

UDRP procedures establish rules for ICANN's accreditation of arbitrators and for the arbitrators' consideration of cases. The rules are meant to distinguish between illegitimate registrations of domain names—cybersquatting and reverse domain-name hijacking—and legitimate ones.[45] The UDRP sets procedures for determining whether there have been acts of bad faith. But most trademark disputes do not entail bad faith: two rights holders may have genuine competing claims to the same domain name. In this situation, the UDRP establishes who has precedence for owning a particular domain name. Under the UDRP, the arbitrator is supposed to transfer the domain name to the complainant only if three conditions are met: (1) the domain name is the same as or confusingly similar to a trademark or service mark held by the complainant; (2) the current domain name holder has no legitimate interest in the domain name; (3) and the domain name has been registered and used in bad faith.[46] In practice, however, critics have charged that these criteria are being interpreted in a way that serves the interests of big business over newcomers and small-business owners.

This issue—the determination of who has rights to domain names—raises questions about whose interests are being protected. Karl Auerbach, formerly the ICANN board member representing North America at large, wrote, "[The UDRP] evolved from WIPO "meetings" that largely were attended by, and held by, those who are advocates of maximum expansion of protections of Intellectual Property. The result was, as one would expect, highly biased toward Intellectual Property protection."[47]

Milton Mueller's research suggests that while the ICANN UDRP guidelines as written are reasonably fair, a flaw in the system of implementation arises from the rule giving the complainant the right to choose which of the approved mediation services will be used. Complainants, usually firms with substantial resources, can forum-shop and choose the mediation services that most favor their position.[48]

Even with the newly introduced top-level domains, prime virtual estate is a scarce commodity. There is a real value to firms obtaining the most advantageous Internet domain name, that is, one that is memorable and closely linked to the company. The same goes for organizations. Stronger protection for holders of famous marks means fewer opportunities for holders of less famous marks and for those who will want domain names in the future. By tying trademark rights to domain-name rights, the public gains the ability to be more certain about whom they are dealing with when they do business on a website. But the public also loses in the inability to hold and access less famous or less commercially important marks.

■ Lack of Consensus and an Opening for Crime

The examples above represent just a few of the many current debates over the extent of intellectual property protection that ought to be granted and the appropriate balance between the interests of the public and those of individuals and corporations. Ironically, the lack of consensus has created an opportunity for pirating and counterfeiting intellectual property.

Because the law-abiding citizen may not see anything wrong in picking up a cheap knockoff of an expensive product or downloading a free version of a newly released feature film, there is a global market for stolen intellectual property. According to experts and news reports, organized crime has moved in, profiting from the willingness of individuals to turn a blind eye toward an intellectual property owner who is a distant other—say, a corporation somewhere in cyberspace. The International Anti-Counterfeiting Coalition notes that "counterfeiting operations are relatively risk-free and offer enormous profits."[49] A report by the secretariats of the United Nations Economic Commission for Europe and the Organization for Security and Cooperation in Europe notes a connection between weak states' inability to police counterfeiting and the opportunity for terrorist groups to prosper.[50]

Although consumers of illegitimate products bear some responsibility, intellectual property owners who demand too many restrictions undermine the legitimacy of their own claims. When the rights provided to innovators and creators are too strong, people ignore them more easily. When the balance is evident—firms receive an appropriate return on their investment, while the public receives understanding, knowledge, or enjoyment—then the bargain holds.

■ Notes

1. World Trade Organization, "Council Approves LDC Decision with Additional Waiver," press release, June 28, 2002 [cited August 19, 2002],

available from www.wto.org/english/news_e/pres02_e/pr301_e.htm; and World Trade Organization, "Declaration on the TRIPS Agreement and Public Health," WT/MIN(01)/DEC/2, Ministerial Conference, Doha, November 14 and 20, 2001[cited August 7, 2002], available from www.wto.org/english/thewto_e/minist_e/min01_e/mindecl_trips_e.htm.

2. As F. M. Scherer points out, "Switzerland, for example, had long granted patents on drug manufacturing processes, but did not award patents on product formulas until 1977. This is a significant difference, since product patents normally provide much stronger barriers to generic imitation than process patents." F. M. Scherer, "Pricing, Profits, and Technological Progress in the Pharmaceutical Industry," *Journal of Economic Perspectives* 7, no. 3 (1993).

3. Sheryl Gay Stolberg, and Jeff Gerth, "In a Drug's Journey to Market: Discovery Is Just the First of Many Steps," *New York Times,* July 23, 2000.

4. Pharmaceutical Research and Manufacturers of America (PhRMA), "The Discovery Process: An Overview" [cited October 1, 2001], available from innovation.phrma.org/dprocess [note: link is no longer available].

5. A similar concern with potential profits serves to encourage pharmaceutical companies to research treatments for HIV/AIDS rather than vaccines to prevent infection. Rachel Glennerster and Michael Kremer, "A Better Way to Spur Medical Research and Development," *Regulation* 23, no. 2 (2000).

6. Pharmaceutical companies also have little incentive to look for cures to rare diseases, whether or not potential customers would have the means to purchase the drugs. There would not be enough customers to recoup the investment in R&D during the period of patent protection. To change the incentive structure, the United States enacted the Orphan Drug Law.

7. Peter J. Neumann and Eileen A. Sandberg, "Trends in Health Care R&D and Technology Innovation: The Pace of Innovation Shows No Sign of Slowing, but More Funding Is Now Drawn from Private-Sector Sources," *Health Affairs* (November–December 1998).

8. Ibid.

9. Linda Stecklein and George Stone, "An NIH Perspective on the Bayh-Dole Act and Invention Reporting Responsibilities," *SRA Journal* 31, no. 2 (1999).

10. Mary Poovey, "The Twenty-First-Century University and the Market: What Price Economic Viability?" *Differences* 12, no. 1 (2001).

11. Glennerster and Kremer, "A Better Way to Spur Medical Research and Development."

12. David Kreling et. al, "Prescription Drug Trends: A Chart Book" (Menlo Park, CA: Kaiser Family Foundation, 2000), p. 52.

13. In the United States, the Orphan Drug Act of 1983 encourages pharmaceutical companies to develop drugs for rare diseases by providing tax deductions for a substantial proportion of the cost of clinical studies and by providing exclusive marketing rights for seven years for the first firm to produce a useful treatment or cure. The drawback of this approach is that subsequent novel drugs that have similar clinical effects are excluded during

this period. Scherer, "Pricing, Profits, and Technological Progress in the Pharmaceutical Industry," p. 99.

14. "Medicines for All, Not Just the Rich," *Bulletin of the World Health Organization* 79, no. 4 (2001).

15. World Health Organization and World Trade Organization Secretariats, Workshop on Differential Pricing and Financing of Essential Drugs, "Executive Summary of the Report," Norwegian Foreign Affairs Ministry, Global Health Council, April 8–11 2001 [cited August 21, 2003], available from www.who.int/medicines/library/edm_general/who-wto-hosbjor/hosbjorexe-eng.pdf.

16. Glennerster and Kremer, "A Better Way to Spur Medical Research and Development."

17. This parallel is drawn by John H. Barton, "Financing of Vaccines," *The Lancet,* April 8, 2000, pp. 1269–1270.

18. A detailed, if polemic, account of the conflicting principles of TRIPS and CBD has been published online by GRAIN, a sustainable development advocacy organization. Genetic Resources Action International (GRAIN), "TRIPS Versus CBD: Conflicts Between the WTO Regime of Intellectual Property Rights and Sustainable Biodiversity Management," *Global Trade and Biodiversity in Conflict,* no. 1, April 1998 [cited October 1, 2001], available from www.grain.org/publications/issue1-en-p.htm.

19. Secretariat of the Convention on Biodiversity, United Nations Environmental Program, Convention on Biodiversity, June 5, 1992 [cited January 25, 2003], available from www.biodiv.org/convention/articles.asp01.

20. Frederick M. Abbott, "TRIPS in Seattle: The Not-So-Surprising Failure and the Future of the TRIPS Agenda," *Berkeley Journal of International Law* 18 (2000); and David Downes, "How Intellectual Property Could Be a Tool to Protect Traditional Knowledge," *Columbia Journal of Environmental Law* 25 (2000).

21. Joris Kocken and Gerda van Roozendall, "The Neem Tree Debate," *Biotechnology and Development Monitor* (1997); and Emily Marden, "The Neem Tree Patent: International Conflict over the Commodification of Life," *Boston College International and Comparative Law Review* 22 (1999): 238–284.

22. Lori Wolfgang, "Patents on Native Technology Challenged," *Science* (1995).

23. Marden, "The Neem Tree Patent," pp. 290–291.

24. Parvathi Menon, "For an 'Evergreen Revolution': Interview with Dr. M.S. Swaminathan." *Frontline (India),* December 25, 1999–2000 [cited August 19, 2002], available from www.flonnet.com/fl1627/16270940.htm; and Action Group on Erosion, Technology, and Concentration (Etc. Group), *Basmati Rice Patent,* 1998 [cited August 19, 2002], available from www.rafi.org/article.asp?newsid=62.

25. Ranjit Devraj, "'Basmati' Patent Win Not Final, Say Food Security Experts." *Third World Network,* October 8, 2000 [cited October 1, 2001], available from www.twnside.org.sg/title/basmati.htm.

26. Ibid.

27. Anupa Prathap Matthew, "Basmati Battle Simmers Down," *Gulf News,* September 5, 2001.

28. This is the basic point made by Dorothy C. Wertz, *Controversial Attempts at Patenting* (February 1, 1999 [cited August 21, 2003]), available from www.genesage.com/professionals/geneletter/archives/controversialattempts.html. Wertz, however, implies that RiceTec has used genetic engineering to splice genes. Information from RiceTec can be found at RiceTec, *Hybrid Seed* [cited August 19, 2002], available from www.ricetec.com/hybrid.htm.

29. Kocken, "The Neem Tree Debate."

30. Biotechnology Industry Organization (BIO), *Primer: Genome and Genetic Research, Patent Protection and 21st Century Medicine* (July 2000 [cited October 5, 2001]); available from www.bio.org/genomics/primer.htm.

31. Ibid.

32. Ibid.

33. Ibid.

34. The strict versus lenient utility standard debate is detailed in John R. Thomas, "An Examination of the Issues Surrounding Biotechnology Patenting and Its Effect Upon Entrepreneurial Companies" (Washington, DC: Library of Congress, Congressional Research Service report for Congress, 2000).

35. American Institute of Physics [Naomi Pasachoff], "Marie Curie and the Science of Radioactivity," website content based on the book of the same title by Naomi Pasachoff (New York: Oxford University Press, 1996) [cited January 25, 2003], available from www.aip.org/history/curie/resbr3.htm. Though the Curies did not patent their work, one element, americium (atomic number 95), was patented by Glenn Seaborg, who was successful in producing and isolating it. Glenn Seaborg, Element 95 and Method of Producing Said Element, U.S. Patent 3,156,523, filed August 23, 1946, and issued November 19, 1964. Americium, unlike radium, is not a product of nature; rather it is a by-product of a nuclear reaction.

36. A related concern comes from the use of medical samples in research. Do we have any right to the properties of our cells? James Boyle tells the fascinating story of John Moore, whose spleen was the source of a cell line patented by the University of California. James Boyle, *Shamans, Software, and Spleens: Law and the Construction of the Information Society* (Cambridge, MA: Harvard University Press, 1996).

37. More information about Cyveillance can be found online at Cyveillance, *Company Information* [cited August 12, 2002], available from www.cyeillance.com.

38. Maria Alicia Gaura, "Church of Scientology Wins $3 Million Ruling," *San Francisco Chronicle,* September 19, 1998; Stephen Fraser, "The Conflict Between the First Amendment and Copyright Law and Its Impact on the Internet," *Cardozo Arts & Entertainment Law Journal* 16 (1998).

39. Jacobs Persinger & Parker [law firm], Letter to Dee Dreslough [e-mail] (April 1, 1997 [cited August 18, 2002]), redacted copy available from www.chilingeffects.org.

40. Viacom Inc.–Paramount Pictures Corporation [attorney writing on behalf of Paramount Pictures Corporation], Letter to David Henderson (July

29, 2001 [cited August 19, 2003]), redacted copy available from www.chilling effects.org/fanfic/notice.cgi?NoticeID=7. The letter specifically charges that Henderson's posting of a synopsis of *Star Trek: First Contact* and *Star Trek*-related photographs as infringements.

41. Napster went out of business in 2002. Napster-like sites and peer-to-peer sites based on applications like Kazaa continue to emerge. Though the music industry continues to litigate against unauthorized distribution, major record labels have begun to use Napster-style technology for fee-based distribution of music. Brad King, "The Day Napster Died" *Wired News,* May 15, 2002 [cited August 19, 2002], available from www.wired.com/news/print/ 9,1294,52540,00.html.

42. Fred Von Lohman, *Peer-to-Peer File Sharing and Copyright Law after Napster* (Electronic Frontier Foundation, January 2003 [cited August 21, 2003]), available from www.eff.org/IP/P2P/20010227_p2p_copyright_ white_paper.html.

43. Electronic Frontier Foundation, *Unintended Consequences: Three Years under the DMCA* ([2001, cited August 19, 2002]), available from www. eff.org/IP/DMCA/20020503_dmca_consequences.pdf.

44. A federal appeals court upheld the initial judge's ruling against Doughney. Declan McCullagh, "Ethical Treatment of PETA Domain," *Wired News,* August 25, 2001 [cited August 19, 2002], available from www.wired. com/news/privacy/0,1848,46313,00.html.

45. Cybersquatting is the registration of a domain name with bad intent, for the purpose of either tricking unsuspecting site visitors or of extorting money from a potential legitimate user. Reverse domain-name hijacking refers to wresting away a domain name from a legitimate user, often by using threats of lawsuits to intimidate a less well financed firm or individual.

46. Internet Corporation for Assigned Names and Numbers (ICANN), Uniform Dispute Resolution Policy, August 26, 1999 [cited August 19, 2002], available from www.icann.org/dndr/udrp/policy.htm.

47. Karl Auerbach, *Answers to IDP Questionnaire* [cited February 1, 2001, available from www.internetdemocracyproject.org/IDPanswersauerbach.htm.

48. Milton Mueller, "Rough Justice: An Analysis of ICANN's Uniform Dispute Resolution Policy" (Convergence Center, Syracuse University School of Information Studies, August 19, 2000).

49. International Anti-Counterfeiting Coalition, "Organized Crime and Product Counterfeiting" [cited August 19, 2002], available from www.iacc. org/teampublish/109_476_1676.cfm. See also Roslyn A. Mazer, "From T-Shirts to Terrorism: That Fake Nike Swoosh May Be Helping to Fund Bin Laden's Network," *Washington Post,* September 30, 2001; and a rebuttal: Naomi Klein, "Comment & Analysis: McWorld and Jihad," *The Guardian (London),* October 5, 2001.

50. United Nations Economic Commission for Europe and Organization for Security and Cooperation in Europe Secretariats, *The Economic Dimension to Security: New Challenges and New Approaches,* April 30, 2002 [cited August 19, 2002], available from www.unece.org/commission/2002/ CRP.1_ECE_session.pdf.

5

Information

Information defines the Information Age we live in. We know lots of facts nowadays, but why do we think that our era is so different from the past? Do we have more or better information, or do we just have "data smog"?[1] Our predecessors no doubt possessed new information. They knew facts, many of which are now lost or forgotten. (Who among us knows the technique for churning butter?) Nevertheless, our times seem different because we are compelled to absorb mountains of facts necessary for living in the twenty-first century. Moreover, information is increasingly valuable within the global economy. Some kinds of information that had once been freely shared are now commodities to be sold or sponsored by advertisers.[2]

Though the English term *information* was in the lexicon as early as the Middle Ages, many date the beginning of the Information Age to 1948, when Claude Shannon wrote about information in his influential paper "The Mathematical Theory of Communication." Shannon's contribution was to work out the fundamental mathematics of a general system in which "an information source produces a message to be communicated" to a receiver. By distinguishing between the *content* of the information (the message) and the information itself, he was able to show that content is irrelevant to the engineering task of transmitting it.[3] This realization paved the way for creating the means to store and transmit information—technologies that work regardless of the actual content being stored or transmitted. (In other words, the principles underlying a database of weather data are the same as those underlying a database of customer purchases. Similarly, weather data and customer data can be dispatched electronically

97

through essentially the same process.) With advances in computer science that followed Shannon's pathbreaking work, efficient means of communicating and storing information became possible, which in turn created an opportunity for usable—and valuable—compilations of information.

Today, information is used more loosely, and the term itself has lost some meaning because it encompasses too much. Here is one definition: information is any change or variation from randomness—the signal, not the noise. By this definition, radio waves emitted by a distant galaxy are information, whether or not an astronomer is observing and recording them. Similarly, the words I speak are information because they are recognizably distinct from random sounds. Information can be a product of the natural environment or of human interaction, irrespective of whether a human observer perceives the signal. (If a tree falls in the forest and no one hears it, the information—sound waves caused by the crashing tree—still exists.)

However, information is of social consequence only when a human is involved as the sender, the recipient, or an intermediary. (If two computers exchange information automatically, a human may neither directly send nor receive the information. Nevertheless, humans serve as intermediaries because they have created the situation in which the communication between the computers is desired.) Albert Borgmann directs our attention to how humans relate information to reality, specifically differentiating between information *about reality,* information *for reality,* and information *as reality.* Information about or for reality refers to the way in which humans interpret signs that tell us something about the world out there. As Borgmann puts it, "A PERSON is informed by a SIGN about some THING."[4] The assumption is that there is some objective reality that can be described using symbols (words being a kind of symbol). When a child comes home soaking wet, the parent may quickly figure out that the kid has been jumping in puddles. In other words, the parent interprets the sign (unexpected wetness) and is informed about the child's puddle-jumping activities. Score-keeping during athletic competitions is another example of information about reality. When a baseball player hits a home run, a fan can record the information about what happened on a scorecard, thereby preserving it for future reference.

Information *for* reality provides a recipe for creating. Borgmann differentiates these two categories this way:

> Gregorio Allegri wrote a score *for* the *Miseree* that was to be per-
> formed in the Sistine Chapel only and was therefore kept secret.
> When the fourteen-year-old Mozart, on having heard the psalm
> once, wrote down the score from memory, it was information *about*
> rather than for the performance of music.[5]

Allegri's musical score set out how the musicians were to create the reality of the music. Mozart's transcription of the music, however, replicated or recorded what he heard. Here is another example: maps contain both information *about* reality and information *for* reality. For example, a highway map of Maryland describes objective reality about where the highways go. A topological map of the same state describes a different aspect of reality: the elevations of locations. The images that comprise the map have been created to represent aspects of the reality of Maryland. But by enabling the map reader to figure out how to get from Point A to Point B, the map is also a way of creating the reality of the journey.

Information *as* reality is a much more intangible thing, something that has become increasingly valuable as a form of property. Information as reality is essentially virtual reality. For instance, L. Jon Wertheim's 2002 *Sports Illustrated* article about Simonya Papova was an exercise in virtual reality creation. Though the story about the statuesque, up-and-coming tennis dynamo was compelling realistic, those who read the entire article discovered that she was nothing more than a computer-generated image, her story an author-generated narrative. The information manifest in the article neither represented reality nor provided instructions for producing reality. The reality in the story was the information itself. Even something as simple as a music CD can be understood as information as reality. When I listen to a recording of a piece of music, I experience the information—the audio record of the music—rather than the performance of the music itself. In the same vein, if I use data from the U.S. Census, the data represent the reality of people's lives (information about reality). But it is the census data itself that I experience. I do not think of Sally on Elm Street and her two children; I think of aggregates that do not exist in the real world but do exist in the analysis of the information itself.

The loss we face in a world filled with information as reality, as Borgmann points out, is that humans gain rich experience when we focus on the real world, not the virtual world. We miss the opportunity to gather information *about* and *for* reality with all or our senses in all of its complexity when we rely on the simplified, digitized version. And yet the simplified, stripped down, coded, and computerized versions of reality represented in large databases *are* useful. By increasing productivity, they have the potential to increase our material wealth, if not our spiritual wealth. Of course, understanding the conditions under which different kinds of information have value to the market and to society is fundamental. How we go from having information about, for, and as reality to acquiring wisdom is a much more difficult issue.

Until recently, information was not considered to be intellectual property. Indeed, one of the distinguishing factors was that intellectual property was not merely a compilation of facts or ideas but rather a creative product. If it is intellectual property, then someone's creativity or innovative ability is embedded in the work, and that creative effort forms the kernel of what is owned. Information, by contrast, existed "out there," independent of the compiler or gatherer.[6] Hence the traditional distinction: whereas intellectual property depends on the genius of some individual or group of individuals, information gathering or compiling can be accomplished by anyone who makes the effort.

Today, this sharp distinction is becoming fuzzy. First, compiling information requires technical creativity (i.e., how should the database be created?). Second, it requires analytical creativity (what kinds of information should be compiled?). Third, it is time-consuming to collect and easily copied. Fourth, because data can be recorded and reproduced with a high degree of fidelity, the resulting high-quality data products are now more valuable than the lower-quality information that used to be available.

Technical creativity and *analytical creativity* refer to the organization of databases and their content. Imagine a company that markets targeted mailing lists. The technical creativity is provided by the people who program the database system. The analytical creativity comes from the marketing or product development staffs—the people who know what kinds of information they need and how they want to be able to manipulate it. The number of technicians, analysts, and other people engaged in knowledge work, and the number of hours they work, mark a significant shift toward increased costs for value-added brainwork.[7] Firms have made a significant investment in producing usable information.

Moreover, technologically speaking, we have better tools to gather, compile, organize, and extract information. New technologies allow us to collect more information of better quality. For example, satellites and airborne instruments image the Earth, its resources, and human activities in ways that no earthbound observer could. Sensitive ground-based information detects seismic disturbances and can distinguish between earthquakes and nuclear explosions. Such distinctions could not be made without the use of these special information-gathering and -analyzing instruments. Genetic information read from DNA, precise locations determined by the global positioning system, and Google searches are additional examples.

Computers are so commonplace today that the changes they have brought are easy to overlook. The way the practice of pharmacy has changed is a prime example of the impact of computerized databases. Prior to the use of computers in pharmacies, when a patient came in to fill a prescription, the pharmacist pulled out the patient's record and added the new medication to the list of medications the patient was taking. It was the pharmacist's responsibility to draw on her knowledge of which drugs can or cannot be taken together to avoid a contraindication or drug interaction that had to be avoided. Nowadays, this process has been routinized and streamlined by computerization.[8] Today's pharmacists have a lot of information about known drug interactions at their fingertips through a computer database. In the old days, a drug recall meant that the pharmacists had to go through their files, patient by patient, looking for those who had received that particular drug and contacting each one. (Or they simply relied on the patients to know what drugs they were taking.) Now pharmacists can pull up the information about who is taking what with just a few keystrokes.

In addition, access to a computerized database allows marketers and others to develop promotional tie-ins, either for health enhancement (i.e., if the pharmacy is cooperating with the health insurer, who has an interest in keeping the patient as healthy as possible) or for additional sales. For example, diabetics might receive information on managing the disease. Known diabetics might also be seen as a target audience for advertisements for new devices that test blood sugar levels. There may be magazines that want their subscriptions, or organizations that want their membership. One example is a continuing education course of the National Community Pharmacists Association, entitled, "Marketing Your Pharmacy Services in the New Millennium." Using a hypothetical Diabetes Day, the course discusses how the pharmacist might market services and products to the targeted group of diabetics. Pharmacists are encouraged to identify patients to receive flyers advertising Diabetes Day by using their "computer database [to] compose a printout of anyone on insulin, or any other type of diabetic agent."[9]

Firms, governments, and organizations frequently assert proprietary claims about the information they have gathered. Although information may not be scarce in its natural form, the costs of gathering information are high enough that the compilation has the characteristic of scarcity. Many people may want aerial maps of a location (e.g., the Drug Enforcement Agency may want the map to figure out who is growing marijuana in the backyard; utilities may want the map to check on power lines; developers might be looking at potential locations for new housing developments; I might want aerial maps because I think they look good on my wall), but not everyone is going to hire a plane and pilot to go up and take the picture. The information—the image of the ground—is there for anyone in the right location (in the air) to see it. But in practical terms, the ability to capture the image is scarce.

The case of drug interactions is also instructive. Theoretically, pharmacists can look up each drug in books (the ubiquitous *Physician's Desk Reference* is simply a database in printed form) that are freely available in the library. They could also survey every drug company routinely to be informed of new interactions that are discovered. They could then develop their own database or rely on memory to check each patient's record against what they know. In practice, of course, it is much more reliable and efficient to use a database that has already been developed. What is scarce is the time needed to compile the information and the technical skill needed to put it in a useable format.

Despite the quasi-property features of information today, neither domestic nor international laws to protect it are fully formed. Some interests seek to transform information into intellectual property, sometimes drawing on laws protecting trade secrets. In other situations, people rely on contract law and refer to proprietary business information. In this arrangement, a person can sign a contract that allows him to use information that I am selling, but he may not transfer that information to anyone else. This is much like a licensing agreement for copyrighted material.

Sorting out the aspects of information property in the twenty-first century is not easy. At no other time in human history have we been able to marshal so much information for so many purposes.

Who owns or otherwise possesses information? What is information, really? How is information different from other forms of knowledge? How does information come to be valuable?

■ Who Has/Owns/Controls Information?

The first questions to ask about information are who has, owns, or controls it, and how is it possessed, owned, or controlled? Information comes in many forms, some of it useful for commercial purposes, some of it purely for intellectual or spiritual needs, some of it necessary or beneficial for national security, some of it solely for personal well-being or satisfaction. Other information is useful for nefarious purposes, ranging from gossip to crime.

Consider some disparate bits of information:

- historical facts such as the names of Christopher Columbus's ship[10] and a list of every interstate conflict in recorded history;[11]
- scientific facts such as the atomic weight of molybdenum[12] and the location of the gene for cystic fibrosis in the human genome;[13]
- personal facts such as your address and your weight;
- other economically, politically, militarily, or socially relevant facts such as a company's client list, the location of the nearest Dairy Queen restaurant,[14] the precise location of Osama bin Laden today,[15] and the translation of the Dead Sea Scrolls.[16]

It seems obvious that these kinds of information have differing importance and vary to the extent that they are (or are not) public goods. Certainly, ownership of information about my weight must differ from information about molybdenum's (atomic) weight, and Dairy Queen locations are different from the location of enemy leaders.

Information can thus be classified as unowned, commercial, or state-controlled.

The Global Information Commons: Unowned Information

Some facts are unowned; they are part of a global information commons. This category includes historical knowledge and other knowledge that one can glean from the teachings of the past, scientific discoveries, patented technological know-how, and traditional knowledge. For example, the names of Christopher Columbus's ships and the atomic weight of molybdenum are readily available from a variety of sources, including encyclopedias and online reference materials.

The culture of science places a high premium on the communication of new knowledge. The scientific method emphasizes the need for experiments to be replicable. Moreover, scientific advances build on prior investigations. Science thus puts a premium on sharing information among the community of scientists. However, since the scientists' reputation rests on the quality of the data, they have an incentive to hold on to information and not release it precipitously. Data must be checked and rechecked for systematic errors and other problems with accuracy and reliability. Also the scientists who conduct an investigation and collect the data want first crack at the analysis of it, especially since the results of data analysis, rather than just data collection, contribute the most to their reputation.

In general, scientists do not have to place information into the public domain until they have confidence in the quality (accuracy, replicability) of their data and have published the results of their analyses. The basic culture of science, though, requires that the information be made public, usually through the publication of the information in peer-reviewed scientific journals, through presentations at professional scientific conferences, and in the sharing of data. Other scientists can then check the accuracy of the data by trying to replicate it, or they can build new knowledge by analyzing the data. The obligation to disseminate is so strong that in hard science fields it is customary for the author (or her institution) to pay to have the scientific article published. In other words, the person providing the knowledge to the global information commons pays to place that information in the public domain.

Increasingly, however, scientists are torn between the long-standing culture of dissemination and the need to keep potentially valuable information secret. This is especially true under the provisions of the Bayh-Dole Act, which encourages universities to commercialize the results of research funded by government grants. Because information today increasingly leads to proprietary information or to a patentable invention, scientists have reason to be more cautious about releasing—or not—information into the public domain. In the absence of property rights in new discoveries, scientists are motivated by their desire for a good reputation and recognition from their peers. This intangible benefit translates into more tangible benefits like higher pay, tenure, promotion, job offers, and the like. But few researchers in basic science fields become wealthy as a result of their efforts. Thus the scientists who are able to commercialize the results of their research receive the greatest monetary rewards. In essence, there is a culture of science that values the creation of new knowledge for the benefit of the world, and there is a competing culture of the market that emphasizes the creation of new knowledge for profit.

Commercial Information

When information is owned it is no longer a public good. Instead, owners use legal and technical means to restrict access to the information, thereby making it excludable. The result is a private good (the information is available to others only at the discretion of the owner) or a club good (the information is available to the members of a group but all others are excluded from access). This is the case with commercial information, which may start as openly available data. A business might begin to build a proprietary database by collecting the names and addresses of its customers. Since the purchaser's name is disclosed whenever a sale is not on a strictly cash basis, the purchaser gives up personal information (her name) at the time of the transaction. Purchasers often voluntarily disclose personal information when they fill out forms that accompany the new purchase. In doing so, purchasers are contributing information to the company's customer information database.

Customers may want to disclose information in this way because they receive a benefit in return. For example, if they need a service or assistance, they can demonstrate that they have purchased the company's product and are entitled to the warranty. Much of the information submitted by purchasers, however, helps the company more than the customer, despite assurances that disclosing information results in better service. The company's real goal is often finding out how to better market its products, and the benefit to the customer is minimal. The company obtains valuable information, which it can use for its own purposes or sell to other companies. By holding the information in its database or data warehouse, the company can make the information, as collected and organized, excludable. The company's computers are protected from trespassers by laws prohibiting unauthorized computer access and by technical means such as firewall software.

MicroStrategy, a firm in northern Virginia, is one example. It depends on analyzing such data to create useable information, or data mining. The company provides software that enables users to build large databases, analyze them, and disseminate the information to other people in the organization, clients, and suppliers. By integrating several computer-oriented functions, the software streamlines the management of very large amounts of data.[17]

Commercial information need not be information about clients, however. It may also refer to other kinds of information. For example, builders and developers may need to know what lies below the surface of a building site. Can a building be built safely here? Where should the oil well be drilled? Geophysical services consultants can answer such questions by providing information about subsurface conditions.[18] Geological information on the location of water and other resources, such as oil, can be collected using new technologies, including remote sensing from airplanes or satellites and surface techniques such as seismic refraction and reflection.[19] Customers for this information include governments as well as private firms. Jordan, for example, with support from the U.S. Agency for International Development, contracted with ARD, Inc., a corporation headquartered in Vermont, for geophysical technical assistance. Commercial information is developed because it has value in a business setting. Either the information is sold, or it is used by the developer for other business purposes.

State-Owned Information

Governments also develop and own proprietary information, which may or may not be commercial. Indeed, state-owned proprietary information can be sold as commercial information property, given away as a public good, or kept secret.

State secrets are bits of information that the state has deemed important to national security or other national interests. In the wake of September 11, voices in Congress and other legislatures in the West urgently called for increased surveillance—in other words, for the intensified collection of data about people's activities—and the use of that data to head off future terrorist attacks.[20]

Government intelligence agencies gather, compile, and organize information in order to conduct analysis. These agencies gather information that is unowned (public source data) and owned (either state secrets or other kinds of information property). Much of their efforts involve collecting information from published sources like newspapers and from radio and TV broadcasts, though other data are gathered through covert activities. The end products of the intelligence analysis are often, but not always, state secrets. The U.S. Central Intelligence Agency, for example, makes a good deal of information widely available through publications and its website. Nevertheless, much of the business of spying involves stealing other countries' or groups' secrets and using those secrets for secret ends.

All states, democratic or not, keep some information secret. Although most information gleaned through espionage is about other governments, spies sometimes collect information about the activities of private firms in the target country. (This access to secret commercial information is sometimes inadvertent, sometimes intentional.) Though most cases of economic espionage involve company insiders providing proprietary information to competitors, governments spy as well. There is nothing new here: in 1792 the British embassy in China conducted economic espionage, collecting information on technologies and processes that greatly benefited British commercial interests.[21] In 1988, the U.S. government and Boeing Corporation charged that France's intelligence agency, the General Directorate for External Security, passed along secret information about Boeing's data on its then-new 747–400 to Airbus, a competing firm.[22] Turnabout was unfair play in 2000, when France charged the United States with using its ability to intercept electronic communications to collect secret commercial information to benefit U.S. firms.[23] Such charges and countercharges continue.

Another problem facing governments is how to deal with secret information that has slipped into the public domain. How to build a nuclear or biological weapon is information that the government would prefer to restrict. One way is to limit what is exported. The United States export restrictions on dual-use technologies covers many high-tech products, including advanced supercomputers and some forms of encryption.[24] The idea behind the export prohibition is not only to deny the actual high-tech equipment to countries but also to keep engineers and scientists in those countries from engaging in reverse engineering.

Much government information, however, is not secret. Though much unclassified information in the past was available to citizens, directly and through public libraries, the trend has been for the government to charge user fees. This shift began during the 1980s, when, during the Conservative administration of Prime Minister Margaret Thatcher in Britain and the Republican administration of Ronald Reagan in the United States, influential politicians advocated reducing government spending and encouraged privatization of as many government services as possible. Many OECD countries with large social welfare programs were feeling the pinch of rising costs for programs. The state of the global economy, prevalent ideas about how economics worked,[25] and the standing of both Reagan and Thatcher made this approach attractive to several governments. New Zealand, for example, adopted wide-ranging economic reforms, beginning in 1984, that led to privatization of government services and deregulation. In doing so, information came to be sold to cover costs and perhaps earn a profit. Meteorological services (see Chapter 6) and air traffic control services were just two of the kinds of information that New Zealand commodified.[26]

In the United States, according to Robert Gellman, federal agencies have been whittling away at the legal guarantees of free access to U.S. government information through "license agreements, royalties for use of data, restrictions on redisclosure of information products, limitations on qualified recipients, and denial of access to digital versions of publicly available data."[27]

But much information is still unowned and provided at no charge by governments. This information can take many forms, including consumer protection information, health information, and legal materials. In the United States, the Freedom of Information Act (FOIA) allows access to any government information that is neither secret (FOIA does not cover classified information) nor private (one cannot use FOIA to obtain someone else's tax returns).[28]

Many international organizations also have an ethos of placing information into the public domain. The United Nations and the World Health Organization, for example, post enormous amounts of information about their activities (resolutions passed, actions taken, budget, etc.) on their websites. Prior to the rise of the Internet, researchers relied on international governmental organizations' documents held in depository libraries. The Internet, of course, makes gaining access to official information much easier.

The ease of access to information provided by some organizations raises suspicions about those that do not offer sufficient information to the public. The World Bank and the International Monetary Fund, in particular, have been criticized for their lack of transparency, that is, their insistence on keeping information secret instead of placing it in the public domain. Both organizations have recently made an effort to be more transparent and to offer more information to the public.

Sharing and Hoarding Information: Alternatives to Markets

A more practical question, though, is what do we do with information once we acquire it? One possibility is to commodify it by buying, selling, or licensing it. These, however, are not the only answers; information can also be shared and hoarded.

Sharing information. Shared information is unowned; it is part of the knowledge commons. In that case, the person with the information has an obligation to make it available to others. Science works this way, as do many social relationships. Take as one example my role as a professor. My salary, according to the university, is based on teaching, research, and service (basically committee work). The teaching component can be divided into the facts and skills that I impart to my students (the content of the teaching), and my time and effort spent actually imparting the facts and skills (the act of teaching). I suggest that my students' tuition pays for the act of teaching, not for the content. After all, they don't *really* need me if they just want the content; they can be autodidacts and educate themselves by doing the reading and thinking. I'm in the classroom to facilitate their learning.

The act of teaching is a service that I choose to sell by agreeing to the conditions of employment set by the university. Facts and skills that I have learned are the content. It would be wrong to intentionally keep students from learning some content that they seek to learn. Just because my students are studying one text does not mean that I can ethically deny them access to another. Moreover, I do not even think of stopping them from communicating what they have learned to others. It is fundamentally good for knowledge to spread.[29]

In some cases, shared information can be conceptualized as owned but given freely and voluntarily as a gift. When two people look at an information-sharing relationship differently, misunderstandings result.

Consider the issue of transfer of technology and knowledge from the Global North to the Global South. The governments and firms in the North have information (the location of resources, for example, gleaned from earth-imaging technologies) that the people of the South could use. Is it the obligation of the North to disclose this information? Or would it be the charitable, gift-giving thing to do with North-owned information property? Back in the late 1970s and early 1980s, the attempts at creating a New International Economic Order and a New International Information Order sought to impose on the countries of the North the obligation to transfer technology— in other words, to disclose information—to countries of the South.[30] In the end, the dominance of the market and the pervasiveness of commodification led to the prevailing view that information property *may* be shared by giving it as a gift, at the discretion of the owner.

Hoarding information. At the other extreme is hoarding information, by which I mean creating information as a club good, available only to those who are members of the group. This is distinct from patenting an invention (at least in theory) because a patent protects a device or process and actually discloses the information about how the device or process works. It is also distinct from copyrighting material because a copyright simply assures that the information cannot be reproduced. A person can still learn as much as he wants from it as long as he doesn't copy it. Hoarding information is more akin to trade secrets (but not all hoarded information is a trade secret). When information is hoarded it is excluded from a global information commons. Hoarded information is property; the owner creates it as property by using secrecy to create artificial scarcity.

Medieval guilds, such as that of the glassmakers of Venice in the thirteenth and fourteenth centuries, are a good illustration of what it means to hoard information.[31] Glassmaking was a complicated technology involving recipes and techniques for combining sand and other ingredients and heating the mixture in three furnaces. The clarity, strength, and quality of Venetian glass—the result of high-quality ingredients and the know-how of the craftsmen—made Venetian glass the finest in its day. To be members of the glassmaking guild (and only members were allowed to make glass), craftsmen were required to take an oath to abide by the rules of the guild. These rules, which covered a variety of subjects, included a prohibition against dealing in stolen or defective glass and regulations on taking and training apprentices, and also specified some aspects of how the famous Venetian glass was made. There was also a specific injunction against making glass outside the borders of Venice. Although there was competition between glassworkers within Venice, the interest of all was served by keeping the art within the city-state. Members of the guild were prohibited from making glass elsewhere because that would introduce the knowledge of the craft to outsiders.[32] The guaranteed quality of the product and the secrecy process benefited the economy of Venice. The community benefited as a whole from its reputation as a source of the highest-quality glass, which was exported to other places in Europe.

There are other examples of hoarding information. Medical information, for example, can mean a patient's specific condition or general knowledge about how to prevent, diagnose, and treat disease. Until recently in North America (and continuing today in other cultures), doctors routinely withheld information from patients about their conditions, especially when the diagnosis was some form of cancer. Physicians, by virtue of their knowledge and their role in making decisions on behalf of patients, possessed power over their patients.[33] Medical information in general was made available only to people in the medical profession, and the language used in professional journal articles made (and still makes) access difficult for those not trained in the field.[34] It is only since the advent of the World Wide Web that large quantities of medical information (some good information, some garbage) have been readily available to laypeople, and physicians are now being trained to reject the role of Hoarder of Knowledge and Maker of Decisions in exchange for the role of patient partner in understanding conditions and making decisions.

The use of special language is an important way for information to be restricted. One could argue that there is a sacred priesthood in scholarship that, laden with jargon and incomprehensible to the untrained, creates superficial value by making the information inaccessible to all but those who are in the club. Increasingly, academics speak only to one another. Even though every writer must make assumptions about how much knowledge the reader brings to the table, it seems that much scholarly writing has fallen into the trap of obfuscation for the sake of seeming erudite. Physicist Alan Sokal skewered this tendency with a practical joke played on the journal *Social Text*. He wrote a paper filled with nonsense but larded with trendy jargon. The journal's editors did not detect the spoof and published the paper, at which point Sokal revealed the hoax.[35] When the use of jargon becomes a way to keep non-Ph.D.'s out of an intellectual dialog, then information is being hoarded.

■ Information as a Commodity

Sharing information and hoarding information are nothing new. Selling information as commodity, however, is a newer activity within the global economy. Until recently compilations of facts have not been protected as property. To explore the emergence of information property, an explanation of the legal context is necessary. I then look at recent developments that have eroded openness.

. . . *Or Not. First, a Look at* Feist, Waterlow, *and* Magill

Europeans and the Americans pursued different policies regarding access to information. In the United States, the predominant idea that facts are not protected as property is seen in *Feist Publications, Inc. v. Rural Telephone Service Co., Inc.* (1991), a well-known U.S. Supreme Court case.[36] The case occurred in Kansas. Rural Telephone Service Company, the local telephone company for several communities, was a public utility. As such it operated under a set of government regulations, including the requirement that it publish a telephone directory. Rural published a directory that consisted of names, addresses, and phone numbers arranged alphabetically[37] for residences and for businesses. But Rural had made the decision to issue separate directories for different telephone service areas. Another company, Feist Publications, saw a business opportunity in creating a single directory for eleven combined telephone service areas. Feist's revenue would come from selling advertisements. Residents would be enticed to use Feist's directory because it covered a larger region.

Feist thought at first that it would be a good idea if the firm licensed the white pages listings from Rural to be included in its new directory. Rural refused. From Rural's perspective, Feist was a competitor for scarce advertising dollars from Kansas businesses. Feist's response was to simply take the information and put it in the new directory. Rural sued Feist for copyright infringement, arguing that Rural had a property right in the alphabetical list of names, addresses, and telephone numbers that Feist was prohibited from copying without permission. Rural based its claim on a property right in the information because of the resources it needed to expend to compile it in the first place (the so-called the sweat-of-the-brow argument). Feist's response: facts are facts, and a compilation that shows no originality in selection (all telephone subscribers in the service areas were included) or organization (alphabetical) should not be considered copyrightable. The U.S. Supreme Court agreed.

Around the same time, similar cases were being argued in Europe; some of the decisions differ from those in Feist. In *Waterlow Directories Limited v. Reed Information Services Limited* the British High Court decided that extracting more than an insubstantial amount of information from a database was infringement, even if the information extracted was not creative or original. This case involved Reed Information Services, which published a legal directory of 12,600 names and addresses of solicitors and organizations. Waterlow Directories Limited copied 1,600 of the names into a computer database for sending solicitations by mail. The court found in favor of Reed, the plaintiff, because Waterlow had appropriated the information unfairly under British law.[38]

A similar case involving access to information concerned an Irish company's publication of TV broadcast schedules. This case, *Radio Telefís Eireann v. Magill,*[39] was decided by the European Court of Justice (ECJ) in 1995; it sets a precedent for all the countries of the European Union. Until recently in Ireland, each TV station compiled and publicized its own broadcast schedule. Magill Publications decided to introduce a new product: the *Magill TV Guide,* which would include a compilation of television stations' scheduled broadcasts for the week. RTE, BBC (both of them TV stations), and ITP (a company publishing the weekly guide for a third station, ITV) sued Magill on the grounds that the publisher violated their copyright in their schedule data. Though the court in Ireland ruled against Magill, the ECJ ultimately ruled—more or less—in its favor. The TV stations, according to the ECJ, were required to license their schedule data to Magill so that it could develop its *TV Guide.* (Magill would have to pay for the license.) The TV stations, the ECJ decided, had been acting like a monopoly by not allowing Magill to access their data. The stations were found to be in violation of a European Union treaty prohibiting anticompetitive behavior.[40]

This ruling did clarify the duties of monopolies or firms with monopoly-like power to provide information that a potential competitor needs in order to enter the market. However, the ruling emphatically did not create an absolute right to free information. And by also deciding that the stations could charge a reasonable fee for access to the schedules, the ECJ ruling implied that the TV stations had a property right in their schedules.[41]

Reacting to the Legal Environments in the United States and Europe

In a global economy that depends on producing data to make money, information sellers have a strong incentive to make sure that laws protect information. They seek a standard of protection consistent with *Waterlow* and *Magill* (supporting rights to information property) rather than *Feist* (favoring public access). One way to achieve that goal is to create a strong property right in information by treaty or other international agreement.[42]

Though the Organization for Economic Cooperation and Development began discussing the question of databases in the early 1980s,[43] the EU was the first to adopt rules protecting the data in databases, regardless of originality or creativity, through Directive 96/9/EC of the European Parliament and of the EU Council of March 11, 1996, on the Legal Protection of Databases. The directive protects any form of database, which it defines as "a collection of independent works, data or other materials arranged in a systematic or methodical way and individually accessible by electronic or other means." The form of the selection or arrangement is protected by copyright. The content—the data in the database—is covered by sui generis (unique, or a new form of) protection. The only requirement for protection is that the database owner show that he has made a "substantial" investment in preventing unauthorized use of the information (extraction or reutilization). The directive provides protection for a period of fifteen years. If any substantial part of the database is added to or revised during that time, the clock starts again and the database owner receives protection for another fifteen years.[44]

Critics of the EU database directive see a shrinking of the global information commons as a result. Unlike copyright and patent laws, which provide finite periods of protection, sui generis protection can be extended without limit, even with only a modest effort by the database owner to update or revise the information. Also, fair use provisions are not included in the directive, a significant omission that limits access to information. This strong protection of data creates complications, especially when research requires the use of data from different sources.

> Data aggregation is also becoming a problem for science. Over the
> past 5 years, academic (for example, Swiss-Prot) and commercial
> biologists [in the EU] have burdened their data with 'pass through'
> rights that place restrictions on data even after they have been
> incorporated into other databases. This creates opportunities for
> gridlock. A U.S. government data provider has had to restrict its
> use of Swiss-Prot data in order to avoid the potential repercussions
> resulting from redistribution.[45]

The EU Database Directive was the model for the database treaty
proposed in the World Intellectual Property Organization. In 1996,
the same year the EU passed its directive, the WIPO secretariat prepared a draft treaty that would have granted expansive new property
rights for compilations of information in databases. In 1998 similar
rules were included in legislation introduced in the U.S. Congress
(the Collections of Information Antipiracy Act, H.R. 2652). These
rights were strongly supported by businesses who depended on producing data of one kind or another. However, strong opposition from
scientific and library organizations has thus far forestalled progress
on a treaty and legislation. Though initially the United States had
supported the WIPO Treaty, it reversed its position and withdrew
support as a result of domestic criticism. The legislation passed the
House but never made it through the Senate. Nevertheless, the issue
is far from dead. According to the American Library Association's
Office of Government Relations, "Efforts to pass [database protec-
tion] detrimental to libraries will continue in the 108th Congress
[2003–2004]."[46]

Consequences of Commodifying Information

Why do proposals to protect commercial databases rankle scholars,
scientists, and librarians? Proposed rules would, according to many
experts, take a public good—information—and transform it into a
private good—a protected database. Opponents to database protection point to the unfair advantage such rules would give to companies
like Reed Elsevier Publishers (a major supporter of protection). This
large multinational firm publishes books, directories, and scientific
journals and provides information services to the legal, business,
government, accounting, and academic markets. Its North American
Legal Markets and U.S. Corporate and Federal Markets divisions
(formerly Lexis and Nexis, respectively) provide important resources
for researchers, students, and librarians.

Indeed, in drafting this book, I frequently used Reed Elsevier products such as LexisNexis Academic, a database of legal, news, and business sources. I do so legally, under the terms of my university's license. For example, I have used the database to obtain information (quoted or paraphrased) from various documents, such as the Supreme Court's decision in *Feist,* as well as from news sources. Under current laws, my use of the database is appropriate, and I am free to profit from book royalties. No matter how much money I earn on this book, taking facts from LexisNexis is not an infringement of Reed Elsevier's copyright. Its copyright protects the construction of the database, the selection and arrangement of the content, the look and feel of the user interface, and the like. But I am free to use the facts in any way I choose. Proposed rules protecting databases, however, might give Reed Elsevier a property right to the information itself (including legal decisions) because the company had gone to the trouble of compiling it. What control might an information owner have over how I am allowed to use the information? Might the owner require me to pay royalties derived from using the information, or even place other limits on the dissemination of my research?

Opponents of copyright protection for information in databases think such outcomes are plausible. William Gardner and Joseph Rosenbaum point out the negative effects of strong database protection, given the complicated relations among government, university, and private-sector research. In their hypothetical example, a university-based scientist, working under a grant from the National Institutes of Health (a government organization), might acquire genetic information from a private company. Suppose the scientist, following the scientific norms of sharing information, provided her colleagues with the results of her research, which included data from a private company. She could be liable under the proposed law because she may have harmed the firm's potential market. Even though a judge might limit the damages awarded to the firm (the researcher, after all, was not selling the data), the firm could still use the suit to deter others from sharing copies of the firm's data. Such rules, if these interpretations are correct, would have a chilling effect on scholarship.[47] Although the scenario presented by Gardner and Rosenbaum is hypothetical, there have been attempts to enforce property rights for information. As discussed in Chapter 1, sports reporting and game scores have already been the subject of this kind of legal wrangling.

In the United States, proponents of protecting databases as a form of property urged the ratification of the WIPO treaty as the first step in establishing rights. Instead of developing national laws and *then* seeking to internationalize them by treaty, this strategy would have imposed a new international norm on the United States. Opponents claimed that strong property rights advocates were trying to make an end-run around the domestic debate. If the United States were to have ratified such a treaty, it would have become the law of the land. The draft WIPO treaty contained provisions that would have gone well beyond Article 10.2 of TRIPS, which states that the data in a database may or may not be owned.[48]

This attempt, however, did not go unnoticed. People with an interest in access to information protested the Clinton administration's advocacy of the treaty in the absence of public debate. Organizations such as the Digital Futures Coalition and the Electronic Freedom Frontier lobbied to convince decisionmakers that the treaty went much too far in providing benefits to individuals at the expense of the public good. Librarians' associations were particularly vocal opponents, as were the major scientific organizations in the United States. Scientists were worried that access to data would be limited by proprietary claims. Librarians argued that protecting information, not merely the fixed form of expression, would constitute an end to fair use. By 1997, the United States had backed down from supporting the treaty (which it had instigated), and the treaty was not adopted. The debate has not died, however, as the issue continues to be raised by firms and individuals supporting it.

■ The Value of Information

The impetus to create property rights in information stems from an understandable interest on the part of businesses: it costs money to gather data. Whether the data consists of legal decisions, telephone numbers, or high and low temperatures around the globe, there is an opportunity cost inherent in every decision to be an information provider. These companies could, after all, invest their resources in other businesses. And the sweat-of-the-brow argument seems inherently fair. Shouldn't the industrious compilers of information be rewarded for their efforts?

Here's an ironic thought: the idea that information has value because it is gathered by the sweat of one's brow parallels Karl Marx's labor theory of value. Marx and scholars following him argued that true value comes from the labor required to produce a commodity.[49]

118 ■ *Knowledge Power*

This interpretation contrasts with the standard capitalist explanation that value is determined by supply and demand. A simple supply-and-demand model does not work for information, of course, because it is not scarce.[50] Once it has been compiled, it cannot be used up. As John Perry Barlow, a songwriter for the Grateful Dead and prominent commentator on Internet policy, writes, "Information is experienced, not possessed."[51]

Being able to control information is a source of power as well as wealth. Under rules mandating strong property rights in facts, those who would be able to control the collection and distribution of facts would be able to determine who could participate in the global economy, polity, and society, and in what way. Owning facts and possessing the ability to prevent others from knowing them can be used as a weapon, given our dependence on information. Imagine any government controlling information about the human rights of all people on this planet as articulated in the United Nations Universal Declaration on Human Rights. Imagine a company withholding information uncovered by its own scientists about the addictive and carcinogenic properties of its product. Imagine if we had the knowledge from seismological models that an earthquake would strike a certain part of Afghanistan at a certain time. How would we use that information? The ability to control the flow of information is an exceptionally important power resource.

■ **Notes**

1. David Shenk, *Data Smog: Surviving the Information Glut,* 1st ed. (San Francisco: Harper'sEdge, 1997).

2. While the material costs of sponsored information, like commercial broadcast television, are paid for by the advertisers, the sponsored content is not truly free to us consumers because we must pay the price of putting up with the advertisements.

3. C. E. Shannon, "A Mathematical Theory of Communication," *Bell System Technical Journal* 27 (1948). See also Albert Borgmann, *Holding on to Reality: The Nature of Information at the Turn of the Millennium* (Chicago: University of Chicago Press, 1999); and Yaneer Bar-Yam, *Concepts in Complex Systems: Information* (New England Complex Systems Institute, 2000) [cited September 13, 2002], available from necsi.org/guide/concepts/information.html.

4. Borgmann, *Holding on to Reality,* p. 18.

5. Ibid., p. 57 (emphasis in original).

6. The distinction between information and intellectual property is highlighted by the category of trade secret, which fits uneasily in the intellectual property category. Trade secrets are valuable only as long as they are not disclosed. Once they are disclosed, they do not have protection as a form of intellectual property. They become information.

7. In the late 1950s, Peter F. Drucker was perhaps the first to emphasize the key role of the professional specialist and professional manager in using knowledge to innovate, thereby shaping the new economy. Peter F. Drucker, *Landmarks of Tomorrow* (New York: Harper, 1959).

8. On routinization of productive activity, see Peter F. Drucker, "Beyond the Information Revolution," *Atlantic Monthly,* October 1999.

9. Julie M. Wickman and Johnathan G. Markquess, Marketing Your Pharmacy Services in the New Millennium, National Community Pharmacists Association, Alexandria Virginia, Program Number 207-000-00-103-H01, June 2000 [cited September 18, 2002], available from www.ncpanet.org/CONTEDU/marketmille.html.

10. The *Nina*, the *Pinta*, and the *Santa Maria* on his first voyage to the New World.

11. Perhaps the closest we get to such a list is the Militarized Interstate Dispute data of the Correlates of War project. See Daniel M. Jones, Stuart A. Bremer, and J. David Singer, "Militarized Interstate Disputes, 1816–1992: Rationale, Coding Rules, and Empirical Patterns," *Conflict Management and Peace Science* 15, no. 2 (1996).

12. The atomic weight is 95.94. C. R Hammond, "The Elements," in *Handbook of Chemistry and Physics,* edited by Robert C. Weast (Cleveland, OH: Chemical Rubber, 1972).

13. Chromosome 7. *Cystic Fibrosis*, vol., *Encyclopedia Britannica Online* [cited January 26, 2003], available from www.search.eb.com/eb/article?eu=28894.

14. Dairy Queen Company, website [cited January 26, 2003], available from www.dairyqueen.com.

15. Your guess is as good as mine and, apparently, as good as the intelligence agencies'.

16. Ann Wells Branscomb devoted a chapter of her book to the question of ownership of translation rights to the Dead Sea Scrolls. See Anne Wells Branscomb, *Who Owns Information? From Privacy to Public Access* (New York: Basic Books, 1994).

17. Microstrategy, website [cited August 19, 2002], available from www.microstrategy.com.

18. Of course, the government may also want to know where water and other resources are, as well, for public purposes. And unfortunately terrorists and other criminals may want to use the information to inflict harm. For the latter reason, the U.S. government took steps to limit access to data on the nation's water supply, which had routinely been available in public libraries, and to detailed maps from the National Imagery and Mapping Agency. Ariana Eunjung Cha, "Risks Prompt U.S. to Limit Access to Data: Security, Rights Advocates Clash over Need to Know," *Washington Post,* February 24, 2002.

19. Seismic refraction surveys involve thumping the ground with special equipment and using sensitive instruments on the surface to sense the seismic wave as it travels through the different materials (rock, sand, water, etc.) below the surface. A description of different geophysical techniques can be found at Northwest Geophysical Associates, Inc., website, January 31, 2002 [cited August 23, 2003], available from www.nga.com.

20. As I will discuss in the chapters on privacy, there is a balance to be struck between surveillance for the public good of security and an individual's right to privacy. Plans for increased surveillance had been in the works prior to the attacks on the World Trade Center and the Pentagon, but much of the discussion had been about the need to use this surveillance to stop crime, particularly drug trafficking.

21. Scott Savitz, "Mission to Beijing: Government-Sponsored CI [Competitive Intelligence] in the 18th Century," *Competitive Intelligence Magazine,* April 1999.

22. Dorothy E. Denning, "Who's Stealing Your Information?" *Information Security,* April 1999 [cited August 16, 2003], available from infosecuritymag.techtarget.com/articles/1999/aprilcover.shtml.

23. BBC News, *France Accuses US of Spying* (February 23, 2000 [cited September 25, 2002]), available from news.bbc.co.uk/1/hi/world/654210.stm.

24. U.S. Department of Commerce, Bureau of Industry and Security, Export Enforcement Program [cited August 20, 2003], available from www.bxa.doc.gov/Enforcement/Default.htm.

25. The contributions of the Chicago School of economic theory, including the contributions of George Stigler and Milton Friedman, are notable here. See Robert Leeson, *The Eclipse of Keynesianism: The Political Economy of the Chicago Counter-Revolution* (New York: Palgrave, 2000).

26. Peter Osborne, "Why the Kiwis Are Doing Better Than the Aussies," *Business Times* (Singapore), December 7, 1994. Other examples are discussed in Shaun Goldfinch, *Remaking New Zealand and Australian Economic Policy: Ideas, Institutions, and Policy Communities* (Washington, DC: Georgetown University Press, 2000). In the United States, the privatization of the postal service has received much attention. U.S. Postal Service, *History of the U.S. Postal Service* [cited September 18, 2002], available from www.usps.com/history/his1.htm.

27. Robert Gellman, "Twin Evils: Government Copyright and Copyright-Like Controls over Government Information," *Syracuse Law Review* 45 (1995), citations omitted.

28. Information released under FOIA is not exactly free. The government agency releasing the information may charge a reasonable fee to cover the labor and photocopy costs. Noncommercial users are charged for time, after two hours, and duplication, after 100 pages. The fee is waived if it does not exceed $14. Commercial users are also charged for "document review" after the first 100 pages. U.S. Department of Justice, *FOIA (Freedom of Information Act) Fees and Waivers* (February 12, 2001 [cited August 23, 2003]), available from www.usdoj.gov/04foia/04_1_2.html.

29. The imperative to spread information, in its various forms, was best captured in a charge Hayward R. Alker Jr. gave to a gathering of his former

doctoral students on the occasion of his retirement from the Massachusetts Institute of Technology: "Go and make me some grandstudents!"

30. Craig Murphy, *The Emergence of the NIEO* (Boulder, CO: Westview, 1984). See also Alan Riding, "New Information Order: Debating Pragmatics," *New York Times,* January 24, 1982; and Anthony Smith, *The Geopolitics of Information: How Western Culture Dominates the World* (New York: Oxford University Press, 1980).

31. Pamela O. Long, *Openness, Secrecy, Authorship: Technical Arts and the Culture of Knowledge from Antiquity to the Renaissance* (Baltimore: Johns Hopkins University Press, 2001), pp. 88–96.

32. Ibid. Of course, there were some guild members who violated the rules, as Long notes. The rules contained provisions for punishments, including fines and restrictions on working.

33. Michel Foucault, *The Birth of the Clinic: An Archaeology of Medical Perception,* 1st American ed., translated by A. M. Sheridan Smith (New York: Pantheon Books, 1973).

34. Decoding the language of medical professionals in order to get help for a child with a rare disease is the theme of *Lorenzo's Oil* (MCA Universal, 1992), a fictionalized account of a Lorenzo Odone, who suffers from adrenleukodystrophy (ALD). See also Barry J. Stith, *The Use of the Movie "Lorenzo's Oil" as a Teaching Tool* [cited September 26, 2002], available from carbon.cudenver.edu/~bstith/loren.htm; and *Myelin Project* website [cited September 26, 2002], available from www.myelin.org.

35. Alan Sokol, "Transgressing Boundaries: Towards a Transformative Hermeneutics of Quantum Gravity," *Social Text* 46 (1996).

36. *Feist Publications, Inc. v. Rural Telephone Service Company,* 499 U.S. 340 (1991).

37. These were typical white pages. Rural also published yellow pages, consisting of business listings arranged by category.

38. Thomas P. Arden, "The Conflicting Treatments of Compilations of Facts under the United States and British Copyright Laws," *American Intellectual Property Law Association Quarterly Journal* 19, no. 4 (1991).

39. *Radio Telefis Eireann (RTE) and Independent Television Publications Ltd (ITP) v. Commission of the European Communities. Competition—Abuse of a Dominant Position—Copyright,* Joined Cases C-241/91 P and C-242/91 P, 1995 ECJ CELEX LEXIS 9006 (1995), 1995 ECJ CELEX LEXIS 9006 (1995).

40. "Broadcasters' Abuse of Dominant Position," *The Times* (London), April 17, 1995. See also "New Legal Tool Could Help Push the TPA [Third Party Access]," *EC Energy Monthly,* May 16, 1995; and Darrell Prescott and Katarzya Buche, "The Convergence of U.S. and European Laws Concerning Compulsory Licensing and Licensing Restrictions," *Mondaq Business Briefing,* April 19, 1999.

41. A similarly influential case happened in the Netherlands in 1991: *Van Dale v. Romme.* Romme took all the entries in a dictionary published by Van Dale and put them in a computer file that could be manipulated in order to find the answers to crossword puzzle clues. Van Dale charged that Romme violated its copyright. Romme's position was that the words were just words.

Eventually Van Dale prevailed (the lexicographers working for the publisher put their creative effort into identifying the words to include), but the case pointed to gaps in the otherwise strong protection for information under Dutch copyright law. P. Brent Hugenholtz, "Chronicle of the Netherlands, Dutch Copyright Law, 1995–2000," *Revue Internationale du Droit d'Auteur* 2001 [cited August 18, 2003], available from www.ivir.nl/publications/ hugenholtz/PBH-RIDA2000.doc.

42. This unhappiness with the degree of legal protections was (and is), I would argue, out of proportion to the real risk faced by information sellers. Even in the United States, where the laws protecting compilations of data are weakest, the information seller still has legal means to protect its information. Trade secret law, unfair business practice prohibitions, and contracts can all be used to protect the seller of information from misappropriation of its product.

43. Karl P. Sauvant, "Transborder Data Flows and the Developing Countries," *International Organization* 37, no. 2 (1983).

44. European Parliament and European Council, Directive 96/9/EC of the European Parliament and of the Council of 11 March 1996 on the Legal Protection of Databases, 1996 [cited January 26, 2003], available from europa.eu.int/ISPO/infosec/legreg/docs/969ec.html.

45. Stephen M. Maurer, P. Bernt Hugenholtz, and Harlan J. Onsrud, "Europe's Database Experiement," *Science,* October 26, 2001.

46. American Library Association, Office of Government Relations, *2003 Copyright Agenda* [cited January 26, 2003], available from www.ala. org/washoff/fairuse06.pdf.

47. William Gardner and Joseph Rosenbaum, "Database Protection and Access to Information," *Science,* August 7, 1998. Similarly, Jonathan Band has argued that the legislation proposed in 1998 would have prohibited a scholar from publishing a book in which she compares data taken from her own collection of data (in this hypothetical example) of criminal prosecution in Alabama with the data of other researchers on criminal prosecutions in North Carolina and Texas. Jonathan Band, *The End of History: Comments on HR 2652* June 16, 1998 [cited January 26, 2003], available from www.arl. org/info/frn/copy/end.html.

48. World Trade Organization, Uruguay Round Agreement: TRIPS, Part II: Standards Concerning the Availability, Scope, and Use of Intellectual Property Rights, Section 1 Copyright and Related Rights, Article 10.2 [1994] [cited September 17, 2002], available from www.wto.org/english/ docs_e/legal_e/27-trips_04_e.htm#1. See also World Trade Organization, *Overview: The TRIPS Agreement* [cited August 21, 2003], available from www.wto.int/english/tratop_e/trips_e/intel2_e.htm.

49. Karl Marx, "Value, Price, and Profit," in *The Portable Karl Marx*, edited by Eugene Kamenka (New York: Penguin Books, 1983 [1865]). An accessible review of Marxian and neo-Marxian writing on this topic can be found in Keith Griffin and John Gurley, "Radical Analyses of Imperialism, the Third World, and the Transition to Socialism: A Survey," *Journal of Economic Literature* 23, no. 3 (1985).

50. To be more precise, information is not scarce once it has been collected. Willing information gatherers and the time they have to do the gathering are scarce.

51. John Perry Barlow, *Selling Wine Without Bottles: The Economy of Mind on the Global Net* (December 13–14, 1993 [cited September 9, 2000]); available from www.eff.org/pub/Publications/John_Perry_Barlow/HTML/idea_economy_article.html.

6

Owning Information
About the Planet

How information is owned and controlled impacts how global society develops, communicates, and builds upon knowledge. Evolving property rights in information affect national and global security, the economy, and the quality of our lives. In this chapter and in Chapter 7, I illustrate these connections by looking at the ownership of information. This chapter focuses on data about the planet.

■ Information About Weather

Throughout human history, philosophers and scientists have blamed climate and weather for human wretchedness and human happiness. Harold Sprout provided a partial list of the proponents of "the proposition that climate . . . affects human behavior and performance": Hippocrates, Aristotle, and Pliny in the ancient world; to Bodin and Montesquieu in sixteenth-century France; and others up through the middle of the twentieth century.[1] People have recorded the weather for millennia,[2] and they have recorded it *systematically* for centuries.[3] These records were once shared freely, a practice that is quickly disappearing.

Early Weather Record Collection

Meteorologists did not have an understanding of the physical processes that caused changes in the weather until the end of the nineteenth century. Until that point, the study of weather and climate consisted almost exclusively of the careful (or not-so-careful) recording of each day's weather. The methods of the science were inductive—this kind of cloud formation usually means rain, the average temperature for the end of February in Chicago is "around freezing."[4] Although all acknowledged the importance of the weather to the safety of ships at sea and the productivity of crops in the fields, collections of weather data could do little to help because the predictive capability of the science was negligible. Yet scientists valued the recording of data, and early on, even before the standardization of thermometers and barometers, "men of science" called for the careful recording of weather data. The purpose was to share the data.

One early example was physician Jacob Jurin, who in 1723 published the article "Invitation to Make Meteorological Observations According to a Common Plan" in *Philosophical Transactions* (London).[5] Jurin noted the availability of new technologies to observe the weather systematically (e.g., thermometers and barometers) and suggested that "distinguished men are as yet unable to ascertain the causes of these changes [in the weather] but love of learning and knowledge will entice them to investigate them where possible." He asked that "educated persons, who want to improve this branch of natural science, . . . collect and diligently note down in a diary, at least once or more often each day," several specific weather variables. In a statement that revealed the unowned nature of weather data, the author described a specific format "to make the diaries readily comparable" and provided a sample. Date and year were the first two columns, height of the barometer and thermometer were in the next two, wind direction and strength were in the fourth, while sky aspect (e.g., "occ. sunshine") and "the amount of rain and melted snowfall in London inches and tenths" were in the last column. He then requested that the observers "send copies of the diaries at the end of each year to the Secretaries of the [British] Royal Society" so that the information could be "brought together with the diary for London arranged by the Royal Society and that a collection of these diaries be communicated in individual years in the Philosophical journals to the public." The theme of sharing information would persist in subsequent international efforts, from decisions at the First International Meteorological Congress in Brussels (1853) through the post–World War II era, under the aegis of the United Nations and the World Meteorological Organization (WMO, starting in 1961).[6]

But Jurin's story is still relevant. Even though few people actually performed observations according to Jurin's exact design, some observations, including some from two observers in the American colonies, were received by the Royal Society and published.[7] Though the existence of instruments to measure temperature and barometric pressure made recording such data possible, the expense prevented widespread collection. When Prince Elector Karl Theodor financed the free distribution of uniform, calibrated instruments through the Meteorological Society of the Palatinate in 1780, more observations, this time from thirty localities, were collected and published. The Reverend Johann Jacob Hemmer and the society provided detailed instructions for using the instruments, which would make the data from different observers more comparable.[8] The patronage of the prince elector suggests that this undertaking conferred a privilege on the data-gatherers rather than a property right to the information. Accepting the instruments, I infer, obligated the recipient to share the data collected with them freely.

Governments and the Collection of Weather Data

Funding the collection of data through patronage of noble benefactors "dried up" with the upheavals of the French Revolution,[9] but networks of observers continued to record weather data. At the First International Meteorological Congress in 1853 scientists from many countries agreed to standardize observations taken on ships at sea, data useful to maritime transport. In 1872 at the Leipzig Conference of Meteorologists an agreement was reached on standardizing observations made on land and on the creation of a permanent body to deal with international weather and climate issues. In 1873 the International Meteorological Organization, the forerunner of the WMO, was founded to coordinate the collection and publication of data.[10] According to Robert White, the information was put into a common pool; governments extracted what they needed.[11]

Edith Brown Weiss notes that 1873 marked the point when governments took an important role in setting rules governing international sharing of weather data, but individual scientists still played a major part. Although delegates to the International Meteorological Congress "were no longer meteorologists in their private capacity," and instead were representing governments at the 1879 congress, a panel of nongovernmental experts was established to set policy on weather data.[12] Weiss suggests that "until 1950, international cooperation in meteorology was largely a non-governmental effort conducted on a voluntary basis."[13]

As these institutional arrangements were evolving, so was the science, and advances in scientific knowledge would have an important effect on the usefulness of weather and climatic data. At the beginning of the twentieth century meteorology began to progress beyond inductive guesses about weather patterns to theories that accounted for the physical causes of weather phenomena. Vilhelm Bjerknes of Norway was a physicist who turned to meteorology and developed physical models of the atmosphere. The work done by Bjerknes and his son, Jacob, along with their associates, changed meteorology by explaining how storms and other phenomena are the result of the interaction of warm and cold air masses. This causal understanding allowed the prediction of weather based on the direction of winds.[14] The information, because of its predictive value, became more valuable. The agricultural sector developed a need to know when weather conditions were favorable for planting, and the development of civil and military aviation created a demand for knowing more about winds aloft. The conjunction of advances in meteorology with other technological and social changes led governments to change the rules for controlling weather data.

Robert Friedman points out that Bjerknes intentionally courted government officials and convinced them of the importance of developing a predictive science of meteorology. This scientist was influential in pointing out to policymakers that they had a national security and an economic security interest in promoting and funding research in this science.[15] Consequently, two instruction rules vied for predominance. Would weather data continue to be unowned, a shared scientific resource freely provided? Or would it be property owned by governments, with access restricted or enabled according to security concerns?

The shift to government ownership of weather data was a recognition that the ability to predict the weather was a strategic resource. Military historians recounted Napoleon's march to Moscow as instructive in the dangers of not understanding expected weather conditions.[16] Government weather bureaus, which were created to provide weather predictions, were situated within militaries. Moreover, military officials speculated on how weather could be used as a strategic weapon. States restricted other states' access to weather data during times of war.

The new scientific knowledge led to proposals for weather modification and attempts to seed clouds for rain, disperse fogs, and the like.[17] Some of these efforts were humanitarian at heart; others were frankly motivated by strategic goals. But the uncertain consequences of such actions led many scientists and policymakers to raise alarms about the potential transnational ramifications of even the most benign attempts. For example, Harold Sprout, writing in 1963, quoted words of caution from a 1955 article by John von Neumann. If weather modification efforts were successful, von Neumann wrote, "the climate of regions and levels of precipitation might be altered. . . . Once such possibilities become actual, they will be exploited." Thus "all experience shows that even smaller technological changes than those now in the cards profoundly transform political and social relationships."[18] In 1969, Rita F. Taubenfeld and Howard J. Taubenfeld wrote of the problems that would result from weather modification and the need for international institutions capable of restraining "international conflicts of interest."[19] John Ruggie optimistically predicted that "collective decision-making systems" would be established to deal with the negative externalities of large-scale weather modification.[20] Nevertheless, the possibility of using weather modification as a weapon prompted governments to keep much of the information classified. It was not until 1977 that the United States and the Soviet Union signed the United Nations treaty banning environmental warfare.[21]

As scientific knowledge about the potential for weather modification grew, the ability to predict the weather improved as well. The rules declaring that an international public good and directing weather services to exchange the data freely coexisted with rules that identified some of meteorological information as secret—owned by the state. For example, even though the United States had secretly experimented with using weather *modification* as a weapon, the United States and Cuba continued to exchange weather *data* through the World Meteorological Organization during the 1962 Cuban Missile Crisis.[22] Because the attempts to seed clouds and cause major rainfall were generally unsuccessful and because a successful activity could potentially cause harm elsewhere, these experiments are no longer commonplace, but governments still maintain their interest in weather.

Meteorologists, including those employed by governments, have long argued for freely shared weather data. These scientists tend to be closely tied, via professional associations and scientific training (i.e., via their epistemic community[23]), to their colleagues. Restricting the dissemination of scientific knowledge, even given the secret purposes of states, tends to go against the scientific grain. As scientists, meteorologists continue to maintain that the main purpose of forecasting is to protect lives and property.[24]

The role of scientists in constructing weather data as an international public good was apparent in the 1960s and 1970s through activity coordinated by the WMO World Weather Watch. With the advent of satellite and computer technologies, better weather data could be collected. These data, along with data from ground sites and weather balloons, could be made more useful because of powerful computing capabilities.

In 1967, the WMO launched an effort to create the Computer Program Library on Numerical Weather Prediction for the World Weather Watch. Helmut Landsberg, a climatologist who was exploring the history of the sharing of weather data in early modern times, was the president of the WMO Commission on Climatology, one of the technical commissions that worked on this effort.[25] Sharing computer programs and coordinating reporting formats were not easily achieved, but the very fact that such coordination was attempted shows how providing a public good—weather data—focused the interaction of government meteorology offices.

Privatization of Weather Services

From the early efforts to harmonize data recording in order to facilitate sharing through the WMO efforts of the mid-1960s and 1970s to today, a major shift occurred. Weather data have become increasingly privatized. The current expanding market for commercial uses of forecasts means weather data is information as reality, a commodity that can be bought and sold. Value-added information (forecasts) as well as raw weather data are being redefined as private property, either owned by states or firms. The reasons for this alteration can be found in the improved science and technology (satellite imaging and computers), increased costs (the costs of developing and maintaining the improved science and technology), and changing dominant political ideology (the Reagan-Thatcher drive toward privatization).

Meteorologists distinguish between raw (unenhanced) data and forecasts that have value added.[26] In the United States, the government has provided raw data as a public good and encouraged the formation of private meteorological consultancies to do value-added microforecasts. A national weather bureau, which was originally created in 1870 as part of the signal corps of the War Department, became a part of the Department of Agriculture in 1891. The Weather Bureau was placed in its current home, the Department of Commerce, in 1940,[27] and demobilized military meteorologists from World War II provided the highly trained human capital to create an industry in specialized forecasting. According to Robert White, firms began to produce detailed information for consumers, services that were beyond the capacity of government. One example is TV forecasts for local stations; another is forecasts for building and construction firms that need to know specific information in order to use materials such as cement properly. To encourage investment in meteorological consultancies, the U.S. government implemented a policy of not charging for the weather information itself and only charging a small fee for the communications hookup. In other words, the data are distributed free, but the medium of transmitting the data is not. European countries generally provided all weather services through a government agency.[28]

The general trend toward privatization of government functions began to have an impact on weather services in the 1980s. After some years of "increasing pressure on government funding for meteorology . . . , together with a government-wide move to 'user-pays' for specialised services, and to more autonomy and accountability for government departments," New Zealand privatized its weather service in 1992.[29] MetService (NZ) Ltd., a state-owned enterprise, is still required to provide basic weather forecasting as a public service, much like the requirements placed on utilities, but it is now a profit-seeking enterprise. In the words of Marco M. Overdale, MetService's Chief Information Officer,

We exploit information on weather
With techniques that grow ever better
Our inspiring environment
And high skill requirement
Make our customers love us forever.[30]

Other states, particularly in Europe, began requiring governmental bureaus to market meteorological consulting services to recoup some of their operating costs. These government bureaus had to become quite entrepreneurial to cover the expense of providing high-quality data from new, more technologically sophisticated satellites.

The state-run European bureaus ended up competing with private U.S. firms exporting consulting services.

Until 1995, U.S. firms received much of the data from European sources for free, via the U.S. government, which acquired the data from the WMO. This meant that a U.S. firm could get free data from a European satellite, manipulate the data to create specialized forecasts, and then market the forecasts in Europe. The European weather bureaus were also trying to market specialized forecasts, but instead of getting the data for free the bureaus were required to recover their costs. The U.S. firms, in essence, were selling Europeans their own data.

In 1995, a debate over proprietary rights to raw data erupted at the WMO. EU countries wanted to create tiers of data, with more basic data remaining a public good and the more detailed data—for which the market is growing—becoming the private property of the state that generated it. The U.S. government, however, advocated reaffirming the notion of weather data as a public good by stressing the value of "free and unrestricted exchange of data and [related] data and products."[31] The compromise, WMO Resolution No. 40, (1) reaffirms the free and unrestricted flow of data; (2) identifies a set of essential data and products that national meteorological services must provide to the WMO at no charge; but (3) finds that "members may be justified in placing conditions on their re-export for commercial purposes outside the receiving country . . . for reasons such as national laws or costs of production."[32] Data from European satellites are now encrypted and provided by special licensing arrangements to those who pay the fee.[33] The U.S. government (or any other government, for that matter) has pledged, under the conditions of the relevant WMO resolution, not to give away data from other countries that might then be reexported back into those countries.[34]

When the tiered data proposal was raised, the U.S. meteorological community was alarmed because, first, many members were engaged in commercial activity, and second, the expectation that raw weather data was a public good (while value-added data was not) was—and continues to be—a deeply held belief.

> Nations would continue to provide free access only to information relating to large-scale weather patterns, such as the movement of storms. But new restrictions would be permitted for the more detailed weather readings needed to make highly localized and time-specific forecasts. Countries could forbid the use of these "tier

2" data by third parties—including the commercial weather services that have risen as potential competitors.[35]

Elbert Friday, who was the director of the U.S. National Weather
Service at this time, asserted that "no one dreamed that the data
[themselves] would take on intrinsic value [as opposed to the value
of the forecast]."[36] The U.S. scientists argued that their activities provided a public good by protecting human life and property. The tier
system would add costs only to the production of localized weather
conditions; but the scientists argued that strictly local conditions can
also harm property and human beings. Restricting access to the tier 2
data could have a negative impact on the comprehensiveness of
weather forecasts.

In interviews I conducted during the negotiations on Resolution
No. 40, meteorologists Robert White, Elbert Friday, and Richard
Hallgren (the executive director of the American Meteorological
Society at the time) pointed out the consequences for less developed
countries if restrictions on the transmission of data were agreed to.
Hallgren asserted: "I am of the opinion and the [American Meteorological Society] is on record stating that the two-tiered system is fundamentally flawed." In his view, and in that of White, the agreement
could easily lead to the untenable position of some developing countries giving all their weather information to industrialized countries,
while industrialized countries will only be giving *some* of their
weather information to developing countries.[37] In other words, developing countries have the technical capacity to collect tier 1 data,
whereas industrialized countries can collect tier 1 and tier 2 data.
Hence a developing country would be obligated to share freely all its
data with the rest of the world while an industrialized country would
only be required to share *some* of its data.[38]

Friday related an incident in which a representative from an
African country approached him and asked to be hooked up to the
satellite communication system (funded by the United States, with
assistance from Canada and Finland) linking Central American and
Caribbean countries to the data, outputs, and forecasts from the U.S.
National Meteorological Computing Center. Unfortunately, because
of the distance involved, connecting the African country would have
been too expensive. It would have been easy for the European Meteorological Consortium to provide the satellite hookup to Africa, but
the Europeans had thus far refused. The consortium would find it

difficult to justify giving away the satellite information to African countries when small European countries were paying for the satellite itself. Friday noted, "I am afraid that increased commercialization and intellectual isolation will end up harming what we're here to do: protect life and property from the weather. Once you start restricting data, those restrictions will spread."[39]

Since then, a continuing problem is the tension between the provisions of Resolution 40 and the goal of using weather data to contribute to sustainable development efforts. The global rules now in place define basic weather data as a public good, detailed weather data as state-owned property, and value-added forecasts as private property.[40] The pooling of data collected on a daily basis around the world by ground stations and satellites creates a global weather information system that provides full coverage of the globe. On the one hand, this global system depends on the willingness of individual countries, through national meteorological services, to share data to protect life and property, to safeguard the environment, and to contribute to sustainable development. Good weather data help countries pursue sustainable development and enables research into global climate change. On the other hand, if information is reexported or otherwise given away in violation of Resolution 40, the entire system of sharing weather may collapse.[41]

■ Information About Regions: Remote-Sensing Data

The next case looks at the use of satellites and other instruments to observe weather and many more aspects of the Earth. *Remote-sensing data* refers to all kinds of data about planet conditions collected by airborne or space-borne sensors.[42] Weather data collected from satellites, airplanes, and weather balloons can now be considered as a special type of remote-sensing data, a category that includes information for observing deforestation, desertification, pollution, and other conditions.[43] In contrast to the collection of weather data per se, which evolved from shared scientific activity of individuals, the collection of Earth remote-sensing data—the imaging of the earth from above—began as a form of espionage. The United States and the Soviet Union used images gleaned from spy satellites and airplanes to gather intelligence. The data were not publicly available for use by individuals or firms, but the collection of the data was a component of the governments' provision of the public good of national security. Thus the outcome—national security—was the public good, but the data remained secret, owned by the government for governmental purposes. The images that constituted the data were not a commodity since there was no legal market for them. Even now, the U.S. government attempts to restrict extremely high-resolution images to military uses.

Civilian Remote Sensing Begins

Civilian applications of remote sensing from satellites developed after the military applications. With the civilian data, the U.S. government (and later other governments) produced data as a public good for use by academic scientists and for commercial activities. In the 1980s, however, as government was jumping on the privatization bandwagon, attempts were made to privatize the production of civilian remote-sensing data. One notable example is the U.S. Landsat program.[44]

In 1965, NASA began the Earth Resources Survey Program in conjunction with the Department of Agriculture and, beginning in 1966, with the Department of Commerce and Department of the Interior.[45] The stated purpose was to explore the use of remote sensing for observing natural resources, with the consequent application of the information to geology, hydrology, geography, and cartography. In 1972 NASA launched Earth Resources Technology Satellite (ERTS 1, later known as Landsat 1). Landsats 2 through 6 have been launched to date (Landsat 6 failed almost immediately after launch). From 1972 to 1974, more than 300 U.S. and foreign investigators received ERTS 1 data.[46] From this beginning until the program was privatized, the data were distributed at the cost of filling the user request.

Beginning of Privatization Efforts

The first tentative steps toward privatization and the emergence of weather as private property came in 1979. President Jimmy Carter, in Presidential Directive 54, announced that all civilian remote-sensing activities from space were to be placed under the authority of the National Oceanographic and Atmospheric Administration (NOAA). The directive further specified the "integration of civilian operational activities under NOAA; [the joint] or coordinated civil/military activities where both parties' objectives can be best met through this approach; [and the separation of] defense activities which have no civilian counterpart." Of special importance was the directive to the Commerce Department "to further private sector opportunities in civil land remote-sensing activities, through joint ventures with industry, a quasi-governmental corporation, leasing, etc., with the goal of eventual operation of these activities by the private sector." Moreover, President Carter directed that the United States would continue "providing LANDSAT data to foreign users and promoting development of complementary and cooperative nationally operated satellite systems so as to increase benefits for all nations."[47]

The Reagan administration, however, had a greater stake in privatization. Instead of a gradual transfer of Landsat operations to the private sector, the Reagan administration advocated quick privatization and an end to government funding. In 1981, the privatization process was initiated when the proposed FY 1982 budget omitted funds for two planned Landsat satellites. Also in 1981, the secretary of commerce was instructed "to determine how to transfer Landsat to the private sector as soon as possible."[48] However, privatization could not proceed as quickly or as cheaply as the administration wished. Three independent studies concluded that it would be impossible to commercialize Landsat operations "in near or long term without substantial government subsidy."[49] In 1984, Congress approved the privatization of Landsat but explicitly decided not to privatize weather satellites. Though both types were engaged in remote sensing, Congress differentiated the two, with weather satellites more clearly providing a public good. Still, Congress required that Landsat data be made available on a nondiscriminatory basis after privatization. This simply meant that any potential user who was willing to pay the price could acquire the data on the same terms as anyone else. The problem with relying on nondiscrimination is that Congress did not restrict the prices that could be charged for Landsat data.

As negotiations proceeded, only the Earth Observation Satellite (EOSAT) Company[50] remained in the bidding,[51] and in 1985 it received a ten-year contract. EOSAT was to operate Landsats 4 and 5 (the only two in operation at that time), build Landsats 6 and 7, and maintain data rights. EOSAT would have "exclusive rights to market Landsat data collected prior to the date of the contract (9/27/85) until the expiration date (7/16/94)," plus "exclusive right to market data collected after 9/27/85 for ten years from the date of acquisition."[52] Though the U.S. government retained title to the data it had produced with taxpayer money, EOSAT was licensed to receive all the revenue from selling the data for a ten-year period. EOSAT was licensed to receive all the revenue from sales of data collected by Landsat satellites operated by the company for ten years from the date that the data were gathered. EOSAT, which was acquired by Space Imaging in 1996, would have exclusive rights to the revenue from an image of Earth collected on, for example, August 9, 1987 (during the period of the contract when EOSAT was to be operating the satellites) until August 9, 1997. After the ten-year period of exclusivity, the archived data would be available for the cost of providing it. EOSAT did not have a copyright on the data, but the exclusive licensing arrangement allowed EOSAT to force its customers into a contractual obligation not to copy or redistribute the data.[53]

To make EOSAT's venture viable, the U.S. government initially promised to provide a subsidy of $250 million; but in 1986 the Reagan administration recommended limiting funding to half that amount. At about the same time, NOAA submitted a plan to Congress that called for only one additional Landsat satellite, a plan Congress rejected "because commitment to only one spacecraft [would] not build confidence in [the] system or make commercialization viable."[54]

In 1987 Congress accepted a NOAA compromise proposal for one additional satellite along with the study of one more. In 1988, Congress released the funding for Landsat 6. Though NOAA did not request operating funds for Landsats 4 and 5 (the two remaining satellites in operation) for FY 1989 (the satellites were past their design life and were expected to fail), Congress decided to add a half a year of funding. By this point, there was a good deal of disagreement among the relevant actors over governmental support for remote sensing data, privatization, and the capacity of EOSAT to be commercially successful.

In 1989 NOAA announced that it had expended its funds for Landsat operations and directed EOSAT to turn off the satellites. The National Space Council, members of Congress, other governments, and foreign and domestic users of the data protested.[55] Interim funding was cobbled together, but EOSAT was not committed to collecting continuous streams of data. Instead, EOSAT collected data "on demand," turning on the satellite when it had a buyer for a certain image. Consequently, the commitment of the entire U.S. remote-sensing program to create a data archive that monitored the Earth and its resources faltered. According to Kathleen Eisenbeis,

> When Congress passed the Landsat Act, it was fearful of losing all civilian remote sensing capability because of aging satellites and the federal budget crisis. To protect users, both foreign and domestic, and to prevent the total loss of Landsat data, the Congressional committees negotiated legislation which required data continuity and nondiscriminatory access. Unintentionally, these benevolent policies enabled EOSAT to produce an intermittent supply of data, the 'acquisition-on-demand' strategy and to set its own profit-maximizing pricing policy.[56]

Renewed Government Oversight and Responsibility

From 1989 to 1992, funding problems for EOSAT continued; its revenues were not sufficient. As a consequence of the failure of privatization, policies on Landsat data became a combination of information provided for the public good (i.e., research), information owned by the government but given away or sold when deemed appropriate, and information that was a private good by virtue of exclusive marketing rights. In 1991 EOSAT relinquished its exclusive rights to market multipectral scanner data, one of the three formats of data from Landsat, after it was two years old.[57] In 1992 National Space Policy Directive No. 5, signed by President George H. W. Bush, reevaluated the role of privatization. In addition to asserting that the policy goal was to "promote and not preclude private sector commercial opportunities in Landsat-type remote sensing," the directive reemphasized the need to provide a consistent and sufficiently comprehensive set of data "to allow comparisons for change detection and characterization." The policy further stated that the U.S. government would "make Landsat data available to meet the needs of national security, global change research, and other federal users." To achieve this latter goal, the government would authorize a differential pricing system, in which the government and researchers within the U.S. Global Change Research Program would receive data at minimal cost.[58] Congress then passed the Land Remote Sensing Policy Act of 1992, which brought more government involvement in operations and in the development of new technologies for Landsat. The new law authorized negotiations with EOSAT on policy for data from Landsat 4 through 6 and specified the development of a new data policy for the proposed Landsat 7 on the basis of "cost of fulfilling user request" for domestic and foreign users.[59]

In April 1995 an agreement between the U.S. government and EOSAT on the cost of data for noncommercial uses by the government and affiliated users was reached. This agreement brought the price down for all. *Affiliated users* are defined as U.S. government agencies; U.S. government contractors; researchers and institutions conducting scientific investigations related to global change funded by, or defined in agreements with, U.S. Committee on Earth and Environmental Sciences member agencies; global change research programs in non-U.S. countries as well as the global change research programs of the WMO, United Nations Environmental Programme, the Intergovernmental Oceanographic Commission, the International Council of Scientific Unions, and the International Social Science Council; other researchers signing a cooperative agreement with the U.S. government involving the use of Landsat data for noncommercial purposes; and nonprofit public-interest entities. As of October 1, 1996, all data are distributed to the U.S. government and its affiliates by the National Satellite Land Remote Sensing Data Archive at the EROS Data Center in the U.S. Geological Survey, Department of the Interior. The restrictions on copying and distributing the data among other U.S. government agencies and affiliates have been eliminated, as long as the use is noncommercial. The general public can acquire data from ten years ago to the present from Space Imaging; older data can be acquired from the EROS Data Center.[60]

Despite efforts to commercialize remote-sensing data, the potential long-term profitability of the industry is not guaranteed. Countries might resist commercialization by developing new technologies to shield countries from the imaging power of remote-sensing instruments. After all, governments will have an important incentive to invest in research and development of technologies that protect their secrets from prying eyes in the sky. Also the demand for remote-sensing data may simply not be as robust as expected. Old-fashioned data-gathering on the ground (near sensing) might yield superior information at lower cost, especially if the price of analyzing and interpreting satellite imagery remains high.[61]

What is absent from political wrangling over commodification versus sharing of remote sensing data, particularly with reference to Landsat, is the paucity of references to international obligations. Foreign users are mentioned as almost an afterthought, though using remote-sensing data to explore *global* change necessarily involves the planet and not just the United States. Moreover, the United States has advocated a policy of Open Skies, which denies that any state has property rights in images of its territory taken from space. Thus the U.S. policy affirms the government's rights and the rights of firms to take and process data about the globe, but it does not add any responsibility to share information, except for the rule of nondiscriminatory access. The United Nations Committee on the Peaceful Uses of Outer Space has debated "a right to primary access to data for the sensed state and for restrictions with regard to the transfer of data" versus nondiscriminatory access. The question has been refined to differentiate between unenhanced (primary) data versus valued-added data (analyzed information), but an international consensus has not emerged.[62] (Under the 1994 agreement, the data themselves are available to other governments and foreign firms; the price depends on the nature of the use.) The Landsat program currently cooperates with several foreign ground stations that can download data,[63] and the United States has used the data and training for making use of the data as part of foreign aid packages.[64]

▪ Location, Location, Location

The third case also concerns the use of satellites for generating data, in this case data about precise locations. It's an old real estate adage: the top three factors in determining the cost of a house are location, location, location. It's not just houses, though. Knowing exact locations has become quite valuable for ships at sea, airplanes aloft, and cars whose drivers tend get lost. Not surprisingly, precise location information is also important to armies. Technology has made receiving information from the Global Positioning System (GPS) relatively inexpensive and accurate. Handheld receivers or units installed in cars can provide the value-added information of how to get where you want to go.

Here's a highly simplified explanation of how GPS works. GPS consists of twenty-four satellites orbiting the Earth, ground stations for tracking the satellites, and receivers. The satellites constantly broadcast their location and the time. Receivers pick up the signal and compare the time stamp on the signal to the actual time that the message reached the receiver. That infinitesimal difference, measured in nanoseconds, can be translated into the distance between the satellite and the receiver. (The radio waves travel at a fixed velocity—the speed of light. Distance equals velocity times the amount of time that it takes for the signal to arrive at the receiver.) With one satellite we can determine the distance between the satellite and the receiver. With signals from two we can narrow the possible area in which the receiver might be located. To fully determine location by triangulation, we need three satellites. The receiver receives the broadcasted radio waves of three satellites and computes its location. Signals received from a fourth satellite allow the receiver to correct for timing discrepancies and make the determination of location more accurate.[65]

GPS was born out of the need for a navigational system that was precise and not dependent on good weather.[66] Though radio navigation began as early as the 1920s, it was not until World War II that radio signals were paired with time information to provide navigation assistance. The first satellite-based radio navigation system was launched in 1959,[67] but it was not until 1978 that the first GPS satellite in the initial test group was launched by the U.S. Air Force, the lead agency. The Air Force eventually launched eleven test satellites (Block I) between 1978 and 1985.

It turned out that the initial test satellites provided useful data for civilian applications as well as for military ones. As the tragic downing of a Korean airliner that had wandered into Soviet airspace showed, civilian aircraft would benefit from knowing exactly where they were. In response to that incident, President Ronald Reagan pledged to make GPS signals available, without charge, to the world as a public service when the system was fully operational. Even with the limited coverage offered by the Block I satellites, though, the surveying industry found that it was able to benefit from GPS signals, especially with innovations that enhanced the accuracy of the satellite information with ground-based information.

In 1989, the first of the full-scale satellites (Block II) were launched.[68] Block II satellites broadcasted two kinds of signals: precision and coarse. A military GPS receiver was equipped to scan for the coarse signal and then tune into the precision signal. Civilian receivers were equipped to receive only the coarse signal. In 1990 the coarse signal was intentionally degraded to prevent enemies equipped with GPS receivers from using that information against the United States. The Selective Availability (SA) system, the name given to the system of degrading the information in the signal, turned out to be problematic.

The 1991 Gulf War demonstrated the usefulness of GPS navigation to armed forces. The system was hailed for making it possible for Coalition troops to find their way over unknown terrain and through sandstorms and other impediments. There was just one problem: the armed forces did not have enough military GPS receivers. The army scrambled to purchase civilian receivers to distribute to troops, but the civilian receivers received only the degraded coarse transmissions rather than the precise transmissions. Since Coalition forces had the technological advantage (the Iraqi army was not known to have a large number of GPS receivers), the United States made the decision to turn off the Selective Availability feature. After the war, SA was restarted.

Quickly, though, the number of civilian applications for GPS technology increased. Moreover, the combination of military and civilian demand for receivers placed U.S. firms in a leadership position in global markets. In 1991 the United States promised to provide GPS coarse data (by inference, degraded coarse data) to the entire world and to provide significant lead time in the event that the United States decided to stop providing GPS services. The most important change came in 1995, when President Bill Clinton discontinued SA, opening up coarse data that was not degraded to civilian receivers. Encrypted Precise Positioning Service (PPS) data are still reserved for the military because these data carry enhancements other than accuracy.[69] The decision to discontinue the signal degradation system came after the recognition that improved data would not provide a significant advantage to an enemy.[70] But as September 11 demonstrated, lethal harm can be caused by relatively low-tech terrorist actions without high-quality navigation data.

The overwhelming benefit from providing data is economic. U.S.-based industries have a lead in developing and marketing applications for GPS information. By encouraging the world to rely on the U.S.-provided information, the U.S. standard becomes the global standard, though the lead is likely to decrease somewhat with global competition. A 1998 report prepared for the U.S. International Trade Administration predicted:

> • Total growth for the [GPS-related product] market is expected to remain robust with an average growth rate of just under 25% during 1998–2003.

- Global sales are on-track to exceed $8 billion by 2000 and could exceed $16 billion by 2003.
- The relative U.S. share of the world market will decrease as a result of GPS consumer products being increasingly sold through multinational consumer product companies.
- During the early portion of the period, Japan's share should expand slightly as a result of increasing car navigation sales, but flatten later in the period as markets saturate.
- In Europe, rapid growth in car navigation is expected throughout the period while the defense market share declines after 2000.
- The consumer GPS market will begin to build rapidly toward the end of the period as lower-priced GPS capabilities are embedded in mass market goods.[71]

We come back to the peculiar truth that the United States has made its information valuable by giving it away. Since slightly less than one-third of the global market in GPS-related products is sold by U.S. firms, the U.S. government benefits from GPS-generated tax revenues and increased employment.[72] The ability to set the standard is a means of controlling the flow of information. By controlling the information as state-owned property (by virtue of owning and controlling the satellites that produce the information), the government is able to determine how that information is treated as property. The United States may continue to reap benefits by providing the signal as a public good, but alternatively the United States might choose to re-create the information as a club good, restricting access by degrading or encrypting the signal. Doing so might be necessary during war for security reasons. Others might see an opportunity for the government to recoup the costs of maintaining the service by charging a fee for access. Another option would be to privatize GPS, as was done with Landsat.

The insecurity that results, along with the desire to create a competitive industry in value-added services and products, has led the European Union to begin developing its own satellite navigation system, Galileo. As Matthias Ruete, director of the EU's Trans-European Networks for Transport program, noted, the GPS system and a similar system used in Russia (GLONASS) are products of their respective militaries. "Their links with defence priorities provide no guarantee of development and dependability for the future. But this future is crucial in determining the development of an integrated European transport sector," he commented.[73] Full deployment of this system is expected by 2008.[74]

EU policymakers are mindful of the consequences of U.S. ownership of satellite navigation data. Although it currently suits U.S.

purposes to provide the data as a public good, such may not always be the case. Moreover, the economic effects of contracting with European firms to develop and launch the satellites and to put the system into operation can provide a boost to the European economy. The information at stake—the location and time signal from the satellite— is not exhaustible. The satellite is, after all, broadcasting the information, and any receiver can pick it up without taking anything away from other receivers. But the very fact that the United States has the ability to restrict access, potentially sealing European competitor firms out of the club, is a source of information insecurity.

■ Data for Both Military and Civilian Purposes

Weather data, remote-sensing data, and global positioning system data all provide information about the planet and are all valuable because of the usefulness of that information in society for military and civilian purposes. How the information is owned—or not— reflects the social negotiation of control over the information. When governments assert ownership the question of control of the information and access to it becomes a security issue. Paradoxically, governments provide the public good of security by restricting access to secret information and providing access to other information. Only in the latter case—when the government releases the information to the public—is the information *itself* a public good. Still, the commodification of information about the planet enables the development of a market for such information products. All of the benefits and drawbacks of private property and club goods apply.

■ Notes

1. Harold Sprout, "Geopolitical Hypotheses in Technological Perspective," *World Politics* 15, no. 2 (1963). Ibn Khaldun could also be added to this list. Ibn Khaldun, *The Muqqadimmah: An Introduction to History,* translated by Franz Rosenthal, *Bollingen Series* (Princeton, NJ: Princeton University Press, 1967).
2. Though I personally assume poetic license on the part of the author, "And rain fell upon the earth for forty days and forty nights" (Genesis 7:12) is a weather report. Perhaps a more persuasive example would be Aristotle's *Meteorologica* (ca. 340 B.C.E.).
3. Systematic collection of weather data requires instruments. According to textbook author Joe R. Eagleman, rain gauges were used in India

around 300 B.C.E., and the wind direction in Athens was determined with a wind vane on the Acropolis in 100 B.C.E. Galileo developed a rudimentary thermometer in 1600, and early work on what later became the barometer was done by Evangelista Torricelli in 1644. In 1646 Blaise Pascal suggested that Torricelli's invention be used to measure atmospheric pressure. An instrument to measure wind speed, an anemometer, was developed in 1667 by Robert Hooke. Scales for the improved thermometer were developed by Fahrenheit in 1714 and Celsius in 1736. Joe R. Eagleman, *Meteorology: The Atmosphere in Action,* 2nd ed. (Belmont: Wadsworth, 1985), pp. 4–7. See also the discussion of Jacob Jurin that follows.

4. W. Ladd Hollist, "Chicago in February?!?," *International Studies Newsletter* 24, no. 5 (1994).

5. Jacob Jurin, "Invitatio Ad Observationes Meteorologicas Communi Consilio Instituendas," in *Royal Society of London Philosophical Transactions* 1723. The typescript article, found in the collection of the papers of Helmut Landsberg, Historical Manuscripts and Archives Department, University of Maryland at College Park Libraries, was sent to Patrick Hughes, Editor, Environmental Data and Information Service (EDIS), National Oceanographic and Atmospheric Administration (NOAA), and was dated May 4, 1979. The cover letter notes that the original publication of Jurin's paper "stimulated the taking of some of the early meteorological observations in England and also the American colonies."

6. Edith Brown Weiss, "International Responses to Weather Modification," *International Organization* 29, no. 3 (1975): 810.

7. Helmut Landsberg notes that records of a few other observers' efforts in the colonies have been found as well. H. E. Landsberg, "An Early Appeal to Weather Observers," (1979), available from Historical Manuscripts and Archives Department, University of Maryland, College Park Libraries. A handwritten note on the typescript indicates that the essay was sent to Patrick Hughes at EDIS-NOAA on May 17, 1979.

8. Ibid. Also see Helmut Landsberg, "An Anniversary: A Bicentennial of International Meteorological Observations," 1980, typescript sent to Dr. N. Taba, editor, WMO Bulletin, available from Historical Manuscripts and Archives Department, University of Maryland, College Park Libraries.

9. Helmut Landsberg, "Historic Weather Data and Early Meteorological Observations," in *Offprints from Paleoclimate Analysis and Modeling,* edited by Alan D. Hecht (Somerset, NJ: John Wiley and Sons, 1985), p. 58. Also see Landsberg, "An Anniversary."

10. Weiss, "International Responses to Weather Modification," p. 809.

11. Robert White, President National Academy of Engineering, interview with the author, September 8, 1994.

12. Weiss, "International Responses to Weather Modification," p. 809.

13. Ibid., pp. 809–810.

14. Robert Marc Friedman, *Appropriating the Weather: Vilhelm Bjerknes and the Construction of a Modern Meteorology* (Ithaca, NY: Cornell University Press, 1989).

15. Ibid.

16. After the U.S. Civil War, Albert J. Meyer, the U.S. Army's chief signal officer, convinced the government to use the telegraph to gather weather

data from military posts across the country. James R. Fleming, *Meteorology in America, 1800–1870* (Baltimore: Johns Hopkins University Press, 1990), pp. 154–155.

17. Research into weather modification in the United States began in 1891 with a $9,000 congressional appropriation to determine if artillery blasts would cause rain. Aerial dispersion, using aircraft, of electrically charged sand to produce rain was attempted between 1921 and 1924 by the Army Air Service. In 1966, the United States tried a weather modification technique, developed by the Naval Ordinance Test Station, over Laos. Subsequently during the Vietnam War, secret weather modification projects targeted against the enemy were conducted beginning in 1967. Charles C. Bates and John F. Fuller, *America's Weather Warriors, 1814–1985* (College Station: Texas A&M University Press, 1986), pp. 141–142 A comprehensive discussion of who did what in weather and climate modification can be found in Edith Brown Weiss, "The Political and Legal Problems of Weather and Climate Modification," Ph.D. dissertation, University of California, Berkeley, 1973.

18. Selected from a more extensive quotation in Sprout, "Geopolitical Hypotheses in Technological Perspective," pp. 199–201, taken from John von Neumann, "Can We Survive Technology?" *Fortune,* June 1955, p. 106.

19. Rita F. Taubenfeld and Howard J. Taubenfeld, "Some International Implications of Weather Modification Activities," *International Organization* 23, no. 4 (1969): 809. See also Eugene Skolnikoff, "Science and Technology: The Implications of International Institutions," *International Organization* 25, no. 4 (1971).

20. Weather modification efforts would result in the recognition of "joint supply and nonappropriability." Collective decisionmaking would allow rational resolution of public problems. John Gerard Ruggie, "Collective Goods and Future International Collaboration," *American Political Science Review* 66, no. 3 (1972): 891.

21. Bates, *America's Weather Warriors.*

22. Robert White, "A Cloud over Weather Cooperation," *Technology Review,* May/June 1994.

23. Peter Haas, "Introduction: Epistemic Communities and International Policy Coordination," *International Organization* 46, no. 1 (1992).

24. Elbert "Joe" Friday, Director, National Weather Service, interview with the author, October 28, 1994.

25. D. A. Davies, WMO Secretary General, "Memorandum to WMO Technical Commission Presidents" (Geneva, December 14, 1970). Ref. P. TC-828, available from Landsberg Papers, Historical Manuscripts and Archives Department, University of Maryland Libraries.

26. Ferd Baer, Professor of Meteorology, University of Maryland, interview with the author, October 26, 1994.

27. National Weather Service, U.S. National Oceanic and Atmospheric Administration, "National Weather Service Celebrates 125th Anniversary," press release, February 3, 1995 [cited August 28, 2003], available from www.erh.noaa.gov/er/gyx/125thsk.html.

28. Robert White, president, National Academy of Enineering, interview with the author.

29. MetService, *About Metservice* [cited January 28, 2003], available from www.metservice.co.nz/corporate/about.asp. MetService (NZ) Ltd. was created out of New Zealand's public national weather service in 1992.

30. For a short while, this limerick appeared on a website, www.met.co.nz/met/about/metservice.html. Marco Overdale writes that he wrote the "limerick in November 1996 after a forecast vision review. We had prepared the usual prose type statement of our aims when the CEO almost parenthetically said it would be neat if we could make this into a limerick or something. About five minutes later I read out the limerick and it was immediately adopted." Marco M. Overdale, September 27, 2002.

31. U.S. Department of State, unclassified telegram from the U.S. Mission in Geneva to the Department of State, June 1995, on file at the Department of State.

32. World Meteorological Organization, "Resolution 40 (CG-XII), WMO Policy and Practice for the Exchange of Meteorological and Related Data and Products Including Guidelines on Relationships in Commercial Meteorological Activities, June 1995," in *World Meteorological Organization, Exchanging Meteorological Data: Guidelines on Relationships in Commercial Meteorological Activities—WMO Policy and Practice.* Report No. 837 (Geneva, Switzerland: WMO, 1996).

33. Robert White, "Report of the Ad Hoc Committee on International Data Exchange," *Bulletin of the American Meteorological Society* 75, no. 4 (1994).

34. World Meteorological Organization, "Resolution 40 (CG-XII) . . . June 1995."

35. White, "A Cloud over Weather Cooperation."

36. Elbert "Joe" Friday, Director, National Weather Service, interview with the author, October 28, 1994.

37. Richard Hallgren, Executive Director, American Meteorological Society, interview with the author, November 7, 1994.

38. White, "A Cloud over Weather Cooperation"; Robert White, president, National Academy of Engineering, interview with the author, September 8, 1994.

39. Elbert "Joe" Friday, interview with the author, October 28, 1994.

40. A geologist has suggested to me that earthquake prediction services will be a future development analogous to the common good raw data/privately owned forecast relationship. Jeanne Sauber Rosenberg, Scientist, NASA/Goddard, personal communication via e-mail, 1994.

41. World Meteorological Organization, Geneva Declaration of the Thirteenth World Meteorological Congress, May, 26 1999 [cited August 21, 2003], available from www.wmo.ch/index-en.html.

42. Usually this refers to conditions on Earth; however, the imaging of conditions on other planets is also a form of remote sensing.

43. The U.S. Geological Survey limits the definition of *remote sensing* to nonphotographic airborne or space-borne sensing. According to the online glossary, *remote sensing* is defined as a "process of detecting or monitoring

an area usually from the air or from space by measuring reflected or emitted radiation. Some satellites carry special instruments while orbiting the Earth to detect the amount of heat being emitted by the planet." U.S. Geological Survey, *Glossary* (October 19, 1999 [cited September 27, 2002]), available from interactive2.usgs.gov/glossary/. However, since photography is a specific case of measuring radiation (i.e., visible light is recorded), the definition I have used is more appropriate.

44. This chronology is taken from Ames Research Center, National Aeronautic and Space Administration (NASA), Earth Science Division, Ecosystem Science and Technology Branch, "Landsat Program Chronology: Major Events in the Landsat Program with Emphasis on the Period Since October 1992," November 4, 1998 [cited August 19, 2003], available from geo.arc.nasa.gov/sge/landsat/lpchron.html.

45. Ibid.

46. Ibid.

47. Jimmy Carter, "Announcement of the President's Decisions Concerning Land Remote-Sensing Activities, November 20, 1979," in *Public Papers of the Presidents of the United States* (Washington, DC: U.S. Government Printing Office, 1980). See also Kathleen M. Eisenbeis, *Privatizing Government Information: The Effects of Policy on Access to Landsat Satellite Data* (Metuchen, NJ: Scarecrow, 1995); and NASA, "Landsat Program Chronology."

48. Eisenbeis, *Privatizing Government Information,* p. 8.

49. NASA, "Landsat Program Chronology."

50. EOSAT was a joint venture between Hughes Aircraft and RCA at the time of the contract.

51. Peter Marsh, "U.S. Satellite Network Goes into a Spin," *Financial Times,* November 23, 1984; Thomas O'Toole, "U.S. To Pay for Landsat's Turnover to Private Industry: Stockman, Congress End Long Dispute over Satellites," *Washington Post,* May 18, 1985.

52. NASA, "Landsat Program Chronology."

53. Eisenbeis, *Privatizing Government Information,* p. 73.

54. NASA, "Landsat Program Chronology."

55. Ibid.

56. Eisenbeis, *Privatizing Government Information,* p. 72.

57. NASA, "Landsat Program Chronology."

58. President George H.W. Bush, *Landsat Remote Sensing Strategy, National Science Policy Directive-5* (February 13, 1992 [cited August 15, 2003]), available from www.hq.nasa.gov/office/codez/new/policy/pddnspd5.html.

59. Land Remote Sensing Policy Act, U.S. Code 15 (1992), §§5601 et seq.

60. National Aeronautics and Space Administration, "Current Status and Summary of Agreement Between Landsat Program Management and EOSAT Corporation on Cost and Reproduction Rights for Landsat 4/5 Thematic Mapper Data," October 1, 1996, last modified May 1, 1997 [cited December 3, 2001], available from geo.arc.nasa.gov/sge/landsat/apr11.html. See also Space Imaging, "Space Imaging and EOSAT Agree on Acquisition," press

release, Thornton, Colorado, November 5, 1996 [cited October 2, 2002], available from www.spaceimaging.com/newsroom/releases/1996/eosat_news.html.

61. Yahya A. Dehqanzada and Ann M. Florini, *Secrets for Sale: How Commercial Satellite Imagery Will Change the World* (Washington, DC: Carnegie Endowment for International Peace, 2000).

62. Horst Fischer, "Basic Principles of International Space Law and Civilian Use of Outer Space," in *Outer Space: A Source of Conflict or Co-Operation,* edited by Bhupendra Jasani (Tokyo: United Nations University Press, in cooperation with the Stockholm International Peace Research Institute, 1991).

63. NASA, "Landsat Program Chronology."

64. Eisenbeis, *Privatizing Government Information,* p. 29.

65. A clear explanation of GPS can be found in an online publication, Aerospace Corporation, *Global Positioning System Primer* (cited October 23, 2001); available from www.aero.org/publications. Documents pertaining to GPS can be found at the U.S. Interagency GPS Executive Board (IGEB) website [cited January 28, 2002], available from www.igeb.gov.

66. Information for this section relies on the account published in Scott Pace et. al, "The Global Positioning System: Assessing National Policies," report prepared for the Executive Office of the President, Office of Science and Technology Policy (Santa Monica, CA: Rand Corporation, 1995).

67. TRANSIT, a Navy satellite.

68. Automated Data Service, U.S. Naval Observatory, *Block II Satellite Information* (August 19, 2003 [cited August 20, 2003]); available from ftp://tycho.usno.navy.mil/pub/gps/gpsb2.txt. The four-year hiatus between the completion of the test series and launch of the first Block II satellite was, in part, a result of the *Challenger* disaster. The Air Force had intended to launch these satellites from a space shuttle. After the loss of *Challenger,* the decision was made to reconfigure the satellites for launch on Delta rockets.

69. United States, Executive Branch, Interagency GPS Executive Board (IGEB), "Frequently Asked Questions About SA Termination," October 15, 2001 [cited September 28, 2002], available from www.igeb.gov/sa/faq.shtml.

70. President William J. Clinton, *Statement by the President Regarding the United States' Decision to Stop Degrading Global Positioning System Accuracy* (May 1, 2000 [cited September 28, 2002]), available from www.ostp.gov/html/0053_2.html.

71. Scott Pace and James E. Wilson, "Global Positioning System: Market Projections and Trends in the Newest Global Information Utility," report prepared for the U.S. Department of Commerce, International Trade Administration, Office of Telecommunications Technologies, 1998.

72. Ibid.

73. Quoted in European Commission, "Galileo: The Challenge of Autonomy," February 2000. *RTD info* 25 [cited October 26, 2001], available from europa.eu.int/comm/research/rtdinfo/en/25/03.html?

74. European Space Agency, "What Is Galileo? Feature on Navigation Satellite Applications," April 5, 2002 [cited September 28, 2002], available from www.esa.int/export/esaSA/GGGMX650NDC_navigation_0.html.

7

Owning Information About People

Next we turn to the increasingly valuable business of owning information about people, in particular the process of using computer routines to comb through large volumes of data to connect certain facts to people or groups of people. If a database has information for many variables on many people, it is possible to look for useful correlations. For example, knowing the buying patterns of bank tellers versus farmers, identifying trends in crime in neighborhoods across a city, and figuring out who is not a good risk for long-term health care insurance all require looking at what usually happens or what people usually do. Data mining is the term used for using computer programs to sift through large computer datasets according to some specified criteria. Data mining to discover or create information about people is a special policy concern.

In many ways, though, data mining is the logical extension of what we do normally in our every day experience: we make connections. Consider old-fashioned, noncomputerized matchmaking. A database containing characteristics of eligible people is stored in the matchmaker's brain. The matchmaker sifts through lots of information about a lot of people, based on a set of search criteria (shared interests, similar sense of humor, etc.) In short, matchmaking is just an inspired form of data mining.

A physician making a diagnosis is also doing some data mining. She collects data, including body temperature, blood pressure, pulse rate, and symptoms. She looks for color of the skin and throat; listens for sounds of the lungs, heart, and intestines; she orders cultures and other laboratory work or x-rays. In all likelihood, most of the information she gathers will be of no consequence. But when a correct diagnosis is made, she is matching some of the data about the patient with what she knows about people with a certain disease or condition. The ability to connect elusive pieces of evidence within a mass of data is the mark of a good diagnostician.

In the case of information about the planet (see Chapter 6), images and observations are often valuable because of what they are: information about and as reality. An image of the location of a natural resource is the equivalent of a map telling the viewer how to find the resource and a reality—the picture itself. The information discussed in this chapter is valuable because of the connections that can be made because of it: the information as reality aspect takes on even greater importance. Data mining technologies make large collections of information increasingly valuable as property. Existing collections of data vary in the extent to which they are owned, and there are examples of data as mixed public-private goods, as government-owned (secret) property, as club goods, and as private goods. Often, a particular set of data will contain some information that is not owned or is provided as a public good and some data that is owned, either by government or by private parties. So I am not making any claims that these categories are pure types. Rather, they are exemplars of the value that information has come to have.

■ Mixed Public and Private Goods

One way to create a profitable information-based industry is to sell the data-mining tools—the software programs needed to analyze public information. The complex programs are information *for* reality; the products of using these programs represent information *as* reality.[1] A Geographic Information System (GIS) is a way to pool many kinds of spatial information so they can be mapped together. Inferences (made using either statistical methods or qualitative evaluation) can be made about relationships (e.g., what tends to be located near what?). This information can be useful for land-use planning and helps planners determine where new schools are needed, whether roads and other infrastructure are lacking, and so on. GIS combines satellite remote-sensing data, GPS data for location, and information available from the ground, such as census data by location. The user can add more data and layer it on top of the preexisting set. Mapping software such as ArcView allows the researcher to extract the desired information and display it on a map. Maps, of course, are not a new form of information. Simply digitizing an old-fashioned map and adding a few features would not be a novelty. Rather, it is the addition of large amounts of data from satellite imaging and other sources to these maps that makes them special.[2]

However, combining satellite imaging and positioning information with census and other data is no simple task. The hodgepodge of datasets containing the required information have different formats and standards. In order to make GIS work, interoperability standards need to be met. The Open GIS Consortium is an industry organization created "to deliver spatial interface specifications that are openly available for global use."[3] Just as standards for videotape and CD technology created the opportunity for market development for those products, a similar synergy is expected (and already realized, to some degree) with the adoption of open source (i.e., unrestricted) interoperability standards for the geographic information system technology. "Open interface specifications," according to the consortium's documentation, allow "content providers, application developers and integrators to focus on delivering more capable products and services to consumers in less time, at less cost, and with more flexibility."[4] For example, by providing information to the public in Topologically Integrated Geographic Encoding and Referencing (TIGER®) format, the U.S. Census Bureau supplies data that can be used by a variety of commercial GIS analysis programs.[5]

This kind of interoperability has value beyond the geographic borders of the United States. The United Nations Conference on Trade and Development has a plan to use GIS data to help developing countries build sustainable transportation systems. Combining GIS with transportation statistics will help develop transportation planning, enable efficient road management, and limit negative effects on the environment. Also, introducing state-of-the-art GIS tools into developing countries transfers technology to the Global South in a positive way.[6]

In the United States, the United Kingdom, and a few other countries, GIS is being used to make policing more effective. Crime mapping allows police analysts to enter information about the locations of crimes, arrests, and calls to police. This information can then be displayed on a map, possibly using census data and other resources to identify other locations of interest (e.g., schools) and other factors (potential variables such as socioeconomic data by census tract). These maps, researchers suggest, can help police identify emerging hot spots for crime. Although it seems as if such information could simply be shared by officers in a morning meeting or over coffee, the specialization of duties, the size of police departments, different shifts, and the like make comprehensive reporting difficult. Kurt Smith, an officer in the operational support administration of the San Diego Police Department, wrote about the role played by crime mapping in improving police efforts against narcotics activity:

> Citizens' complaints of narcotics activity often result in calls for service that are dispatched to patrol officers. These calls, often an indicator of a neighborhood in distress, are valuable for problem solving and are a potential source of intelligence. Often, however, detectives are not aware of the calls dispatched to patrol, and officers overlook the opportunity to pursue related calls or develop information from callers. CityMap [software that uses GIS data for mapping], at a glance, allows personnel to see where dispatched narcotics calls have occurred. . . . Clusters of calls are evaluated and compared to narcotics arrests, jump-starting the problem solving process and encouraging the appreciation of the value of what may seem to be "just another dope call."[7]

The analysis software allows the creation of a new kind of information—the map—which is information about and as reality.[8] And the property (in map form) owned by a governmental authority may in fact be copyrighted.[9] Thus intellectual property and information property are evident in all phases of the development of GIS. The software used to create maps is copyrighted or patented.[10] The names of the companies producing the software and the names of the software products are trademarked. Although some mapping data can be accessed for free, additional information may be proprietary. The final map products may also be owned as information property. In the case of crime mapping and many other GIS applications, a private-sector industry has emerged around the government-provided public good of geographic data. As with GPS, the market for GIS software (and thus the mapping data they produce) depends on government-provided data. The privatization of national weather services and the commodification of weather data suggests that the raw data provided by governments (census data, crime data, remote sensing data, etc.) may eventually be commodified as well.

▪ Secret Data: Carnivore, Echelon, and Related Government-Owned Systems

Governments in the United States and elsewhere are in the business of collecting information. How much intelligence they collect inside versus outside the country depends on the type of regime and the extent to which laws and political cultures allow government to gather information and maintain it. Intelligence comes in many forms, including high-resolution data from military satellites and airplanes, as well as direct observation of people's activities. This information is gathered for domestic policing, defense of national security, and other purposes. Indeed, in countries where human rights are not as protected by laws limiting the gathering and use of information, intelligence is an essential tool used for identifying and persecuting dissenters.

Even among democracies there are differences in the ways governments can legitimately collect and hold onto information. Common wisdom has it that Americans tend to be especially cautious about protecting their independence from government oversight, and the United States has many laws (including constitutional guarantees against unlawful search and seizure) to limit the government's collection and use of data. Civil libertarians react very negatively to the idea of a national identity card, such as those issued in many European countries.[11] Americans tend not to like the idea that one number could link together all the government's information about them. That sentiment may be changing, though, as Americans realize that social security numbers, which are keys to a good deal of private information, are being used as de facto government identity cards. Also, in the wake of September 11, there may be an increased willingness to accept more government monitoring of people's lives. Western Europeans, experts generally say, are more willing to allow governments to gather and maintain information. They put strict limits on the use of information with laws, including a European Union directive on the protection of personal information.[12]

But recall the witch hunts of the House Un-American Activities Committee during the McCarthy era, a stain on the U.S. record of protecting civil rights. In those days, communism was the perceived threat to the United States. Today, insecurity—the result of terrorism as well as everyday crimes—forces Americans to weigh the freedom from government surveillance against increased government surveillance that (falsely?) promises increased security. The USA PATRIOT Act (officially: the United and Strengthening America by Providing Appropriate Tools Required to Intercept and Obstruct Terrorism Act), was quickly passed in the wake of September 11. The Patriot Act increases the ability of law enforcement agencies to collect information, and it erodes some of the protections of judicial oversight that would provide a safety net for civil liberties protection.[13]

Carnivore and Echelon are two government programs designed to gather information and make it useful to governments. Both programs have been widely criticized by civil libertarians and others concerned about abuse of governmental powers and the extent to which governments are allowed to conduct surveillance. Carnivore is not a secret project. Echelon, a U.S.-led international collaboration among the Anglo alliance states (United States, Great Britain, Canada, New Zealand, and Australia), remains secret in most of its details, with the U.S. government continuing to deny its existence even while the other governments admit it.

Carnivore

Carnivore is a system to intercept messages traveling on the Internet. The FBI, armed with a court order, can attach a tapping device at an Internet service provider's point of access to the Internet. According to the FBI's website, the "tap produces an exact copy of all data at the access point." The kinds of data collected by Carnivore include e-mail messages and other information that the target has received. These data are then passed through a filter, and only those data that match the search criteria that agents have set are retained. All other data (such as innocent bystanders' private information) is to be deleted rather than recorded. The suspect's communications are then sent via telephone line and modem to another computer at an FBI office. It is on this computer that analysis of the communication (e.g., rebuilding data packets so that full text messages can be read) is conducted.

To safeguard the privacy rights of individuals, there are limits to the ways Carnivore can be used. Carnivore is a form of electronic surveillance and, as such, must be used in accordance with Title III of the Omnibus Crime Control and Safe Streets Act of 1968. The Carnivore system can be set up to collect either of two kinds of information, analogous to (1) collecting the numbers of incoming and outgoing phone calls on a tapped phone and (2) recording entire conversations. By statute, the FBI is required to produce a higher degree of justification to collect full text information than simply the *To:* and *From:* data in message headers. The FBI must also minimize the amount of innocent bystanders' information it collects. When a court decides to allow the FBI to install a Carnivore tap, it issues an order specifying the limitations on data collection and the requirements for judicial review, as well as an order for the ISP to comply. Though in some cases the order to the ISP may omit the name of the target, as well as the reason for the investigation, such information may become known under some circumstances. Only under very unusual circumstances (immediate danger) can a Carnivore tap be employed without a court order, and in that case the court must be notified within forty-eight hours.[14]

Are these safeguards sufficient to protect the rights of people to communicate freely without unwarranted surveillance? Many claim that it is not. A review commissioned by the Department of Justice on the whole evaluated Carnivore positively, though it recommended some improvements to protect the public. These include providing a means for auditing the actions of individual FBI personnel using the system to provide individual accountability and to increase the security of the equipment placed on-site at the ISP. Also the report recommends that all data collected be marked with filter settings (in other words, the search criteria) by which it was collected. This would ensure that only information needed for the court-ordered purposes is being collected.[15]

Some civil liberties advocates do not believe that these recommendations are sufficient. The extent to which judicial oversight protects the public, for example, depends on how lenient a court is in granting the FBI permission to surveil. One concern is that FBI agents may be able to shop for lenient judges. Moreover, the existing protections do not really protect the public from FBI malfeasance. By controlling filtering, agents can choose to extract more data about more people, going beyond the intent of the original court order. Given the current lack of oversight and accountability, it would be difficult to hold agents responsible for overzealous collection.[16] How much information does the government have a right to collect, own, and use?

Echelon

Echelon is potentially even more powerful. It is a secret data-collection system used by the United States, the United Kingdom, Canada, New

Zealand, and Australia. Little is known about this system, because details remain classified. However, according to several advocacy organizations, government statements, and news reports,[17] it seems that Echelon collects massive amounts of international communications and screens them for intelligence. By screening voice and data transmissions via telephone lines, satellite, and the Internet (e.g., for keywords, phrases, addresses, and telephone numbers) intelligence agencies can search for communications relevant to national security. Large-scale government surveillance of communications for security purposes is nothing new. Signals intelligence (SIGINT) has been an important component of intelligence gathering. In the United States, civil liberties are protected by laws that prevent the intelligence agencies from intentionally collecting and holding data on U.S. persons (citizens and legal residents, as well as legal persons, i.e., corporations) unless there is a compelling reason to think the target is involved in something that threatens national security.[18]

Echelon, according to Jeffrey Richelson, refers specifically to a unique system linking National Security Agency (NSA) computers with those of counterpart organizations in the other countries. The computers are equipped with the Dictionary program, which compares specified keywords against the large quantity of information gathered. The Echelon network allows each security organization to specify keywords; when the computer detects a match, it sends the data to the requesting country's computer automatically. This is a significant innovation. "Before Echelon appeared in the 1970s," Richelson notes,

> the agencies shared intelligence, but they usually processed and analyzed the intercepted communications. As a result, most exchanges involved finished reports rather than raw intercepts. Echelon, on the other hand, is an integrated network that allows the agencies to specify which intercepts are of interest and to receive them automatically via computer.[19]

There are many positive elements to this approach: computers using artificial intelligence programs sift through vast amounts of information, ignore communications that are of no interest, and hold on to information with national security implications. Using computers to conduct data mining in some ways protects people's privacy, especially when the only alternative is to sift through data using human analysts. Human analysts cannot be forced to forget stray bits of unnecessary information collected in their memories. Computers can be instructed to delete unneeded information.

So what is the downside? Civil libertarians worry that governments simply have too much power to collect information and too little incentive not to. The American Civil Liberties Union and the Electronic Privacy Information Center, along with the Omega Foundation and the British Cyber-Rights and Cyber-Liberties organization, publish an online resource, Echelonwatch.[20] The purpose of this website is to warn of the potential threat to civil liberties of the Echelon system, which could be used to spy on private citizens. In 1998, for example, an article in the *Washington Post* reported that the NSA admitted to "holding 1,056 pages of classified information about the late Princess Diana, inspiring a flurry of sensational headlines . . . across London's tabloids." The article cited an unnamed intelligence official who said "that the references to Diana in intercepted conversations were 'incidental.'" The NSA's admission was made in response to a Freedom of Information Act request for classified information about Princess Diana, a request the NSA denied for national security reasons. According to an intelligence official, the national security risk was that releasing information about her would reveal how it was collected.[21]

Echelon and other secret intelligence gathering projects are controlled by a small group of people, and there is little real accountability because reports about them are not released to the public. Oversight is limited to the House and Senate Comittees on Intelligence, and judicial review is restricted to special secret courts established under the provisions of the Foreign Intelligence Surveillance Act to deal with legal questions involving classified material. In August 2002, one of these secret courts, the Foreign Intelligence Surveillance Court, ruled against the administration's plans to implement the Patriot Act because of significant threats to citizens' civil liberties. Surprisingly, the court released a public report on its decision. Despite the unusual public protest by a secret court, the decision was overturned by the Foreign Intelligence Surveillance Court of Review on appeal.

Other concerns remain as well. For example, French companies and individuals have accused the United States of using Echelon for industrial espionage.[22] Also, the United States and its Echelon partners are not the only governments using computer surveillance technology. Several countries maintain significant operations, including, according to Echelonwatch, surveillance of private communications. China uses computer surveillance technologies to spy on internal dissidents and foreigners.[23] Surveillance and control of Internet communications are a significant risk to human rights.[24]

The conundrum comes back to the tension between security and liberty. The more data the government owns and is allowed to keep secret, the more security we may have. But when the state scoops up large quantities of data, stores that data, and uses it for its own purposes, that act of the government is a taking. The government is, in essence, utilizing its right of eminent domain to take information property from people without compensation. That is a violation of our liberty. But the reason ostensibly is to protect security. Given the imminent threat of additional terrorist attacks, perhaps the use of eminent domain is necessary. The state, after all, has a responsibility to provide physical security to the lawful inhabitants of the country. This tension will not be easily resolved. Despite the emotional need to take action following September 11, citizens must continue to debate the proper balance between security and liberty.

■ Data as a Club Good: Iceland's Human Data

Our next case similarly involves government taking of information, but the information is being made available for a fee. In December 1998 the Icelandic government made international headlines when it decided to license the entire population's genetic and medical information to a company that in turn would have the right to sell it to research groups and pharmaceutical companies. In essence, this decision creates a new club for information property, made available only to those who pay membership dues.

Iceland is an excellent laboratory for genetic research. Researchers look for genes that are associated (and perhaps cause) particular health conditions. To do this, they compare the DNA of people who have a condition with each other and with people who do not have the condition. If the afflicted people tend to have a certain pattern in the DNA at one location on a chromosome, and the people who are not afflicted tend not to have that pattern, then the location of the pattern and the pattern itself provide an important clue about the condition. Researchers can develop procedures that lead to early detection, treatment, and possibly a cure. If researchers can figure out what the suspect gene does, then they are that much closer to a treatment or a cure.

The difficulty in this process is the enormous variability of DNA. It is difficult to sift through all the variations and find the ones that tend to mark a particular condition. But if researchers are able to draw genetic samples from a more homogeneous population, it becomes easier to identify the genetic patterns. The Icelandic population is remarkably homogenous. Hrobjartur Jonatansson notes that "Icelanders descended from ninth and tenth century Norse settlers and were almost completely isolated from the rest of the world until the beginning of the Twentieth Century." And despite some foreign influence due to the British army's occupation of the island country during World War II, Iceland has not experienced the diverse immigration patterns seen in Denmark and Sweden.[25]

Other elements make Iceland's genetic and medical information attractive as a commodity. Icelanders are particularly interested in genealogy, and there are extensive databases available that detail who begat whom. According to *The Economist,* deCODE Genetics, the company that received the exclusive license to the genetic and medical information, "has built a genealogical data-base that traces the ancestry and family connections of almost three-quarters of the 750,000 Icelanders who have ever lived."[26] In addition, the government has long provided health care, so it possesses health-care records for all Icelanders over several decades.[27] And finally, there is the serendipitous role played by Kari Stefansson, an entrepreneurial Icelander with medical degrees from the University of Iceland and experience as a professor of neurology, neuropathology, and neuroscience at Harvard University, who is the cofounder, president, and CEO of deCODE Genetics.

So what do the researchers at deCODE actually do? The company is inputting all the information (for deceased and living persons) into a database. For a living person, the database will be updated when new information (e.g., a new diagnosis) becomes available. Though the database does not include names, a code system will allow researchers to link new information to a person's records. Added to this health information will be information from tissue samples provided by individuals and public domain genealogical information. Except for the tissue samples, the information is gathered without asking for specific consent. It is possible to opt out and have one's information removed, but those people who do not file the special paperwork required to opt out "are presumed to give consent." This category includes the deceased, newborns, and the mentally ill.[28] deCODE is paying the government of Iceland $12 million for the exclusive twelve-year license. The company has signed an exclusive contract with Hoffman-LaRoche, in which Hoffman-LaRoche will pay $200 million "for exclusive access to the database to probe the genetic origins of 12 common diseases." One source says that the contract includes an agreement on the part of Hoffman-La Roche "to supply Icelanders free of charge with any medicines that result from their research."[29]

DeCODE's strategy of re-creating the raw data into a scarce and excludable commodity includes working with partner firms like Hoffman-La Roche and Genmab. These firms will collaborate on creating new products, such as methods of diagnosis and drug therapies (Hoffman La-Roche), as well as new antibody therapeutic products and clinical tools that predict how a particular patient is likely to respond to a particular drug (Genmab). At the core of the project is the Database Subscription and Consulting Services being developed by deCODE. According to the company's business model,

> deCODE expects to develop and operate the deCODE Combined Data Processing system [DCDP]. The DCDP is intended to cross-reference non-personally identifiable healthcare information on the Icelandic population in the Icelandic Health Sector Database (IHD) with genealogy data and genetic data obtained through informed consent. We are currently developing new mathematical algorithms in order to be able to extract further knowledge from the DCDP. Services we plan to offer to future subscribers of the DCDP will include gene discovery and drug target validation, as well as analytical support for disease management, pharmacogenomic, and health management programs.[30]

Limiting the exchange of data to partners and subscribers transforms Iceland's data into a club good. Only those willing to pay for access, either by agreeing to share profits or by paying a subscription fee, will have access. Moreover, once the data have been mined and used to create knowledge, "deCODE plans to continue to leverage the power of [its database searching technology] to generate new proprietary knowledge about the connections between genes and disease."[31] This statement reflects the company's position that the prudent business move is to take scientific discoveries and new knowledge about the natural world and transform that information into property.

Several criticisms have been raised about the nature of the deal. The opt-out provision (as opposed to an opt-in provision) means that participation is assumed. To the extent that the data do not link individuals to their health histories, using medical records is not considered problematic. Custom and accepted professional ethical standards allow the use of anonymous personal information for research. But if someone can find enough clues in the data to identify an individual, then there is a real problem.

Suppose that a database contained the subject's town, gender, profession, cause of death of parents, along with other variables (history of illicit drug use, treatment for sexually transmitted disease, family history of schizophrenia, etc.). It might be easy to identify subjects. Now suppose that someone wanted to use the database for inappropriate purposes, perhaps curiosity, perhaps something more nefarious. In a population as small as Iceland's, it would be fairly easy to identify someone. And stripping the database of all potential links to real-person names would be extraordinarily difficult.

Even if Icelanders consent, how well informed is that consent? Do they know how that information will be used? One might disclose private health information to help find a cure for a serious disease, but few would be willing to provide such information for less noble causes, especially if it meant lining the pockets of a pharmaceutical giant or supporting an unstated ideological agenda. Once Icelanders consent to be included in the database, will they be able to track how their information is being used? Will they be able to keep tabs all new topics of research?

This raises yet another point: Who benefits? Has the government of Iceland benefited the public good or the private good of deCODE? Do Icelanders have some property right in health information that would entitle them to compensation? Will scientists not associated with deCODE be able to conduct related research? The agreement is an interesting experiment if nothing else, part of the trend toward privatizing government information. It is too soon to predict the results.

▪ Data as a Private Good: Data Owned by Firms and Others

Firms and other organizations generate a lot of data. In recent years, firms have turned to mining their own proprietary databases. Most public attention has been focused on the retention of data about customers, but companies also collect data about their own products, their employees, or the companies they do business with.

The interesting aspect is that the information itself has become a valued property. A mailing list is nothing more than a mailing list. The value is in the information it contains: potential customers and their addresses. There is nothing new about selling mailing lists or about keeping careful records. But today computers are able to combine large datasets into a single database—a data warehouse—that can be mined to extract commercially useful information. To create a data warehouse, the firm (or other organization) combines all the different databases, restructures them so that they can be compatible, and cleans the data to get rid of the inevitable bad entries.[32]

For-profit organizations are not alone in their collection, use, and valuing of information. Think about the data that a university collects. University offices of institutional research routinely mine data, combining information on names, student ID numbers, home addresses, courses enrolled in, grades, credit hours completed, campus addresses, roommates' names, meal plan usage, and more. University administrators extract information of value to the institution, helping it provide a better educational experience for existing students or helping it recruit new students. The concerns raised by personal information databases maintained by the for-profit and nonprofit sectors are similar: what information is collected, how safely is it stored, what use is it put to? But there is, I believe, an additional wrinkle with nonprofits. Consumers tend to be a bit more wary of the private sector than they are of nonprofits. While consumers are likely to assume that a firm is fundamentally self-interested and has little concern for the well-being of the consumers or their data, they tend to be a bit more sanguine about the motives and expected behavior of nonprofits. It may be unwise, however, to assume that one's personal data is safe in the hands of the university or other nonprofit.

The process of creating a data warehouse and then using technology to mine useful information is known as *knowledge discovery from data,*[33] an increasingly important marketing tool for business. Data mining helps firms target scarce advertising dollars in the most effective way. Targeting advertising toward people who are likely to respond positively saves money. Data mining also helps firms look for changes in the market or in consumer behavior. Looking for unexpected patterns is the technique used by the securities sector for self-regulation. But potential malfeasance is a real possibility here, as rumors (whether true or not), unethical traders, and misinformation can create havoc. Stock markets cannot function unless the customers believe in their integrity.

In many countries, including the United States, the securities industry—brokers and dealers in securities (stocks and bonds)—is self-regulating. That is, the government delegates to a private organization the responsibility for enforcing regulations to protect investors. In the United States, the National Association of Securities Dealers (NASD) is tasked with making sure that the market operates properly and that when unethical traders manipulate the market they are detected and penalized. The NASD Regulation's Advanced Detection System is used to monitor purchases and sales on the NASDAQ stock market. The system can "identify suspicious sequences of trading or quoting activity that can signal a potential violation." Since dealers themselves are supposed to watch out for improper trading, NASD Regulation is developing "real-time monitoring to help them fulfill their self-regulation duties. The system is designed to alert exchange operators or traders that they have just executed a problematic trade—in time for them to take immediate corrective action." The idea is to help maintain consumer confidence in markets. Once dealers are able to catch and correct their own mistakes, the NASD "can focus on getting the few truly bad actors in the industry either to respect the rules or get out of the business."[34]

Perhaps even more interesting is the NASD's plan to market its oversight technology to markets around the world. As more countries develop domestic stock markets to complement their newly marketizing economies, having the knowledge to create a trustworthy system of self-regulation can mean the difference between consumer investment and consumer flight. The NASD projects that there is a return to be made in providing the information about how to conduct data mining for self-regulation. The goal is for "markets to operate more like Wall Street and less like Las Vegas."[35]

Nevertheless, data mining is not a panacea. Its value depends on the veracity and accuracy of the data and on whether techniques are used properly: garbage in, garbage out. Intentional manipulation of the market undermines the usefulness of data mining for self-regulation. Nevertheless, one representative of a data mining software firm claimed that careful use of his company's software would have alerted securities dealers to Enron's pattern of reckless and unethical behavior before the problem became severe.[36] Good data analysis software will never be sufficient for predicting business disasters, of course; good, complete data will be needed as well.[37] Yet another intangible product of the human mind will also be needed: integrity.

▪ Digitized Personal Information

Information increasingly is owned as public goods, club goods, private goods, and as combinations of these. The reason is that computers are able to store and manipulate large databases at low cost. Although less knowledge remains in the commons as knowledge becomes increasingly commodified, advances in computer technology allow people to create new information that has been hidden until now.

The ability of computers to manipulate data stands in contrast to the old-fashioned methods, using one's brain and some index cards to make useful connections and find patterns. The owner of digitized information property stored in a computer has more control over the property than we have over the information in our brains. Information coded into a digital format understood by computers is more easily mined to discover new knowledge, more easily transmitted, more easily deleted, and more securely retained than information coded into human memories. The flexibility of digitized data raises concerns about potential violations of privacy, as well as holding out hope for potential means of protecting privacy.

■ Notes

1. Albert Borgmann, *Holding on to Reality: The Nature of Information at the Turn of the Millennium* (Chicago: University of Chicago Press, 1999), pp. 171–177.

2. Ibid.

3. Open GIS Consortium, *Vision, Mission, and Values* (October 7, 2002 [cited August 19, 2003]), available from www.opengis.org/info/vm.htm.

4. Ibid.

5. Open GIS Consortium, press release, September 27, 2002 [cited October 4, 2002], available from www.opengis.org/pressrm/pressrelease/200209023.CIPI2.htm.

6. UNESCO, Economic Commission for Europe, Inland Transport Committee, Working Party on Transport Statistics. Geographic Information Systems (GIS) in Transport Statistics, Preparations for a Workshop on GIS in Urban Transport and Land Use Planning (Spring 2001, Tunis), note by the Secretariat, TRANS/WP.6/2000/8, August 16, 2000 [cited August 16, 2003], available from www.unece.org/trans/main/wp6/pdfdocs/2000-8e.pdf.

7. Kurt Smith, "Mapping Narcotics Activity Information: Linking Patrol and Investigations," *Crime Mapping News,* Fall 2001, p. 4.

8. Borgmann, *Holding on to Reality,* p. 171.

9. Copyright ownership of maps reproduced in an article by Craig Shephard, a GIS development officer with the London Borough of Harrow Community Safety Unit, is retained by the British government. Craig Shephard, "Crime and Disorder Partnership Targets Durg and Alcohol-Related Crime: London Borough of Harrow (UK)," *Crime Mapping News,* Fall 2001.

10. Even when software owners use open interface specifications, the software would still be protected as intellectual property.

11. Belgium, Portugal, and Spain require government issued ID cards. The other EU countries have varying requirements concerning ID cards. Helen Carter, "Used in Europe since the Last Century." *The Guardian Unlimited,* July 4, 2002 [cited Ocotober 5, 2002], available from society. guardian.co.uk/policy/story/0,8108,749018,00.html.

12. European Parliament and European Council, Directive 95/46/EC of the European Parliament and of the Council of 24 October 1995 on the Protection of Individuals with Regard to the Processing of Personal Data and on the Free Movement of Such Data, L 281, November 23, 1995, Official Journal 31–50 [cited November 22, 2002], available from europa.eu.int/ smartapi/cgi/sga_doc?smartapi!celexapi!prod!CELEXnumdoc&lg=EN& numdoc=31995L0046&model=guichett.

13. David McGuire, "Civil Liberties Groups Want Patriot Act Info," *washingtonpost.com,* August 21, 2002 [cited October 5, 2002], available from www.washingtonpost.com/ac2/wp-dyn?pagename=article&node=&contentId =A61618-2002Jul12&notFound=true.

14. Stephen P. Smith et. al, *Independent Review of the Carnivore System,* Final Report for the United States Department of Justice by the IIT Research Institute under Contract No. 00-C-038 (December 8, 2000 [cited August 20, 2003]), available from /www.usdoj.gov/jmd/publications/carniv_ final.pdf.

15. Ibid.

16. See, for example, American Civil Liberties Union, "ACLU Comments Regarding Carnivore Review Team Draft Report 2000" [cited October 6, 2002], available from www.aclu.org/news/2000/carnivore_comments.html.

17. EchelonWatch, website [cited October 6, 2002], available from www.echelonwatch.org. See also European Parliament, "Report on the Existence of a Global System for the Interception of Private and Commercial Communications (Echelon Interception System)," 2001/2098 (INI), final, A5-0264/2001, July 11, 2001 [cited October 6, 2002], available from www. europarl.eu.int/tempcom/echelon/pdf/rapport_echelon_en.pdf.

18. The Foreign Intelligence Surveillance Act (FISA) and President Reagan's Executive Order 12333 are the most relevant rules. Foreign Intelligence Surveillance Act, U.S. Code 50, 1978, §§1801, et seq.; and President Ronald Reagan, United States Intelligence Activities, Executive Order 12333, December 4, 1981 [cited August 20, 2003], available from www.reagan.utexas.edu/ resource/speeches/1981/120481d.htm. The legal requirements and restrictions in the rules were referenced by National Security Administration director Michael V. Hayden, "Remarks Before the House Permanent Select Committee on Intelligence," April 12, 2000 [cited November 7, 2001], available from www.gwu.edu/~nsarchiv/NSAEBB/NSAEBB23/22-01.htm.

19. Jeffrey Richelson, "Desperately Seeking Signals," *Bulletin of the Atomic Scientists* 56, no. 2 (2000).

20. Echelonwatch, www.echelonwatch.org.

21. Vernon Loeb, "NSA Admits to Spying on Princess Diana," *Washington Post,* December 12, 1998.

22. Richard Barry, "Echelon: The French Fight Back" *ZDNET UK News,* June 29, 2000 [cited October 6, 2002], available from news.zdnet.co. uk/story/0,,s2079852,00.html.

23. Echelonwatch, Echelon's Counterparts, July 30, 2001 [cited October 7, 2001], available from www.aclu.org/Echelonwatch/networks.html.

24. Human Rights Watch, Special Issues and Campaigns, "Freedom of Expression on the Internet," 1999 [cited October 6, 2002], available from www.hrw.org/worldreport99/special/internet.html; and Global Internet Liberty Campaign, website [cited October 6, 2002], available from www.gilc.org.

25. Hrobajartur Jonatansson, "Iceland's Health Sector Database: A Significant Head Start in the Search for Biological Grail or an Irreversible Error?" *American Journal of Law and Medicine* 26, no. 1 (2000), citing *Iceland, 874–1974,* Handbook Published by the Central Bank of Iceland on the Occasion of the Eleventh Centenary of the Settlement of Iceland, 1975.

26. "Norse Code," *The Economist,* December 5, 1998.

27. Ibid. *The Economist* (1998) places the initial date in the 1940s. Jonatansson claims that the records go back to 1915. In addition he notes that the government has been working on computerizing the health care system, especially since a 1997 directive was issued. Jonatansson, "Iceland's Health Sector Database."

28. Colin Woodard, "Tempest in Iceland's Gene Pool," *Christian Science Monitor,* June 30, 2000.

29. Andy Soghlan, "Selling the Family Secrets," *New Scientist*, December 5, 1998.

30. deCode, *Statement,* 2001 [cited November 12, 2001]); available from www.deCode.com/company/model [note: link is no longer available].

31. deCode, press release, November 7, 2001 [cited November 12, 2001], available from www.decode.com/news/releasees/item.chtm?id=20141.

32. John A. Chopoorian et. al, "Mind Your Business by Minding Your Data," *S.A.M. Advanced Management Journal* 66, no. 2 (2001).

33. Described more fully, this is a process consisting of an iterative sequence of data cleaning, data integration, data selection, data transformation, data mining, pattern evaluation, and knowledge presentation. See Jiawei Han, "Data Mining" (1999 [cited August 17, 2003]), available from ftp.fas.sfu.ca/pub/cs/han/pdf/ency99.pdf; and Rhonda Delmater and Monte Hancock, *Data Mining Explained: A Manager's Guide to Customer-Centric Business Intelligence* (Boston: Digital, 2001).

34. Robert R. Glauber, "Keynote Remarks," the Annual Conference of the Securities Industry Association Compliance and Legal Division, Orlando, Florida (March 19, 2001 [cited November 14, 2001]), available from www.nasdr.com/1420/glauber-02.asp.

35. Ibid.

36. John Soat, "IT Confidential," *Infoweek.Com* (2002 [cited October 7, 2003]); available from www.informationweek.com/story/IWK20020419S0026.

37. Robert X. Cringely, "Invisible Giant: How SAS Solves Business Problems Most Companies Don't Even Know They Have" (April 11, 2002 [cited October 7, 2002]); available from www.pbs.org/cringely/pulpit/pulpit20020411.html.

8

Privacy

The commodification of information and the technology to manipulate it presents global society with a problem: the threat to privacy. In this chapter, I examine privacy, the third leg of the knowledge triad (intellectual property and information being the other two). I first develop a conceptualization of privacy that focuses on the role played by information flows to and from the individual. Privacy can be understood as a space filled with information. The space surrounds the person, and the person herself is the gatekeeper. Individuals exercise power when they successfully control the flow of their personal information. Chapters 9 and 10 examine privacy violations and privacy protections, respectively.

■ Privacy as an Information Space

We intuitively imagine that everyone is surrounded by a sort of privacy bubble, a space that contains personal information.[1] I formalize this widely shared intuition by emphasizing the information content of the space and the role played by the individual as gatekeeper, controlling the flow of information outward *and* inward. Gatekeepers who are successful receive desired information and communicate information outward at will. They also prevent the unwanted disclosure of information or the unwanted intrusion of information.

John Hollander describes this space as a "zone . . . that one carries about with one (and that, today, can be said to extend to disembodied information *about* one)."[2] Information in a patient's file at the physician's office, though not physically close to the patient, is still within the patient's information space. The idea of privacy as an imagined space is ingrained in the tropes we automatically invoke when we speak. When we say that we need our space or when we complain that someone or something gets too close, we are making a claim that privacy can be understood to be a space around the person.[3] We make a similar claim when we speak of an invasion of privacy. The metaphor alludes to a hostile incursion into a territory. The phrase signifies that the individual's sovereign control over her information space has been attacked.

The definition of privacy as an information space is also consistent with definitions drawing on the idea of privacy as separation from others and freedom from surveillance. Such a definition of privacy is implicit in the very influential article published in 1890 by law partners Samuel Warren and Louis D. Brandeis (who later became a U.S. Supreme Court justice). If a right to privacy is the right to be left alone, as they stated,[4] then privacy must be the "aloneness," the separation from others.[5] A contemporary extension of this definition is set forth by Jeffrey Rosen, who conceptualizes privacy as that which ought not to be observed or disclosed without permission. Privacy is a zone in which we are protected from an "unwanted gaze."[6] Similarly, Amitai Etzioni, views privacy "as the realm in which an actor (either a person or a group, such as a couple) can legitimately act *without disclosure* and accountability to others."[7] Control of the flow of information is the theme that ties these definitions together. *What* is known and *who* is allowed to know matters. Unlike definitions that conflate privacy with autonomy, privacy does not involve being able to do what one wants; rather it means being able to control the flow of information about what one does or what one is like.

■ Personal Information: Content of the Information Space

The reason we care about controlling the borders of this information space is that it contains personal information. According to Richard Murphy, personal information, loosely defined, is "any data about an individual that is identifiable to the individual."[8] I take a somewhat more expansive view by relaxing what is meant by "about an individual." As I use it here, *personal information* is data about a person (a person's attributes such as her eye color or his salary) or information a person has (the person's knowledge, ideas, emotions, and beliefs). Only by taking into account information a person has can we make sense of the privacy problem caused by the intrusion of unwanted information (e.g., pornography or spam). Spam violates our privacy because it forces upon us information that we don't want. There is, of course, considerable overlap between information about a person and information that a person has. Information concerning a person's religion, for example, is information about him and information he has about his own beliefs.

Whatever the piece of personal information, information flows across an individual's privacy boundary when someone or some other entity comes to know something. Inwardly flowing information means that the individual gains some bit of knowledge. Outwardly flowing information means that someone else gains some bit of knowledge about the individual. Information flows require cognition and a relationship between two or more knowing people. Information can be said to flow when someone or some other entity is made to know of something about someone else. The flow can be accomplished by communicating information through words. For example, when an individual tells someone her telephone number, she is sending information about herself out of her privacy zone to another person. To receive information, a person may use any of the senses, but we most commonly think of hearing and vision. If a person hears or sees someone say or do something—if the subject has been surveilled—then information about the action has flowed from the subject to the recipient.

■ From the Completely Private Inner Self to the Intimate Circle

Personal information varies in the degree to which we can control how it flows. We imagine our private information space as being tightly protected or very personal at the core, more porous or open farther out. At the core of an individual is the most private aspect of ourselves, what Antonio Damasio calls "core consciousness" or "core self."[9] The core self is wholly interior—the completely private "I." Only I can feel my inner sense that I am the I who feels my feelings.[10] No one can invade my core self, and I cannot choose to share it. Other people cannot observe how I feel my feelings.

Moving outward from the core of a person's privacy zone, the individual chooses to share information with others based on the nature of the relationship. The more intimate the relationship, by definition, the less information that is kept sequestered from the other person. We commonly assume that the members of a household together form a unit within the private domain. That is, the members of the household are relatively open to each other, but as a unit they are walled off by the privacy boundary from others.[11] A little farther out is a person's circle of friends. Less information is probably exchanged with friends than with family, but friends may exchange different information, including some not disclosed to family members. And of course all relationships are dynamic, and we have multiple, overlapping relationships. The line between disclosed and private, revealed, and hidden shifts constantly.[12]

■ Gatekeepers Controlling the Flow of Personal Information

As we navigate among the relationships in our lives, we constantly act as gatekeepers, sometimes allowing personal information to flow in or out, sometimes restricting it. As a gatekeeper, each individual routinely and continuously makes what Alan Westin refers to as claims determining "when, how, and to what extent information about them is communicated to others."[13] "This, also, involves . . . what uses will be made of it by others."[14]

The flow of personal information refers to how information moves to and from the individual, from and to someone or something else. In a perfect world (at least from an individualistic ideal type), an individual would be able to

- keep all personal information that she wants to remain private from unwanted disclosure;
- obtain all information that she believes she ought to have;
- prevent unwanted information from entering her information space; and
- disseminate any personal information to others as she chooses.

At the other ideal-type extreme, in a completely dystopian world, an individual would

- be forced to disclose all personal information;
- not receive information he wants;
- be forced to take in information he does not want to know; and
- be prevented from communicating information to others.

Of course, the real world lies somewhere between these poles. Moreover, an individual must be seen in relation to others, including individuals, groups, and institutions such as governments and firms. The information that one person wants to receive may be information that someone else does not wish to disclose. Everyone faces a tangled web of interactions and relationships when trying to control the flow of personal information.

▪ Privacy Rights

As gatekeepers, we depend on privacy rights to help us control the flow of personal information. The right to privacy has been constructed as a human right and as a property right.[15] By examining the problem of controlling the flow of personal information across the privacy boundary, we can see a close connection.

Consider first the property right: personal information is a kind of information. As information has become commodified, there has been a greater legal recognition of property rights for proprietary information. However, personal information has material value and may be property owned by the data collector (see Chapter 7); but the value does not accrue to the person the information describes. The knowledge I have about my shopping habits is not a source of profit for me.[16] I gain no appreciable benefit. But that data, combined with similar data from a few thousand other consumers, becomes a valuable databank for a marketing firm. Similarly, knowing what airplane trips I have taken does not make me any more secure. But some argue that if the government had information about the travel records of millions of people, a real, if diffuse, benefit (increased security) would result.

There is an apparent inconsistency here: my personal information can become someone else's property. My personal information has no material value—only emotional or psychological value—to me, but it may have significant material value—and no emotional or psychological value—to some other. The resolution of the inconsistency can be found by closely examining the differences between an individual's personal information and intellectual property or proprietary information. In assigning property rights to owners of intellectual property and proprietary information, society draws on the metaphor of chattel—something owned that can be moved. Information property is something of a natural extension of intellectual property. Both are intangible, but they can be moved, at least in metaphorical terms: when a copyright is sold, it "goes to" the new owner. Even more telling, intellectual property and information property are both products of work. Intellectual property commodifies the mental work of creating and innovating; information property commodifies sweat of the brow—the effort expended by the individual or firm to compile the information in a usable format.

The right to privacy, in contrast, more naturally draws on the metaphor of real property. Real property is attached to the land and fixed in geographic space. The category includes the land itself, buildings on it, and things permanently attached to the buildings. The metaphor is not perfect: a person's real estate is land, with a fixed address that can be located on a map. A person's privacy is constantly changing as the person moves from one relationship to the next. That is the nature of the contingent, dynamic public-private boundary. Real property can be posted with a no-trespassing sign at the property line. The border of one's private zone is more difficult to mark and to patrol.[17]

Despite these discrepancies, the property right for real estate provides an apt analogy. Even though we constantly negotiate the location of the public-private boundary, and even though some things inside that boundary (e.g., a person's house) actually exist in real space, no one can wall off all of his private life and keep it free from trespassers. Intellectual property is stolen, but privacy is violated. Just as the property line separates what is owned by the landowner from what is not, the privacy boundary separates personal information from public information.

It is at this point that the property-rights and human-rights conceptualizations of privacy rights come together. The information space that is privacy is attached to the person. A person's right to control the privacy boundary is like the rights that a person has over her own body. Indeed, privacy is as attached to the person as an arm or a kidney. Furthermore, people own their persons: they possess and use the physical and information manifestations of themselves. As

John Locke wrote, "Every man has a property in his own person; this no body has a right to but himself."[18] All humans have this fundamental (albeit conditional) property right in themselves. Assaults on privacy, like assaults on the body, are violations of human rights.[19] Thus the right to privacy is a property right as well as a human right; an assault violates the individual's right to one's own person as property, as well as the fundamental human right of protecting the individual from violence. Social norms and laws protecting these rights enhance individuals' power to control flows of personal information.

▪ Exercising Privacy Rights: Locating the Boundary

To control the flow of information across the border between our personal space and the public domain, we must know where the border is, either the physical border or the border that exists in our mind. Physical borders are easier to detect. The boundaries of real estate are the most obvious signs of where one's privacy begins. A fence or wall marks physical separateness from the rest of the world and the psychological separateness that keeps others out of our personal space. English law is famous for establishing the idea that a man's home is his castle, that he is sovereign within the confines of the walls of his own house; and laws commonly limit the circumstances under which one's physical domain can be entered by others. For a country to be free, there must be appropriate limits on the authority of the police or any other government agency to breach the privacy boundary.

Fences and walls are not the only physical demarcations of the border. The exterior of a car also marks a boundary between public and private, as does the exterior of a purse, briefcase, or backpack. Clothing keeps some parts of the body private, while other parts are on public display. In some cases, though, people use clothing to communicate personal information. Boy Scouts often wear uniforms or other insignia that identify membership in the organization to other Boy Scouts and to the public at large.

Context

Context becomes important, as when we are at the beach versus the office. Although laws may not differ—walking down Main Street in a bikini is not a criminal offense in this country—social rules most definitely do. Someone walking down Main Street in a bikini will be stared at and singled out for having transgressed the boundary between what is to be seen and what is to be hidden. In Jerusalem, the boundary between public and private shifts from neighborhood to neighborhood. A tourist wandering into an ultra orthodox neighborhood in clothes that are too revealing puts herself in danger of expressions of disapproval, even physical harm, because she has unwittingly breached the boundary.[20] The social rules of traditional cultures often have requirements for dress. For some cultures, modesty requires that the boundary between public and private is shifted so that less of a person's body is revealed in the public domain.

The boundary between public and private can also be located in intangible ideas about what is off-limits. We are all socialized to know the rules differentiating public and private settings, so we sense a difference between a discreet telephone call and words shouted down the street. This is particularly true in countries where the populace enjoys civil liberties and has a reasonable expectation that conversations are not subject to surveillance.[21]

So if a person broadcasts a message by shouting where others can hear, she has done something public, even if the message is intended for a single person. If she telephones discretely (speaking into the receiver, at low volume), she has done something private. Of course, private telephone calls were not always exclusively private, since a human operator was required to place the call. Although social norms of etiquette would prevent a trustworthy operator from revealing who was calling whom or what they said, the operator could not avoid knowing who called whom. Moreover, even the most considerate user of a party line telephone would occasionally unavoidably end up knowing something of what was said to whom by someone sharing the line. With the shift to automated switching and the demise of the party line, the impersonality of the telephone system allowed the location of the privacy boundary to shift. Now we have a reasonable expectation that telephone conversations are private. When that boundary is being shifted yet again for some reason, we are often informed. (Sometimes the law requires that we be informed.)

The location of the boundary applies as well to discussions about the privacy of online communications. Cyberspace may confound attempts to maintain the privacy boundary because technological innovations and accidents can thwart gatekeeping. Nowadays, savvy computer users understand that computer communications are not truly private unless certain extra steps are taken. This applies to commercial and noncommercial communications, to passive website viewing, and to the active sending and receiving of information. People are learning, often through extreme embarrassment, that e-mail messages meant for a single person can mistakenly be sent to an entire list of people. Even though communicating via the Internet is still new to many, society is coming to recognize that, without special attention to protecting communications, the porosity of the public-private boundary in cyberspace makes Internet communications potentially more public than letters sent by regular mail.

The Passage of Time and the Erosion of the Privacy Boundary

The passage of time also changes the privacy boundary, eroding it altogether or shifting its location. Personal information about the deceased is less private than personal information about the living, and personal information about those who have been deceased a long time is less private still. Anthropologists and archeologists depend on this relationship between time and decreased privacy. Those who literally dig up information about the past would not consider this to be an invasion of privacy; they assume that the information residing in ancient ruins is available for study and analysis. Because of the passage of time, the information is no longer tied to a person who can assert privacy rights over it. Even the body of the individual has, in some cases, ceased to stay within the private domain. Skeletal remains have been taken from their locations and brought to museums.

There is a problem, however. The view that the passage of time erodes the individual's privacy right is not universal. Indigenous people have protested what they understand to be a confiscation of sacred (and hence private) human remains. In 1990, the United States enacted the Native American Graves Protection and Repatriation Act,[22] which shifted the boundary back toward increasing the size of the private domain for what were once living, breathing people of this land. Since that time, museums, the scholarly community, and indigenous people have come to a broader consensus about the conditions under which it is appropriate to display objects and remains.[23] The discussions continue, though; and debates over the disposition of very ancient remains (e.g., Kennewick Man[24]) suggest that the farther removed in time a person's life was from ours, the less he is deemed a *person* whose inferred wishes can be called upon in locating the private-public boundary.

A much shorter passage of time can also have an effect. A U.S. president while in office has a good deal of latitude in keeping personal papers private because to disclose such information would have a negative impact on his ability to conduct affairs of state. However, once he leaves office and becomes a private person, are his papers still private, or should they be part of the public domain? Does the passage of time diminish the papers' private qualities?

Until President Franklin Roosevelt established the first presidential library for his own papers in 1939, presidential papers remained private and were not routinely archived. Although some materials have been recovered by the government, "many materials," notes the information presented by the National Archives and Records Administration, "have been lost or deliberately destroyed."[25] Presidents, it was assumed, owned their papers and could dispose of them as they chose. In other words, these papers were considered to be private personal information. After President Roosevelt took the initial step of donating his papers to the federal government, President Harry Truman did the same. In 1955, the Presidential Libraries Act formalized an arrangement in which libraries were to be built with private and nonfederal government funds.

But it was the criminal activities of the U.S. administration under President Richard Nixon that brought a sea change in expectations about presidential papers and other materials. Until 1978, presidential papers (memoranda, notes, internal policy statements, and other papers written to and received by the president during his time in office) were controlled by the president who received or issued them, and only custom dictated that they be archived.[26] To balance the public's right to know with the president's right to privacy, the Presidential Records Act of 1978 relied on the effects of time and the general understanding that older materials are more public than newer materials. Under the Presidential Records Act, which went into effect in 1981, "a citizen could request to review some presidential papers five years after the end of a presidency, or ask for all but the most sensitive records after 12 years."[27]

According to the timing of this legislation, President Ronald Reagan was to be the first president whose papers (except those exempted for national security reasons) were to be issued. However, the information release has not gone according to legislative plan[28]; the administration of George W. Bush delayed the release of the Reagan-era documents.[29] On November 1, 2001, President Bush signed an executive order requiring the consent of both the sitting president and the former president before the former president's papers are to be made public. Whether this political maneuver will serve to negate the effect of time and to shift back the boundary between public and private, reinstating a pre-Roosevelt conception of ownership of presidential papers, remains an open question.

■ Legitimate and Illegitimate Boundary Crossings

Locating the privacy boundary in the socially optimal place would require a careful balancing of the need of the individual against the needs of the state, the community, and other individuals.[30] In our quotidian lives, privacy is breached often, sometimes legitimately, sometimes illegitimately. Intruding into the privacy zone to regulate, extracting information from the privacy zone, and pushing information from the privacy zone into the public are neither exhaustive nor mutually exclusive categories of boundary crossings. The examples below are illustrative of the kinds of trade-offs involved in finding the proper balance.

Intrusions into the Private Domain to Regulate

Sometimes the government, another person, or an institution intrudes into the privacy zone to regulate actions or relationships. There are many legitimate reasons for such intrusions. For example, the government can demand the disclosure of personal incomes to levy income taxes. State agencies legitimately intrude into the private family relationship if there is suspected child abuse, for the public has an interest in the safety of children. Child abuse is a violation of law and public morals, and the suspected abusers forfeit the right to prevent public scrutiny of their privacy because of the overriding social concern for the well-being of children. However, some unfortunate families have found that certain rare medical conditions, such as osteogenesis imperfecta (brittle bone disease), can be misdiagnosed as child abuse, and their privacy invaded unfairly, if not illegitimately.

Less than half a century ago, many U.S. states also asserted that controlling conjugal relations between husband and wife was a legitimate intrusion for the public interest. Laws prohibiting the use of contraceptives were not uncommon. The 1965 U.S. Supreme Court decision in *Griswold v. Connecticut* established for the first time that the state was not allowed to intrude into "the sacred precincts of marital bedrooms." In essence, the decision overturning the Connecticut law delegitimated intrusion to regulate married couples' family planning.[31]

Sexual behavior is also regulated by laws, still enforced in many places in the world, making homosexual behavior illegal. Not until 2003 did the U.S. Supreme Court overturn a law banning sodomy.[32] Those who support such laws and believe homosexual acts to be sinful generally argue that, even when conducted in private, such behaviors have a detrimental effect on society. The public's surveillance of the private domain of individuals (homes and bedrooms), from that perspective, is legitimate for the preservation of social mores. For those who disagree, such laws are bigoted and an illegitimate excuse for invading privacy.

Firms and institutions also intrude into our private information space to regulate behavior. Insurance companies and homeowners' associations are two examples of nongovernmental regulators. Regulation by insurance companies is most obvious and burdensome in the case of health care. The company has access to personal information about patients' medical status and the medications they take. Some insurance companies try to convince the patient's physician that a particular drug is more cost-effective than the one originally prescribed, and only considerable effort on the part of the physician will result in coverage, if coverage is granted at all (see Chapter 9).

Like insurance companies, homeowners' associations use information to regulate behavior to protect the bottom line. Unlike insurance companies, which regulate behavior to limit expenditures, homeowners' associates regulate behavior to preserve the value of their investment. Homes in a well-ordered neighborhood, many argue, are more aesthetically pleasing and more highly valued than homes without a governing association. The information communicated by the look of each house is what is at stake here; homeowners are not free to show others information about their tastes in architecture and landscaping. Homeowners' associations can regulate the color of residents' houses, the position of basketball hoops, the size and style of new fences, and anything else included in neighborhood covenants. Picky review boards can prevent homeowners from remodeling or saddle them with substantial costs for redesigning plans to meet neighborhood standards. Of course, one could theoretically vote with one's dollars to avoid such regulatory activities. We could pay out of our own pockets for the health care services, and we could search for a neighborhood without restrictive covenants. But in practical terms it is difficult to opt out of these arrangements.

Extracting Information from the Privacy Zone

Government, businesses, and the nonprofit sector extract information from the private domain. Some of the passage of information is essential for transactions and is therefore legitimate. Employers must have access to employees' social security numbers, for example, in order to report earnings and pay taxes, according to the law's requirement. Banks and other financial institutions may also need social security numbers to report customers' gains. In many other cases, the passage of information is not essential. Neither a physician, nor a credit card issuer, nor a university needs to know social security numbers. The trend of using them as multipurpose identification numbers goes against the purpose of the system and contributes to the prevalence of identity theft.[33] Asking patrons to disclose their social security number without cause is an example of an illegitimate use.

People are increasingly concerned about the extent to which information about them is extracted from the private domain.[34] Once information leaves the secrecy of the private domain, it is easy for any recipient to transfer the information to a third party. Contractual agreements can limit the diffusion of personal information, but people must often remember to opt out by explicitly stating that they do not want information shared with others. The increasing value of information when subjected to data mining increases the incentive for extracting more data from the private domain.

Sometimes, the public claims a right to know certain kinds of private information for the good of the public.[35] Etzioni cites the example of Megan's Law, legislation created in response to, and named in memory of, Megan Kanka of New Jersey, a seven-year old who had been brutally raped and murdered by Jesse Timmedequas. Timmedequas had been released from prison and treatment for sex offenders after a six-year sentence.[36] When he settled in Megan's community, no one knew of his past. Implicit in this law, which gives the public access to information on the whereabouts of sex offenders, is that had the parents known a sex offender was residing nearby, they would have taken extraordinary efforts to protect their child. Proponents of the law claim that publicizing Timmedequas's past is necessary for the community's security. It is important to note here that Timmedequas's conviction for sexual assaults and his status as a former convict was public information. However, since we do not routinely run background checks on new neighbors, the issue is whether *publicizing* information in connection to his new address is necessary for the public good or an unwarranted invasion of a former convict's private domain.[37] On the one hand are the rights of former convicts who have sincerely changed; on the other hand are the justifiable concerns of neighbors.

More recently, the surveillance of charities and associations with suspected terrorist ties raised a similar question. Does the public interest in countering terrorism trump the public's right to freedom of association? How strong must the evidence of the charity's malfeasance be before official action is taken?[38] Surveillance of groups in this way raises questions about the surveillance of people who in some way interact with those groups. Investigations the harken to the McCarthy era—ascribing guilt by association—would extract information about individuals and make it public. Any person attending a meeting could become a target of the state.

After September 11, citizens have been more vigilant and willing to report suspicious behavior. In the course of everyday life, we might pick up a private information about neighbors. We might accidentally overhear a conversation. Manners—that set of social rules that makes society liveable—would normally forbid us from revealing the content of what we heard. Courtesy would plug the leak in the privacy boundary. Now, the U.S. government requests that citizens observe and report. For example, the Department of Justice, in association with the Department of Homeland Security and other government agencies, attempted to implement Operation TIPS, a "national system for concerned workers to report suspicious activity."[39] The plan was to ask citizens to use chance observations to extract more information from the private domains of their neighbors. The question of how to protect civil rights while expanding surveillance of society continues to be debated.

Pushing Information from
the Private Zone into the Public

Finally, we come to the ability of the individual to push information from the private domain into public view. This aspect of control over the public-private boundary is often dismissed as unimportant, and a good deal of the debate seems silly. Take the example of Brandi Chastain, the U.S. women's soccer player who scored the winning overtime goal in the 1999 Women's World Cup Final. By taking off her shirt to reveal her sports bra as a victory gesture, she was communicating information about herself (the appearance of part of her body) that is commonly kept private. Despite news coverage of the event, its importance was negligible.

Of much greater importance is the human rights question: Are people free to information to the public? Freedom of speech and of assembly are closely connected to the right to autonomy and to being able to communicate personal information as one wishes. Consider societies in which women's movements are highly constrained and in which women are forced to cover their bodies fully. This continues to be the situation in Afghanistan, particularly outside the cities, and in Saudi Arabia. When women are prevented from being heard or seen in public, they are sequestered, they are compelled to endure an enforced privacy.[40]

Focusing on the ability to put information into the public domain also untangles some conflated positions on gay rights. The don't ask, don't tell policy of the U.S. military asserts the rights of homosexual servicepeople to keep their orientation hidden in the private zone. The government, the policy asserts, will not try to extract the information by intruding into the private zone of recruits and soldiers. Many people who consider themselves to be liberal on the issue of gay rights agree with this policy: what people do in the privacy of their own homes is nobody's business.

This reasoning, however, only addresses the privacy questions of intruding into the private domain to extract information and to regulate behavior. What is omitted is the right of the individual to make something known to the community. Most people are able to flaunt their sexual orientation in public if they so wish, and many do so. When a man and a woman walk down the street holding hands—which is socially acceptable—they announce their heterosexuality. Because heterosexuality seems normal to the heterosexual majority, this public statement of heterosexual orientation raises not a single eyebrow. We are not even conscious that such an act is a projection of private information into the public domain. Don't ask, don't tell policies deny homosexuals the right to reveal information about their private attachments to the public.[41] In almost all U.S. communities, two men walking hand in hand would be shunned. "What does your husband do?" is an innocent question to ask a heterosexual woman. New acquaintances would not think twice about asking this, and marital status is often disclosed by the signifier of a wedding ring. So strong are social norms discouraging the disclosure of same-sex relationships that we don't even have a language to ask the question in anything but the most awkward of ways.

Similar silencing effects can be seen in the way society treats the disabled, who remain unseen, even by those who would want to help. In essence, there are barriers to disabled people who want to make information about themselves (opinions, appearance, goals, etc.) public. Do-gooders are derided by the disability rights community as people who want to tell those with disabilities what they ought to want instead of accepting the ability of people with handicaps to articulate what they, in fact, do want. Do-gooders force their information into the private zone, saying, in effect, "Here—this is what you want." Disabled activists would rather place their own information into the public zone: "Here—this is what *we* want." Some paternalistic charities, disabled rights advocates claim, infantilize the disabled, giving the able-bodied adult a justification for intruding into the private zone of the disabled. Activists argue that casting people with muscular dystrophy as Jerry's Kids[42] reaffirms the popular belief that the disabled must be cared for, which ends up silencing the disabled, whose interests are subconsciously dismissed as childish.

The disabled face many barriers preventing their full participation in public life. In some cultures, the disabled are cared for while hidden at home, as if the fact of disability were somehow shameful.[43] The idea that a disabled person could leave the private domain and engage in the world of commerce and politics simply does not arise. In other cases, economic disadvantages create barriers to getting needed adaptive technologies. A wheelchair allows a disabled person to exit the private zone and be seen in public only if she can afford the wheelchair and only if the sidewalks and buildings can accommodate her. And even when a person successfully enters public view, she is often not recognized or spoken to.

The justifications for legitimately broaching the public-private boundary change over time, across cultures, and across real and virtual space. As information about people increases in value, the human and property rights that protect our personal information are challenged by the requirements of the market.

■ Privacy in the Information Age

I want to restate the central irony: we do not own our personal information, yet our personal information matters deeply to us. We want to protect privacy, which is to say that we want to control the flow of personal information into and out of the privacy zone. Rules governing the ability to control the flow of information are privacy rights, and they are dynamic and contingent upon multiple factors, including situation and relationships, culture, interests of others, ad infinitum. Considering personal information, like the physical body, as an intrinsic part of the person leads to the conclusion that the right to privacy is fundamental as both a property right and as a human right. Yet this right is not absolute and can never be so.

People continuously negotiate what information to share and withhold. Or they negotiate if they are able to, and otherwise accept conditions forced upon them. Negotiations are fraught with power inequalities and expectations of mutuality. If I wish to prevent personal information from being disclosed, whether I am successful depends on the power I have to bar the door and the power that the other has to break it down. We are most powerful when we are able to maintain the separation between ourselves and others as we choose, opening the door to let information in or send it out, preventing unwanted information from coming in and stopping unwanted leakage of information to the outside.

The globalized economy and the material value of information complicates our efforts to maintain control over flows of personal information. More of our personal information is in demand for commercial purposes, and we are more in demand as recipients of information. Moreover, that demand is global, and domestic laws are often ineffective in stopping violations of privacy.

■ Notes

1. A discussion of the various approaches to privacy and their shortcomings is addressed in Diane Zimmerman, "Requiem for a Heavyweight: A

Farewell to Warren and Brandeis's Privacy Tort," *Cornell Law Review* 68 (1983). See also Amitai Etzioni, *The Limits of Privacy* (New York: Basic Books, 1999); and Anne Wells Branscomb, *Who Owns Information? From Privacy to Public Access* (New York: Basic Books, 1994).

2. John Hollander, "The Language of Privacy," *Social Resarch* 68, no. 1 (2001): 8–9.

3. Fatos Lubonja, "Privacy in a Totalitarian Regime," *Social Research* 68, no. 1 (2001).

4. Samuel Warren, and Louis D. Brandeis, "The Right to Privacy," *Harvard Law Review* 4 (1890).

5. In my view, it is erroneous to equate Warren and Brandeis's right to be left alone with privacy. Rather, the right to be left alone is a *right*. Privacy would exist even in the absence of a right to it.

6. Jeffrey Rosen, *The Unwanted Gaze: The Destruction of Privacy in America,* 1st ed. (New York: Random House, 2000).

7. Etzioni, *The Limits of Privacy,* p. 196 (emphases changed).

8. Richard S. Murphy, "Property Rights in Personal Information: An Economic Defense of Privacy," *Georgetown Law Journal* 84 (1996): 2383.

9. Antonio R. Damasio, *The Feeling of What Happens: Body and Emotion in the Making of Consciousness,* 1st ed. (New York: Harcourt Brace, 1999); and Antonio R. Damasio, personal communication via e-mail, March 3, 2003.

10. Damasio identifies core consciousness and extended consciousness (core consciousness plus the ability to remember the past and anticipate the future) as necessary for the creation of the autobiographical self—the I who has a personal history and relationships with others. Forming relationships with others requires self-awareness and awareness of the environment. Distinguishing between public and private is part of this awareness.

11. Patricia Boling notes that U.S. courts have sometimes defined privacy as familial attachment. Patricia Boling, "Privacy as Autonomy vs. Privacy as Familial Attachment," *Policy Studies Review* 13, no. 1/2 (1994).

12. Jeffrey Rosen, "Out of Context: The Purposes of Privacy," *Social Research* 68, no. 1 (2001).

13. Alan Westin, *Privacy and Freedom* (New York: Atheneum, 1967), p. 7.

14. Alan Westin, "Social and Political Dimensions of Privacy," *Journal of Social Issues* 59, no. 2 (2003).

15. Richard S. Murphy, "Property Rights in Personal Information: An Economic Defense of Privacy," *Georgetown Law Journal* 84 (1996), advocates defining privacy rights as property rights. Pamela Samuelson, "A New Kind of Privacy? Regulating Uses of Personal Data in the Global Information Economy," *California Law Review* 87 (1999), rejects this position. Samuelson adheres to a much stricter, legal understanding of property and property rights than I. Something (like personal information) becomes commodified (ownable) when it is bought or sold. I see something that has been commodified as a form of property. In this case, access to one's privacy is sometimes up for sale. Having the right to sell it or to choose not to sell it is a mark of property rights. Property rights are often incomplete and, indeed, may be very tightly

constrained. The human rights component, most evident in international and European legal formulations, connects personal information to life; hence the French phrase, *la vie privee* carries the connotation of the totality of one's life, not just a small corner of it. A right to privacy derives from a right to life. Article 12 of the Universal Declaration of Human Rights codifies the individual's right to be left alone. It states: "No one shall be subjected to arbitrary interference with his privacy, family, home or correspondence, nor to attacks upon his honour and reputation. Everyone has the right to the protection of the law against such interference or attacks." United Nations, Universal Declaration of Human Rights, 1948 [cited October 20, 2003], available from www.un.org/Overview/rights.html. The European Union's Charter of Fundamental Rights contains more expansive rights, which specifically refer to both the right to left alone and the right to have a say in how one's personal information is used. See the discussion in Chapter 10 of this book.

16. I am ignoring the special case of discounts and special offers given in exchange for permission to collect such personal data.

17. Physical space is also a component of the privacy zone, just not the sole component. As Avishai Margalit notes, "To a large extent, the politics of privacy is the politics of space. The space is the home. It provides a private retreat from the outside world." Avishai Margalit, "Privacy in Decent Society," *Social Research* 68, no. 1 (2001): 258.

18. John Locke, *Two Treatises of Government* (1690), chap. 5, sec. 27.

19. I am referring to illegitimate violations of the person. There are innumerable legitimate reasons for actions such as legal police investigations.

20. Margalit relates a similar anecdote about the confrontation between ultra orthodox and secular Israeli notions of the location of the privacy boundary. Margalit, "Privacy in Decent Society."

21. Having introduced telephone conversations, however, I have to add a caveat. The now ubiquitous practice of holding loud cellular telephone conversations just about anywhere means that half a conversation is routinely shouted down the street, so to speak.

22. *Native American Graves Protection and Repatriation Act,* Public Law 101–601, *U.S. Statutes at Large* 104 (1990): 3048.

23. Cultural artifacts can be considered *cultural property*, a category not well protected by traditional intellectual property laws. The problem for proponents of cultural property rights is that a cultural artifact—a pottery shard—usually does not have an identifiable author/artist. Communities linked by self-identification claim title to cultural artifacts, but the law is not well-suited for dealing with communal ownership. In this discussion, I am highlighting the privacy aspect of the debate over cultural property rights. To the extent that a communal group, such as a tribe, can claim to draw a boundary separating the private and public domains, taking objects out of the private domain and putting them in the public constitutes a breach of the boundary. Stephen Kinzer, "Saving Our Treasures: Homecoming for the Totem Poles," *UNESCO Courier,* April 2001, pp. 28–29.

24. National Park Service, U.S. Department of the Interior, Archeology and Ethnography Program, National Center for Cultural Resources,

"Kennewick Man," September 11, 2002 [cited October 12, 2002], available from www.cr.nps.gov/aad/kennewick.

25. U.S. National Archives and Records Administration, "Presidential Libraries: A Brief History" [cited August 20, 2003], available from www.archives.gov/presidential_libraries/about/history.html.

26. During the Watergate scandal, President Richard Nixon claimed that the tape recordings of telephone conversations and written records from the White House were his private property. The Presidential Recordings and Materials Preservation Act of 1974 was the congressional response. This law required that all of the materials relevant to the Nixon administration's abuse of governmental power and the Watergate scandal be deposited with the National Archives and Records Administration and made available to the public. U.S. National Archives and Records Administration, "About Nixon Presidential Materials" (August 6, 2001 [cited December 3, 2001]), available from www.archives.gov/nixon/about_nixon/about_nixon.html.

27. Richard Reeves, "Writing History to Executive Order," *New York Times,* November 16, 2001. Reeves, the author of this editorial, is a historian.

28. President Reagan set the stage for blocking the shift of the public-private boundary on January 18, 1989, immediately before he left office. Executive Order No. 12667 gave "himself as 'former president' and 'the incumbent president,' whoever that might be 12 years hence, the right to take 30 days to review previously restricted papers the Archives wanted to make public." Either the former or the incumbent president would be allowed to invoke executive privilege to avoid making any or all of the documents public. Reagan's executive order further allowed the White House to extend the period of review. George Lardner Jr., "Release of Reagan Documents Put on Hold: White House Reviewing Secret Papers, Some Dealing with Current Bush Officials," *Washington Post,* June 10, 2001.

29. Bush administration White House Counsel Alberto Gonzales ordered a ninety-day extension of the restrictions in order to conduct a review, then ordered an additional seventy-day extension. In June 2001, White House spokesperson Anne Womack provided assurance that the review would be completed by August 31. Larder, "Release of Reagan Documents"; see also Christopher Marquis, "White House Again Delays Reagan Files' Release," *New York Times,* September 1, 2001.

30. The social construction of the best balance is mediated by culture, the challenges of the particular historical moment, and other public and private concerns. See Westin, *Privacy and Freedom,* pp. 13–18, for a review of the anthropological findings on this point.

31. *Griswold v. Connecticut,* 381 U.S. 479 (1965).

32. *Lawrence v. Texas,* 123 S. Ct. 2472 (2003).

33. James B. Lockhart III, Deputy Commissioner, Social Security Administration, *Testimony Before the House Ways and Means Subcommittee on Social Security and the House Judiciary Subcommittee on Immigration, Border Security and Claims, on Preserving the Integrity of Social Security Numbers and Preventing Their Misuse by Terrorists and Identity Thieves* (September 19, 2002 [cited October 12, 2002]), available from www.ssa.gov/policy/congcomm/testimony_091902.html.

34. *Businessweek/Harris Poll: A Growing Threat* (March 20, 2000 [cited October 12, 2002]), available from www.businessweek.com/2000/00_ 12/b3673010.htm.

35. Etzioni, *The Limits of Privacy*. This provocative book raises questions about when it becomes legitimate to extract information. When does the public interest in knowing take precedence over the individual's right to prevent information from flowing out from his control? He lists four criteria that should guide public debate: (1) Is there a compelling need for corrective action? (2) Can the "goal . . . be achieved without recalibrating privacy" [shifting the boundary, in the terms I use]? (3) What is the least intrusive intervention that would achieve the correct balance? (4) Should there be "changes in law and public policy [that would treat or ameliorate the] undesirable side effects of intervention?" Etzioni, *The Limits of Privacy*, pp. 184–186.

36. Ibid., pp. 43–74; and Bruce Fein and Edward Martone, "Megan's Law," *American Bar Association Journal* 81 (1995): 38.

37. Etzioni's solution is unusual, but it highlights the role of the public-private boundary. He would transfer sex offenders who have completed their sentences to protected villages in which they would be allowed to "lead normal lives aside from the requirement that they stay put." Etzioni, *The Limits of Privacy*. This version of a leper colony expands former convicts' domain of privacy in some ways (they would not be under the constant surveillance of the prison or the mental institution) by making the privacy boundary a wall between them and the rest of the community. At the same time, however, privacy is diminished as (1) the rest of the community recognizes their status because of their residence in this protected environment, and (2) they are restrained in their ability to push out from the private domain.

38. A good deal of evidence suggests that the Holy Land Foundation has been actively supporting the terrorist organization Hamas. The foundation claims that any assistance given by it to the widows and orphans of suicide bombers was incidental and not intentional support for acts of terrorism. As of this writing, the U.S. Court of Appeals has upheld the government's decision to freeze the Holy Land Foundation's assets because of the foundation's ties to Hamas. Sam Hananel, "Decision Upheld to Freeze Assets of Texas Charity," Associated Press, State and Local Wire, June 20, 2003.

39. Citizen Corps, *Operation Tips Factsheet* [cited October 12, 2002], available from www.citizencorps.gov/tips.html [note: link is no longer available]. Under the terms of the final version of the Homeland Security Act, the implementation of TIPS was prohibited. Nat Hentoff, "The Death of Operation Tips: Volunteer Spying Corps Dismissed," *Village Voice*, December 13, 2002 [cited August 17, 2003], available from www.villagevoice.com/issues/0251/hentoff.php.

40. When the woman chooses to cover herself, however, she is successfully acting as a gatekeeper, protecting her personal information from unwanted disclosure. The interpretation of this choice is complicated, though, by the question of whether social pressure allows a woman freedom of choice, and then by the question of whether anyone anywhere has actual freedom of choice in the absence of social pressure.

41. Avishai Margalit defines the difference between outing and coming out: "Outing is an invasion of privacy. Coming out of the closet is a decision by an agent to redraw his or her own line as to what is private and what is public." Margalit, "Privacy in Decent Society," p. 265.

42. Amy Hasbrouck, "Annual Orgy of Pity and Distortion: Jerry Lewis's Telethon of Stereotypes and Paternalism Might Do More Harm Than Good," *The Gazette,* September 1, 2001; and Tracy Boyd, "Advocates Protest MDA Telethon," iCan News Service, August 28, 2001 [cited October, 12 2002], available from www.ican.com/news/fullpage.cfm/articleid/486C7BE6-578C-43D3-B57D1A7CAE47F061/cx/news.nonprofit_news/article.cfm.

43. United Nations Economic and Social Commission for Asia and the Pacific, "Hidden Sisters: Women and Girls with Disabilities in the Asian and Pacific Region," ST/ESCAP/1548, 1995 [cited October 15, 2002], available from www.unescap.org/decade/wwd1.htm; and Deborah Stienstra, "Disabling Globalization: Rethinking Global Political Economy with a Disability Lens," *Global Society* 16, no. 2 (2002).

9

Violating the Public-Private Border

ontrolling personal information is hard work. The location of the boundary, and reasons for breaching it, are part of a dynamic relationship. Our own desires, social norms, formal law, resources, and technological capabilities all play a role in explaining how much control we have over personal information property. This chapter deals with these issues. It addresses (1) how others trespass privacy boundaries by taking information we do not wish to reveal or by forcing upon us information we do not want; and (2) how information can be sequestered by preventing people from putting information into public view and by suppressing access to what ought to be public information.

■ Trespasses: Breaches of the Public-Private Boundary

A *trespass* occurs when personal information is taken without consent and when information is forced upon an individual who does not want it. People are likely to feel violated when personal information has been extracted. The boundary separating the private from the public has been broken—someone has forced open the gate. People are also likely to feel violated when undesired information (e.g., a computer virus) is thrust into the private sphere. Once again, the gate has been broken down, but in the case of intrusions, victims cannot prevent information from entering their personal territory.

191

Controlling the Flow of Information Outward

First, we look at cases where personal information is revealed. The problem of controlling the flow of information outward includes (1) personal information that is taken from us without our permission; and (2) personal information that is taken with our permission but is then used for purposes we had not agreed to.

We are concerned with what happens to personal information we give in confidence for a specific purpose. In many cases, information technology and the ubiquity of digitized flows of data increase the difficulty of maintaining control. When personal information is revealed, it may be by mistake or intentional.

It's important to remember that violating privacy is easy—it does not require complex information technologies; old-fashioned gossip does the trick. I do not include slander or unsubstantiated rumors.[1] Rather I am referring to titillating tidbits of accurate information that a person would have a reasonable expectation of keeping within a certain privacy boundary but that someone has spread outside that boundary.

The role of technology. The challenge today is multiple modes of communication. Moreover, information can be stored, retrieved, and retransmitted instantaneously. The earlier discussion of data mining shows how easy it is, given new technologies, to make usable and valuable data out of bits of information. Whenever information can be converted into digital format,[2] any information retrieved from an individual's private sphere for any purpose can be combined with other information to further breach individual privacy.

Though it is not necessarily easy or cheap to create digitized data, it is easy and cheap to store, retrieve, and retransmit the information. Much depends on the personal preferences of individuals. A diabetic might be pleased that his pharmacy traded his name, address, and record of taking insulin to Company B because Company B sends information on new products that will help him manage his blood sugar. Another person might find such disclosure just plain spooky. Controlling the flow of personal information is more complicated given the advent of digital technologies. There are more opportunities for dissemination of personal data, including intentionally criminal acts. There are different degrees of privacy breaches.

Mistakes. Most breaches of privacy are probably accidental. Though mistakes happen often, the dissemination of incorrect information can have devastating effects on a person's life. A *Washington Post* article detailed the case of Bronti Kelly, whose wallet and identity were stolen in 1990. When the thief, who was using Kelly's name, was arrested, the record of the arrest was added to the database of arrest records maintained by the police, to the Stores Protective Association (SPA) database, and likely to other databases as well. The SPA database is used by companies conducting checks of employees and potential employees. Firms would reasonably want to avoid hiring known or suspected criminals. The real Kelly, who worked in sales, suddenly found himself getting fired from job after job until he realized that he was being confused with the criminal. Although the SPA had given him a document stating that he was not the Bronti Kelly who was arrested, it is not possible to expunge the false information from all databases. The Los Angeles Police Department, for example, reportedly refused to delete his name from their arrest records. According to the real Kelly (the police would not respond to a reporter's question), it was important to keep a record of the arrest because the false Kelly might once again be arrested for a crime. Kelly has no assurance that he has tracked down all the false information maintained about him. It is impossible to eliminate false information contained in a database that you don't even know exists.[3]

Software glitches and the unintentional acts of individuals using the Internet can result in mistaken release of private information. One infamous case was the public posting of children's highly confidential psychological evaluations.[4] Does digital technology really make a difference in this case? Digital technology, by making information flow more easily, makes mistakes easier as well.

Intentional release and unanticipated consequences. Information might be used for purposes not necessarily anticipated by the individual. And in some cases, the use of the data is not necessarily illegitimate. Credit bureaus exist because companies want to know about customers who have a history of defaulting on loans. Companies inform credit bureaus of problems with customer accounts, such as late or missed payments. The information in a credit file is owned by the credit bureau, not by the consumer. Consumers will generally expect potential loan providers to have access to personal credit information. What is probably unanticipated is that some day a potential employer might also gain access to the same information. Employers use credit histories to help determine whether a potential employee is a good hire.

Similarly, insurance companies need information about health. The question is, what will they do with that information? Insurance companies routinely contribute information to the Medical Information Bureau (MIB). Like a credit bureau, MIB receives reports from others (member insurance companies, in this case) and compiles the information so that it is available to other member insurance companies who request it. An individual must sign a waiver before the MIB will release the information. Information about an individual's medical conditions and, in some cases, about hazardous hobbies and driving records is coded and stored. A code stays on a person's record for seven years, then is purged. (Of course, if a person has a chronic condition, like diabetes, the diagnosis of diabetes from seven years ago would be removed, but evidence of the condition would be found in subsequent treatments and prescriptions.)

MIB, which is a nonprofit industry association of insurance companies from the United States, Canada, and other countries, contends that its database is necessary to prevent fraudulent applications for health, disability, long-term care, and life insurance. When a person applies for a new insurance policy, MIB compares the information disclosed by the customer on the application form with the information stored in MIB's database. Any discrepancies are flagged for the insurance company to investigate before deciding whether to issue a policy. This entire procedure is disclosed in the application process.[5] The unanticipated use of personal information comes at an earlier stage. When people go to the doctor for help with a problem, they are not necessarily thinking about whether, five years from now, that office visit will make it more difficult to buy life insurance. Some people who are aware of this problem, and who have the means, decide to opt out of using medical insurance to pay for certain health care. They would rather pay out of pocket for psychological or psychiatric care, for example, than have evidence of a psychiatric diagnosis on their MIB record.

Although MIB has been operating since 1902, the advent of computer technology has changed the landscape. Information can be maintained easily, and existing technologies can be employed to provide security for the data. Moreover, information can be pooled so that the insurance industry can use the data for actuarial analysis, the results of which can then be used to identify risky and less risky customers.

MIB conducts actuarial analysis through its subsidiary, Knowledge Services, a fee-based service. In other words, MIB makes money by using its database, which is comprised of people's personal information. As with credit bureaus, individuals have a right to inspect their files for a fee (waived for those whose application for credit or insurance has been denied) and ask that mistakes be corrected, but the valuable personal information in MIB's files is owned by MIB. The individual cannot take back the information.

MIB and credit bureaus have received a great deal of public attention and, as a result, are required by law to follow certain procedures to allow individuals access to information about themselves and about securing the data. Other repositories of data do not necessarily operate this way. We routinely disclose information to register on websites, get grocery discount cards, and so on. In exchange we hope for some benefit. Trustworthy firms specify how the personal information will be used and whether it will be shared with others, but the disclosure is often buried in the fine print.

In the case of information theft, personal information is stolen. Personal information held by someone else (as in the case of information disclosed in exchange for a discount card), is not under the individual's direct protection and control. Although a home can be broken into, the owner can control the locks and security systems in place. When people give personal information to the government, a bank, a grocery store, or a website they rely on others to secure the data. This is true for transmittal, storage, and use. When I make a purchase from an online bookstore, I trust it to provide a secure Internet connection. I also trust it to protect my information. I am assuming no hacker will be able to access the store's computer to steal my financial information or view my tastes in literature.

Criminal activities. Theft of private information, especially financial information, was a serious problem even before the birth of e-commerce. Before credit card companies realized the importance of limiting access to card numbers, any sales transaction usually involved imprinting the number on several pieces of paper (including carbon paper). Copies were often discarded, and crooks could easily find valid credit card numbers and other information just by going through the trash.

Though innovations in how charges are processed provides some safeguards, thieves can still obtain personal information from discarded receipts, preapproved credit card junk mail, and by observing someone using an ATM card and PIN.[6] And the fact that credit card numbers are stored by e-businesses allows hackers to use flaws in online security to collect data.

It's ironic that some of the most powerful people in the world cannot guarantee the security of their personal information once given to another party. This was revealed by an awkward snafu at the January 2001 meeting of the World Economic Forum in Davos, Switzerland. The computer-savvy offenders stole the credit card details, cell phone numbers, and addresses of private residences of many of the global elites at the meeting, including Bill Gates, George Soros, Yasser Arafat, and Yoshiro Mori. The hackers apparently wanted to provide the information to *SonntagsZeitung,* a Swiss newspaper, in order to embarrass or inconvenience these prominent people.[7] To be fair, the protesters claimed not to be ordinary thieves; their motivation was apparently political, not monetary. Nevertheless, they broke into a computer system and stole information, making it widely available. A computer consultant was arrested in late February 2001 in connection with the crime.[8]

The rich and famous are not the only victims of hacking. CD Universe, an online music store, and Egghead.com, an online software vendor, were both—along with their customers—victims of hackers. In 1999, CD Universe revealed that more than 300,000 credit card numbers had been lost.[9] According to the FBI's National Infrastructure Protection Center (NIPC), organized hacker groups in Russia and Ukraine have attacked more than forty firms by exploiting security breaches in e-commerce systems. Many of the incursions have taken advantage of a known flaw in Microsoft Windows NT. The companies simply neglected to use the security patch (available for free from the manufacturer) to update their systems. These organized hackers (really, data hijackers) seem more interested in extorting money from the firms by threatening to disclose their clients' information unless a ransom is paid. The breach of consumers' privacy happens only when the firm decides not to give in. As of March 8, 2001, the NIPC was reporting that more than 1 million credit card numbers had been stolen.[10]

The problem continues.[11] In November 2001, Playboy.com announced that it had been the victim of a computer crime. Customers received e-mail containing their names and credit card information from "ingreslock 1524," a group that claimed responsibility for the breach of security. The message reportedly advised Playboy.com customers: "Do not trust companies with your details online."[12] The following month, Reuters News Service reported that CCBill, a company that processes credit card transactions for websites, was the victim of a major hack that threatened the security of its customers' data.[13]

The investigation of these crimes is difficult because the Internet facilitates international communication—and thus transnational crime. Companies are reluctant to report that they have been the victims of attacks, as the publicity would probably focus on why they didn't protect the data in the first place. They are often concerned that customers and investors will lose confidence if it becomes known that security was violated.[14] And so the situation becomes a vicious circle, with authorities not being able to investigate crimes they don't know about, which allows criminals to continue committing crimes, which the companies won't report to the authorities, who are then not being able to investigate the crimes, and so on. In addition, investigations are complicated by their transnational character. Russian and Ukrainian computer hackers, in particular, have been identified as culprits in several cases. There is no existing procedure to conduct transnational investigations of cybercrime.[15]

Getting really *personal: genetic data.* New techniques for gathering and storing genetic data raise particular concerns. Information in the form of tissue (e.g., blood samples) and digitized descriptions of DNA sequences provide intimate information about a person's physical body. Such information resides far inside the public-private boundary. In the case of DNA data banking, information about the sequence of adenine, guanine, cytosine, and thymine in an individual's DNA can be stored as a string of letters (A-G-C-T) in computer files. In DNA banking, tissue samples, each of which contains DNA that can be read to record the A-G-C-T sequence, is maintained. Genetic data can be used for medical purposes, criminal investigations, paternity suits, determining insurance premiums, and so on. In the case of Iceland, genetic data are mined for research into genetic origins of disease and potential drug therapies.

DNA banking and DNA data banking store different amounts of genetic information. Currently, *DNA data banking* refers to keeping information about the DNA letter sequences from a particular chunk of DNA. For example, genetic analysis can look for variants of the genome at the sites of the BRCA1 and BRCA2 genes to look for the pattern associated with an increased risk of breast cancer. Forensic DNA databanks would record the chunks of DNA that tend to identify people uniquely.[16] At present, deciphering an entire genome and recording it would be too time-consuming and expensive, though more efficient and less costly techniques are under development.[17] Despite the relatively small amount of genetic information available for each person in a DNA data bank, the ease with which the information can be shared and compiled with other datasets makes DNA data banking particularly attractive. *DNA banking,* by contrast, requires the preservation of tissue samples. The upside of DNA banking is that the entire genome is stored; one could, in theory, analyze the sample to determine the sequence of letters for whichever chunk of DNA was needed.

One problematic aspect of maintaining this information is what it reveals about the individual's close relatives. If a woman tests positive for a gene associated with breast cancer, it means that someone knowing that information would know the odds of her sister carrying the gene as well. Since insurance companies are in the business of taking risk, they want as much information as possible to help them evaluate that risk.

The insurance industry is reacting to this and is beginning to make the case that they deserve more personal information. At the Medical Information Bureau's website, the following statement can be found; it is worth quoting at length:

> Insurance companies today underwrite risks based totally upon information which they can currently obtain from:
>
> • blood, urine, and lab findings;
> • current medical history records;
> • some basic family history information;
> • financial information justifying the amount being applied for; and
> • vocation and avocation risk information.
>
> What concerns the insurance industry is a time in the not-too-distant future when persons who are applying for any form of insurance will have information that due to "privacy" concerns will not be available to insurance carriers. Persons then may be trying to obtain insurance coverage specifically because they have knowledge that their risk of developing a particular medical problem, condition, or disease, is much greater than the general population as a whole.
> In insurance terms, this is known as "anti-selection."[18]

To the extent that this statement represents the position of the insurance industry as a whole, the future may see increasing pressure on people to release genetic information about themselves or their family. It is in the insurance industry's interest to shift the public-private boundary toward more disclosure so that they can make rational business decisions. Individuals want to be sure that any genetic information they obtain does not go to the MIB.

Thus, an example of antiselection for the insurance industry would be rational behavior for the consumer. Will we see the day when insurance companies make eligibility for policies contingent on taking certain genetic tests? If so, the public-private boundary will have shifted immeasurably.

A felony conviction is a sure way to lose control. All U.S. states now collect tissue samples from convicted felons (sometimes limited to sex offenders) and bank the uniquely identifying sequences.[19] The FBI coordinates the exchange of forensic DNA data through the Combined DNA Identification System, which facilitates tracking down criminals who have crossed state lines. In Britain, the government is working toward including "a substantial portion of the country's population" in the DNA databank. The police may collect tissue samples (hair or saliva or other nonintimate samples) for anyone who has been charged with a crime (a recordable offense). In addition, manhunts for criminals have led to mass sampling of men who are voluntarily coming forward to "'rule themselves out' as suspects."[20] As Jean McEwen notes, nationwide collection of DNA profiles could make solving many crimes much easier. "On the other hand, a population-wide DNA databank could fundamentally alter the relationship between individuals and the state, essentially turning us into a nation of suspects."[21] Moreover, if a DNA profile is overly similar to that of an actual perpetrator (perhaps an evil twin), then the wrong person might be implicated.[22]

Several questions arise from forensic DNA data banking. First, how can we maintain the presumption of innocence when DNA data seem to be of overwhelming import? Are we willing to give up control over genetic information in order to increase the efficiency and certainty of police investigations? Are we concerned that data and samples banked for other purposes will migrate (with or without a search warrant) to a forensic data bank? And if all this becomes common, as in Britain, will we be certain that the databanks are secure from intentional and unintentional dissemination of the data? These are concerns for mature democratic societies. The temptations faced by governments in countries where democratic institutions are weaker will be greater still.

Controlling the Flow of Information Inward: Intrusions

The public-private boundary can also be breached in the inward direction, that is, from the public toward the private sphere. Information can be pushed into the private sphere, and people can be made to know something or have some information that they did not ask for and that they do not want.

This is a problematic category, as it is difficult for one person to guess what another may or may not want to know. The field of marketing depends on telling people what they should want to know, even if they don't. Other intrusions may be unwanted but sanctioned by law, as in when law enforcement investigates a crime. We would call that intrusion legitimate when it takes place in the context of well-functioning governance that protects civil liberties.

But one thing is clear: there are opportunities for bad-faith and abusive breaches of privacy. When the information is unwanted, then we feel that our privacy has been invaded. In the classic book *1984*, George Orwell described the insertion of information across the public-private boundary as part of a despotic government's method of controlling the population.

> The voice came from an oblong metal plaque like a dulled mirror which formed part of the surface of the right-hand wall. Winston turned a switch and the voice sank somewhat, though the words were still distinguishable. The instrument (the telescreen, it was called) could be dimmed, but there was no way of shutting it off completely.[23]

All day and all night, in Orwell's dystopia, the telescreen stays on, transmitting the propaganda necessary to keep the population in check, as well as spying continually.

In modern democratic societies, we live far from this Orwellian world, yet our zone of privacy can be breached by the government, by firms and other organizations, and by individuals. As a condition of living in society, people get information they might not want— from the noise of an inconsiderate neighbor, to the smells of a polluting factory, to government exhortations about the national security threat level.

Mistakes. Information often intrudes into private spheres by mistake. Anyone who has ever mistakenly hit the "Reply to All" button, rather than the "Reply to Sender" button, when responding to an e-mail knows how easy it is to send information to someone who does not want it. Another example is preapproved credit card offers, especially when they are addressed to a child or household pet. In these cases the card issuer has used a mailing list that includes unwanted entries. Since companies are not able to routinely clean up mailing lists, mistakes are common. This adds risk where there had been none for the consumer. If a thief steals the preapproved credit card from a mailbox, the intended recipient might become a victim of identity fraud.[24]

The most direct harm may result from unwanted information. In some cultures, for example, the medical custom is to withhold information about a serious illness from the patient, in the belief that knowing how dire the situation is will worsen the condition. A health care worker who does not understand the culture of an immigrant he is treating may cause immense anguish by revealing the information about the condition. In Japan, for example,

> The doctor-patient relationship can be called paternalistic in many cases; informed consent and advance directives have not yet been well established and vitally important medical information is not always fully disclosed because a considerable number of doctors and patient families think that truth-telling harms patients.[25]

In general, though, mistakes that send unwanted information to a person are not particularly severe trespasses.

Intentional intrusions, unintended consequences. Information can be sent with benign intentions but have unintended consequences. Websites send a cookie, a small text file with some information needed or wanted by the website to interact with the user, onto the hard drive of the user's computer.

The website owner fully intends for the cookie to leave information on the visitor's computer. As long as the user's browser is set to accept cookies, the assumption is that she is willing to receive them. Unintended consequences—privacy trespasses that the website did not intend—can come in two ways. First, the information a computer reveals to the website could be taken from the website's database (an example of extracting information). Second, the cookie, provides a record of online activity. If a website visitor is carrying on an illicit virtual romance in a chat room or is patronizing pornographic sites, cookies may betray him. If the visitor is suspected of a crime, cookies might provide evidence of his activities. This is an unintended consequence because cookies are only intended to provide information back to the sending site; they are not intended to provide information to anyone else. However, it is possible that a third party—the suspicious spouse or law enforcement, for example—could get the information in the cookie.

Moreover, physical access to computers may not be necessary. In May 2000, Microsoft released a patch for a bug in its Internet Explorer browser that would allow hackers to gain remote access to cookies. This flaw would allow a hacker to obtain information about what websites a person has visited, as well as other information the cookies had stored.[26] How quickly users will have learned of the problem and the need to install the patch is not clear. By having information in the cookie intrude into the website visitor's private space, cookie-sending websites create the opportunity for personal information to be uncovered by a third party.

Intentional intrusions, intended consequences. In other cases, intruding into private spheres is intentional. The intent may be to annoy, to do harm, or possibly to do good. Unwanted junk mail is merely annoying, but computer viruses that destroy valuable files are harmful. Law enforcement's use of computer viruses is open to question. This section looks at some examples of unwanted, intentional intrusions.

Computer cookies can be used intentionally to create profiles of individual consumers.[27] This uncovering of information is made possible by the insertion of information onto the consumer's computer. The company can use that information to track websites visited by the user and other data.[28] Spam, e-mail advertisements, and other messages sent to a list of recipients are intrusions. Unsolicited commercial e-mail is the electronic equivalent of junk mail and telephone solicitations.[29] As many privacy and consumer advocates point out, however, spam has a more negative effect.[30] People pay for their time online, and time spent identifying and deleting spam is money wasted. In addition, much of what is distributed is offensive to many people—pornographic images and advertisements for adult sites and services—and some claim that an alarming number of unsolicited e-mails come from people interested primarily in defrauding gullible customers.[31]

Nevertheless, trying to restrict spam runs straight into guarantees of free speech: people and firms have a right to drum up business through advertising. But when is their advertising intruding into the private sphere of the consumer? When have they trespassed? These questions are currently being debated in many countries and in international forums such as the OECD.[32]

A particularly noxious form of intrusion is the computer virus transmitted via communications media (diskettes, e-mail, or http headers from a website one has accessed). Information in the form of computer code is placed on the victim's computer. Most of the information available on the social costs of viruses relates to losses suffered by firms. For example, a PricewaterhouseCoopers survey of 4,900 information technology professionals in thirty nations found that in 2000 alone "39,363 human years of productivity would be lost worldwide because of viruses."[33] The damage caused to privacy by computer viruses is vandalism—trespassing into a victim's personal territory and causing damage to personal information (files on the computer).[34]

Computer viruses and worms place undesired information inside the recipient's privacy sphere. In the case of worms and e-mail viruses, the malignant code uses the victim's computer to breach someone else's privacy boundary. These infections spread quickly and widely. The May 2000 Love Bug epidemic began with code written in the Philippines.

And so we are now accustomed to thinking of viruses as unpleasant, costly, and criminal intrusions. Can information be forced inside the privacy boundary for legitimate purposes? In 1999 the FBI was investigating Niodemo S. Scarfo Jr. for organized criminal violations, but Scarfo stymied investigators by encrypting the files on his computer. The investigators sought and received a court order that allowed them to enter Scarfo's business covertly to place a keystroke logging program on his computer.[35] Eventually, Scarfo typed the password for the encryption program, which the keystroke logger captured, and the investigators were able to decrypt some incriminating files.[36] The program used by the FBI is the same sort of program marketed to employers for monitoring workers and to parents for monitoring children.[37] In the Scarfo case, the FBI, under the aegis of a court order, breached the physical privacy boundary—the actual space in which Scarfo's company operated and the actual computer itself—to insert a piece of information covertly onto Scarfo's computer.

Physical intrusion is not necessary if the keystroke logging program can be sent via a trojan horse. A trojan horse can contain instructions to communicate the log back, a method used by criminals to find confidential information such as passwords on victims' computers. Fighting fire with fire, the FBI apparently also intends to use this method, but for investigating crimes. On November 20, 2000, MSNBC reporter Bob Sullivan reported that the FBI is creating a computer virus that sits on the target's computer and silently logs the keystrokes of any passwords and login IDs that are typed. This virus, dubbed Magic Lantern, is supposedly designed to evade the problem of suspected criminals using widely available encryption technology to keep their communications and files private.[38] No further information on Magic Lantern has been released to date by the FBI.[39] This has led to a great deal of speculation about what it can and cannot do and the legal frameworks that will constrain its use and protect civil liberties.

■ Sequestering Information: Prohibiting the Flow of Information Across the Public-Private Boundary

Information can also be sequestered, that is, prevented from flowing across the boundary. In this case, the boundary serves as a wall, preventing a person from accessing the public and preventing a person from knowing about what ought to be public. The sequestering of information can be a fundamental violation of civil liberties and fair market practices and can work in either of two directions. First, flows of information outward can be prohibited; second, flows of information inward can be prohibited.

Prohibited Outflows of Personal Information: Violations of Freedom of Speech and Related Rights

When the state prevents the individual from speaking freely in public or in some other way providing information about himself, that person is being sequestered into the private domain. The seclusion of women in some Muslim societies exemplifies this kind of violation of privacy. So does the social stigma that prevents gays, lesbians, bisexuals, and transgendered people from revealing their sexuality in public. What role does information technology play in enabling the prohibition of outflows of information?

We do know that information technology can enable those who are oppressed to have a voice in the world.[40] However, the technology can be used to achieve the opposite end: to help authoritarian regimes keep control of their populations. Many countries limit access to the Internet, preventing people from being heard, putting their information into the public, and getting information. According to a report by Leonard Sussman of Freedom House, state control of Internet communications is becoming more widespread. In Russia, for example, speech is chilled because "the successor to the KGB began forcing [ISPs] to install surveillance equipment. Security services can now monitor Internet communications without a court order." In Burma, the government hacks into computers when it suspects that they are being used to receive or send forbidden messages.[41]

Cuba is another country that uses a restrictive policy on Internet access. According to Taylor C. Boas, the association of the Internet with U.S. policy interests has provided Fidel Castro a rationale for limiting access to online communication despite the economic benefits that increased connectivity might bring. Only 2,000 computers can access the web directly, and Cubans are allowed to access the web or use e-mail only at work,[42] where they can be closely watched.

Access is also restricted in the Arab world, with prewar Iraq and Libya providing the greatest restrictions. Jordan is more liberal, and Jordanians wanting access need not register or get a special license. Other Arab countries fall on the spectrum somewhere between.[43] But the specter of surveillance remains; individuals are limited in the kind of information they can project into public view. When people do not censor themselves, they may face serious consequences. For example, Sayyid 'Alawi Sayyid Sharaf, a Bahraini telecommunications engineer, "spent more than a year in jail on suspicion of e-mailing 'political' information to dissidents abroad."[44]

This situation is not much different in some other countries, including Singapore and China. Singapore's suppression or, at the very least, chilling of citizens' speech extends to websites, such as TalkingCock (a satirical site) and sintercom (which had been, apparently, a site for political discussion not connected with any particular candidate but that does not seem to be operating now). In July 2001, the Singapore Broadcasting Authority informed these websites that they would have to register with the government. The content providers would be responsible for making sure that everything on the site, including online discussions, would not be "against the public interest, public order or national harmony; or . . . [offensive to] good taste or decency."[45] China's approach, in slight contrast, has been to focus on limiting who has access to the Internet and maintaining governmental control over the infrastructure. It is much easier and much less costly for individuals to use networking technology within China (the access networks) than to access the global Internet. The government controls all international Internet connections and strongly encourages local traffic over international.[46]

For better or worse, limitations on speech and the ability to take information from the private sphere into the public are not solely characteristics of authoritarian regimes. Democratic countries also wrestle with these issues. For example, the U.S. Child Online Protection Act (COPA) seeks to prevent children from accessing pornographic or otherwise objectionable materials. However, such rules may be overly restrictive of adults' freedom of speech. Indeed, the constitutionality of COPA was argued before the U.S. Supreme Court in March 2004. Other countries have also tried to find the proper balance between the right to free speech and the right to avoid unwanted information. German laws require that ISPs take down websites that intend to be offensive. The Australian legislature is considering measures that would make posting material unsuitable for children illegal.[47]

Moreover, since September 11 political sites are subject to increased scrutiny and, in some cases, are being shut down. In Britain, authorities arrested Sulayman Balal Zainulabidin on suspicion of terrorist activity. He was the owner of a website containing material directed toward an extremist Muslim audience, including information on weapons training courses and "Islamic Threat Management." German authorities arrested a Muslim ("Talip T.") on charges of belonging to a terrorist organization. The prosecutor's office cited Talip T.'s homepage, which contained content supporting terrorism, as evidence against him. And it is not just the government that is scrutinizing content. ISPs are increasingly wary about providing services to extremist groups. Lycos Europe NV, for example, monitors its websites and removes sites with terrorist-related content.[48] (Of course, given the nature of the Internet, websites that have been shut down often relocate to another ISP.)

Suppression of Information and Failures of Transparency

The flipside is the suppression of information and failures of transparency, that is, people are denied access to information that they

may not even know they need. This category includes not only traditional forms of government censorship, but also the actions of others
who hold information that ought to be disclosed as judged by ethical
(and sometimes legal) requirements.

Recently, news reports uncovered research projects in which
human subjects were not sufficiently informed about the inherent dangers, an unethical suppression of information.[49] Key to protecting
human subjects is the notion of informed consent. Only when a person is made aware of all the known possible consequences of a particular research protocol can she decide whether to participate. Moreover, the World Medical Association's Helsinki Declaration requires
careful attention to informing the subjects themselves. It states:

> In any research on human beings, each potential subject must be
> adequately informed of the aims, methods, sources of funding, any
> possible conflicts of interest, institutional affiliations of the re-
> searcher, the anticipated benefits and potential risks of the study
> and the discomfort it may entail. The subject should be informed of
> the right to abstain from participation in the study or to withdraw
> consent to participate at any time without reprisal.[50]

People must be adequately informed in language they can understand—translated into the language they speak, with jargon eliminated or explained clearly. Researchers are required to disclose all
information that may be relevant so that the potential subject's decision is truly informed.

How well informed research subjects actually are has been scru-
tinized in the public debate over the obligation not to sequester information. Another controversy concerns pharmaceutical company
Pfizer's research project testing the efficacy of Trovan, an antibiotic,
in Nigeria. Critics argue that Pfizer researchers did not obtain
informed consent from the parents of the participants, that parents
were not told of the risks, and that parents were not told of alternative treatments for their children. Pfizer denies the allegations and
asserts that the research was conducted in a manner consistent with
Nigerian law. In addition to a class-action lawsuit that is currently
pending, there is an unconfirmed report that the U.S. Food and Drug
Administration has opened a criminal investigation.[51]

Communications media, including the Internet, promise to allevi-
ate some of the problems caused by lack of access to information by
making information more easily available. The solution to suppression

by one source is to find information in another source. However, governments are often able to impede access by censoring various media.

China, Singapore, and the Arab world are often seen as emblematic of authoritarian governments' suppression of information.[52] China tries to maintain tight control on access to the global Internet, in part by having the operators of cybercafes be responsible for making sure that customers do not visit unapproved websites.[53] A typical justification of censorship is that offered by advocates of Singapore's approach:

> From a Western, especially American, perspective, censorship is difficult if not impossible to defend. But the position of the Singapore government and indeed even the citizenry is that there are good reasons for censorship. The government believes that there is anecdotal evidence to suggest that media can have negative effects on consumers, it is therefore wiser to err on the side of caution through censorship. There have also been incidents in the past where media reports have caused racial riots and bloodshed: the 1950 Maria Hertogh riots, the 1964 riots during Prophet Mohammad's birthday, and the 1969 riot spillover from Malaysia. These riots have been blamed on uninhibited reporting and are often cited as examples of how the press can incite racial and ethnic violence.[54]

Of course, whether the people actually prefer some degree of censorship is an empirical question not easily answered—given the existence of censorship. But even in societies that prize freedom of expression, governments draw the line at what kind of information can acceptably and legally be sought. Hate speech and pornography—especially child pornography—are the two types of information that are most likely to be suppressed. The definitions, of course, are exceedingly political, the subject of legislation and litigation.[55]

Access to bad speech raises a final issue. In some cases, the intentional substitution of false information in place of the truth is a means of suppressing true information. This, of course, is propaganda. When people are repeatedly and authoritatively given misinformation, they will believe the falsehoods, especially when they have no means of independently falsifying the specious claims and when the claims fit into preconceived ideas and biases. For instance, the Tobacco Institute, the research organization funded by the tobacco industry, continued to produce information suggesting that smoking was less harmful than it was, despite overwhelming evidence to the contrary.[56] Medical quackery depends on the ability of incorrect but optimistic information to crowd out sober, but perhaps more pessimistic, analyses. False information also serves political purposes, such as the fomenting of hatred or distrust of one's enemies. On September 17, 2001, Al-Manar, a Lebanese TV station associated with the terrorist organization Hezbollah, reported that Israel was behind the attack on the World Trade Center. On September 18, a website called *Information Times* posted an article with the headline "4,000 JEWS DID NOT GO TO WORK AT WTC ON SEPT. 11." The webpage address was forwarded via e-mail and widely disseminated. According to Bryan Curtis, writing for the online magazine *Slate*, *Information Times* is supposedly edited by Syed Adeeb, who lists his address as the National Press Club, 549 15th Street, NW, Washington, DC 20045.[57] This is an excellent example of the Internet scam of pretexting. The National Press Club denies having a tenant by that name, the e-mail address listed for Abeed bounces, and there's no telephone listing for either Syed Abeed or the *Information Times* in the Washington, DC, telephone book. Nevertheless, the story spread quickly through the Muslim world, repeated in mosques, newspapers, and in the street. In the presence of such pervasive false information, many Muslims rejected the compelling videotape evidence that Osama bin Laden and Al-Qaeda were behind the attacks on September 11. In this way, false information works on human psyches to inhibit access to truth. When we uncritically accept false information, we help sequester ourselves and prevent ourselves from gathering information.

▪ Individuals' Privacy Interests

Human beings—natural persons—have privacy interests. We want to control our personal information space, our private sphere, by controlling the boundary that separates it from others. Yet our desire for control is countered by society's desire for control, something that is more or less prominent, depending on the nature of the society. And so each of us enters into negotiations over the location of our privacy boundary and its porosity with all of our social interactions. We feel invaded when others, mistakenly or not, reveal personal information and/or force information upon us. We are suppressed when personal information is sequestered, when we are kept from expressing ourselves freely, and when we are prevented from obtaining information to add to our private horde of knowledge.

The four types of transgressions of the public-private boundary are: *taking information from the individual, pushing information onto the individual, preventing the individual from pushing information out,* and *preventing the individual from taking information in.* The legitimacy or illegitimacy of these transgressions depends on society's acceptance of rules about access to personal information, the free flow of information, and freedom of speech. As a society, we seek to find appropriate balances between the interests of the community and the interests of the individual. As complicated as this deliberation is within a single country, communications via the global Internet have made finding the balance a worldwide concern.

In Chapter 10, we look at ways in which individuals, governments, and firms try to limit transgressions of the public-private boundary.

■ Notes

1. See Wolf Bleek, "Witchcraft, Gossip, and Death: A Social Drama," *Man* [New Series] 11, no. 4 (1976), for a discussion of gossip as slander.

2. Digitized data has been transformed into a series of zeroes and ones, which can subsequently be reconverted into something that human beings can comprehend.

3. Rajiv Chandrasekaran, "Doors Fling Open to Public Records," *Washington Post,* March 8, 1998.

4. In November 2001 a University of Montana psychology graduate student, who had been working on an internship at Children's Hospital of St. Paul, was apparently given permission to copy computer files containing patient evaluations, as long as she removed the identifying information in them. Though she stripped some of the evaluations of names and other identifiers, too much identifying information remained. When she electronically transferred those files back to her home institution's computer system, the files somehow ended up on a public website. An anonymous informer then told a local TV station. The station informed the university, and the files were taken down. Information on this case comes from three sources: Maura Lerner and Josephine Morcotty, "A Computer Mistake, and Medical Records Hit the Internet," *Star Tribune* (Minneapolis/St. Paul), November 8. 2001; Bryan O'Connor, "Administration Seeks Answers to U. Montana's Web Site Security Breach," U-Wire University Wire, November 7. 2001; and University of Montana–Missoula, "UM Reviews Procedures to Safeguard Web Site," press release, November 12, 2001 [cited August 21, 2003], available from www.umt.edu/urelations/releases/default.asp?section=Webfolo.

5. Medical Information Bureau, website [cited December 19, 2001], available from www.mib.com/html/mib_and_privacy.html.

6. I should add that credit card issuers make an appropriate use of the confidential information that the customer of necessity shares with them (i.e., from

whom she is purchasing, where the point of sale is, how much the customer normally spends, etc.) to determine if a particular sale seems odd enough to warrant further investigation. Of course this can, at times, be frustrating. My credit card was once disabled because of a possible fraud watch when I tried to rent a cell phone in the airport of a foreign country. The credit card company did not expect me to be in the foreign country; its computer system concluded there was a good chance that my credit card had been stolen.

7. "Hackers Got into Davos System," CNN.com/World, February 23, 2001 [cited December 18, 2001], available from www.cnn.com/2001/WORLD/europe/02/04/davos.hackers; and Charlotte Denny, "Hackers Hold Sway for Now," *The Guardian,* March 29, 2001.

8. "Police Arrest Davos Hacking Suspect," CNN.com/World, February 23, 2001 [cited December 18, 2001], available from www.cnn.com/2001/WORLD/europe/02/23/davos.hack.

9. Robert Lemos and Ben Charney, "Egghead Cracked: Data at risk," *ZDNet News,* December 22, 2000 [cited December 18, 2001] available from http://zdnet.com.com/2100-11-526642.html. In the case of Egghead.com, the intrusion into a database containing the credit card numbers of 3.7 million customers was costly for the company and for the card issuers, even though experts ultimately determined customers' information was probably not stolen. The break-in required a security investigation as well as cancellation and reissuing of customers' credit cards. Robert Lemos, "Analysts: Egghead's Inquiry Cost Millions," *ZDNet News,* January 8, 2001 [cited February 28, 2004], available from zdnet.com.com/2100-11-527001.html.

10. National Infrastructure Protection Commission, U.S. Department of Justice, Federal Bureau of Investigation, press release, NPIC Advisory 01-003, March 8, 2001 [cited December 18, 2001], available from www.nipc.gov/pressroom/pressrel/nipc030801.htm.

11. The problem is not just theft of financial information. Hackers have breached people's privacy by breaking into their e-mail accounts. In August 1999, Microsoft's free e-mail service, Hotmail, was the target. Hackers created several websites through which anyone could simply enter a Hotmail username without a password and get full access to the account. Robin Lloyd, "Status of Hotmail Privacy Unclear," *CNN Interactive,* August 30, 1999 [cited December 19, 2001], available from www.cnn.com/TECH/computing/9908/30/hotmail.06/index.html.

12. "Playboy.Com Web Site Hacked," *Reuters Newswire,* November 21, 2001 [cited February 8, 2002], available from www.usatoday.com/life/cyber/tech/2001/11/21/playboy-hacked.htm.

13. "Hack Preps Servers for Future Attacks," Reuters News Service, December 21, 2001 [cited December 22, 2001], available from www.zdnet.com/zdnn/stories/news/0,45865100990,00.html?chkpt-zdnn_mh_mac [note: link is no longer available].

14. Matt Richtel, "New Economy: In an Era of Tighter Security, How Much Cyberfreedom Are We Willing to Surrender," *New York Times,* December 3, 2001.

15. Louise I. Shelley, "Crime and Corruption in the Digital Age," *Journal of International Affairs* 51, no. 2 (1998).

16. "The DNA identification profiles that most forensic DNA data banks are creating for their data banks are based on restriction fragment length polymorphism (RFLP) analysis techniques, which focus only on segments of the DNA that do not code for structural proteins and thus (apart from their ability to identify individuals uniquely) are genetically uninformative." Jean McEwen, "DNA Data Banks," in *Genetic Secrets: Protecting Privacy and Confidentiality in the Genetic Era,* edited by Mark A. Rothstein (New Haven, CT: Yale University Press, 1997), p. 237.

17. Erika Jonietz, "Personal Genomes: Individual Sequencing Could Be Around the Corner," *Technology Review,* October 2001, p. 30.

18. Medical Information Bureau, "MIB and Privacy" [cited December 19, 2001], available from www.mib.com/html/mib_and_privacy.

19. Henry T. Greely, "The Revolution in Human Genetics: Implications for Human Societies," *South Carolina Law Review* 42 (2001).

20. McEwen, "DNA Data Banks," pp. 235–236.

21. Ibid., p. 236, citing Andrea DeGorgey, "The Advent of DNA Databanks: Implications for Information Privacy," *American Journal of Law and Medicine* 16 (1990): 381–398.

22. McEwen, "DNA Data Banks," p. 237.

23. George Orwell, *1984* (New York: Harcourt Brace and Company, 1949), p. 6.

24. Unsolicited mail inserted into an unsuspecting victim's mailbox can present a serious problem whether or not the intended recipient is correctly identified. Each direct mailing label contains a great deal of encoded data. For example, one company's new homeowner mailing list labels contain (in addition to the name and address of the home buyer): whether the dwelling is a townhouse or condominium (as opposed to a single family house); the recording date of the deed; the amount of the loan; the loan type; the purchase amount; the telephone number of the dwelling; the lender; and whether or not street mail delivery is yet available to that address. Martin Goodside, Executive, Homeowners' Marketing Services, Inc., telephone interview with the author and personal communication via mail, October 2002. Though this information is gleaned through publicly available sources, having the information compiled in this way may enable identity theft.

25. Atsushi Asai et. al, "Doctors' and Nurses' Attitudes Towards and Experiences of Voluntary Euthanasia: Survey of Members of the Japanese Association of Palliative Medicine," *Journal of Medical Ethics* 27, no. 5 (2001): 328, citing R. Ishiwata and A. Saka, "The Physician-Patient Relationship and Medical Ethics in Japan," *Cambridge Quarterly of Healthcare Ethics* 3 (1994): 60–66; and A. Asai, "Barriers to Informed Consent in Japan," *Eubios Journal of Asian and International Bioethics* 6 (1996).

26. Microsoft Technet, "Patch Available for 'Frame Domain Verification,' 'Unauthorized Cookie Access,' and 'Malformed Component Attribute' Vulnerabilities," Microsoft Security Bulletin (MS00-0033, May 17, 2000 [cited October 5, 2002], available from www.microsoft.com/technet/treeview/default.asp?url=/technet/security/bulletin/ms00-033.asp.

27. This practice, promoted by companies like DoubleClick and made possible by data-mining technologies, has prompted a good deal of public reaction. By placing cookies on a user's computer, DoubleClick can keep

track of information about a person surfing the web, including the advertisements she has seen, the operating system of her computer, the Internet protocol address of the computer she is using (which, depending on how her Internet service is provided, may be dynamically assigned, i.e., may be programmed to change rather than remain static), and any information she has sent to a DoubleClick advertiser, such as her name and preferences (e.g., she prefers to have packages shipped by FedEx). The data from the cookies can be combined with other data. For example, DoubleClick may combine the database it acquired when it bought Abacus Direct Corporation, a marketing information firm, with sales and other commercial information from other firms to create a very complete profile of the consumer via "collaborative filtering." MSNBC, "How Your Identity Gets Stolen" [cited December 27, 2001], available from www.msnbc.com/news/660096.asp?cp1=1.

28. Comments by David Banisar, deputy director of Privacy International, quoted in Will Roger, "Activists Charge Doubleclick Double Cross: Web Users Have Lost Privacy with the Drop of a Cookie, They Say," *USATODAY.com,* June 7, 2000 [cited October 15, 2002], available from www.usatoday.com/life/cyber/tech/cth211.htm.

29. Not all spam is commercial, however. Any bulk e-mailing, such as online surveys, can be viewed by the recipients as spam. Hyunyi Cho and Robert LaRose, "Privacy Issues in Internet Surveys," *Social Science Computer Review* 14, no. 4 (1999).

30. This view is shared broadly by privacy advocates and is expressed on organizational websites, including: Electronic Privacy Information Center, "Spam—Unsolicited Commercial E-Mail," May 21, 2003 [cited August 16, 2003], available from www.epic.org/privacy/junk_mail/spam/default.html; and Junkbusters, "Junk Mail Headlines: How You Can Gain Control of Your Mailbox," October 10, 2002 [cited August 18, 2003], available from www.junkbusters.com/junkmail.html. The view can also be found in the print news media: for example, Stephen H. Wildstrom, "It's Time to Can the Spam," *Business Week,* March 12, 2001, p. 24. The concern about the costs and intrusiveness of spam are also raised by Sabra-Anne Kelin, "State Regulation of Unsolicited Commercial E-Mail," *Berkeley Technology Law Journal* 16 (2001); and by R. A. Spinello, "Ethical Reflections on the Problem of Spam," *Ethics and Information Technology* 1, no. 3 (1999).

31. As U.S. Federal Trade Commission chairman Timothy J. Muris noted, "Since 1998, the FTC has maintained a special electronic mailbox to which Internet customers can forward spam. This database currently receives 10,000 new pieces of spam every day." Timothy J. Muris, "Protecting Consumers' Privacy: 2002 and Beyond," remarks presented at the Privacy 2001 Conference, Cleveland, Ohio, October 4, 2001 [cited December 26, 2001], available from www.ftc.gov/speeches/muris/privisp1002.htm.

32. OECD, "OECD Work on Spam" [cited February 29, 2004], available from http://www.oecd.org/department/0,2688,en_2649_22555297_1_1_1_1_1,00.html.

33. John Leyden, "Hackers and Viruses to Cost Business $1.6tn," *Vunet.com,* November 7, 2000 [cited December 26, 2001], available from www.vnunet.com/news/1106282.

34. This culture was described well by Katie Hafner and Matthew Lyon, *Where Wizards Stay up Late: The Origins of the Internet* (New York: Simon & Schuster, 1996).

35. Some of the legal wrangling in this case has concerned whether the court order received by the investigators was sufficient or whether they should have obtained an electronic communications wiretap order, which is more difficult to get.

36. John Schwartz, "F.B.I. Use of New Technology to Gather Evidence Challenge," *New York Times,* July 30, 2001.

37. Two such programs are Spector and eBlaster, which retailed for $49.95 and $59.95, respectively, in 2000. Surveillance by suspicious spouses may actually be the most frequent use for these programs. Alex Pham, "The Spies Among Us Are a Keyboard Away: Tracking Software Raises Sticky Legal, Ethical Issues," *Boston Globe,* July 5, 2000.

38. Bob Sullivan, "FBI Software Cracks Encryption Wall; 'Magic Lantern' Part of a New 'Enhanced Carnivore Project," *MSNBC.com,* November 20, 2001 [cited December 27, 2001], available from www.msnbc.com/news/660096.asp?0na=x21017M32#TOP.

39. Norman Kirk Singleton, Legislative Director for Congressman Ron Paul, "FBI Refuses to Tell Congress Aide About 'Classified' Magic Lantern," Politech Listserv, December 20, 2001, available from archive, www.politechbot.com/p-02955.html.

40. Jamie F. Metzl, "Information Technology and Human Rigths," *Human Rights Quarterly* 18, no. 4 (1996); and Ithiel de Sola Pool, *Technologies of Freedom* (Cambridge, MA: Harvard University Press, 1983).

41. Leonard R. Sussman [Freedom House], *Censor Dot Gov: The Internet and Press Freedom 2000* (2000 [cited January 1 2002]), available from www.freedomhouse.org/pfs2000/sussman.html.

42. Taylor C. Boas, "The Dictator's Dilemma? The Internet and U.S. Policy toward Cuba," *Washington Quarterly* 23, no. 3 (2002).

43. Marcus F. Franda, *Launching into Cyberspace: Internet Development and Politics in Five World Regions* (Boulder, CO: Lynne Rienner, 2002).

44. Human Rights Watch, "The Internet in the Mideast and North Africa: Free Expression and Censorship," June 1999 [cited January 1, 2002], available from www.hrw.org/advocacy/internet/mena/int-mena.htm.

45. Declan McCullagh, "Singapore Political Website Closes After Government Demands," Politech Listserv, August 17, 2001, available from archive, www.politechbot.com/p-02406.html.

46. Zixiang (Alex) Tan, William Foster, and Seymour Goodman, "China's State-Coordinated Internet Infrastructure," *Communications of the ACM* 42, no. 6 (1999).

47. U.S. Federal Trade Commission, "New Rule Will Protect Privacy of Children On-Line," press release, October 20, 1999 [cited October 16, 2002], available from www.ftc.gov/opa/1999/9910/childfinal.htm. The German case is discussed in Marc Le Menestrel, Mark Hunter, and Henri-Claude de Bettignies, "Internet E-Ethics in Confrontation with an Activist's Agenda: Yahoo! On Trial," *Journal of Business Ethics* 39, nos. 1–2 (2002).

See also Michael Rogers and Norman Oder, "Australia Passes Filtering Law," *Library Journal* 124, no. 13 (1999).

48. Stephanie and Gautam Naik Gruner, "Extremist Sites Under Heightened Scrutiny," *Wall Street Journal Online,* October 7, 2001 [cited August 17, 2003], available from www.zdnet.com/zdnn.

49. Researchers are required by law and by ethical code to protect the people who are their research subjects. An overview can be found in U.S. Department of Health and Human Services, Office of Human Research Protections, *IRB [Institutional Review Board] Guidebook* June 21, 2001 [cited August 20, 2003], available from http://ohrp.osophs.dhhs.gov/irb/irb_guidebook.htm. Blame for recent deaths of research subjects Jesse Gelsinger at the University of Pennsylvania and Ellen Roche at Johns Hopkins University has focused on the failure to disclose information, both to the monitoring Institutional Review Board and to the subject. (Both cases have been settled.) These stories are unpleasantly reminiscent of the tales of the infamous Tuskegee syphilis experiment, conducted between 1932 and 1972, in which the U.S. Public Health Service investigated what would happen to men who were left untreated for infection with syphilis. Tuskegee Syphilis Study Legacy Committee, "A Request for Redress of the Wrongs of Tuskegee," May 26, 1996 [cited January 2, 2002], available from www.med.virginia.edu/hs-library/historical/apology/report.html.

50. The World Medical Association, Declaration of Helsinki: Ethical Principles for Medical Research Involving Human Subjects, October 6, 2002 [cited August 21, 2003], available from www.wma.net/e/policy/b3.htm. The declaration further requires the establishment of independent ethics committees (institutional review boards) to oversee disclosure and other human subjects protections.

51. Joe Stephens, "Pfizer Experiment Spurs Criminal Probe," *Washington Post,* September 8, 2001.

52. Sussman, *Censor Dot Gov.*

53. Also known as Reporters Sans Frontiers. Reporters Without Borders, website [cited August 19, 2003], available from www.rsf.fr/rubrique.php3?id_rubrique=20.

54. Peng Hwa and Berlinda Nadarajan Ang, "Censorship and the Internet: A Singapore Perspective," *Communications of the ACM* 36, no. 9 (1996): 72–73.

55. Ron Scherer, "Computer-Created Child Pornography Stymies Police," *Christian Science Monitor,* February 7, 2001.

56. C. Stephen Redhead, "Tobacco Master Settlement Agreement (1998): Overview, Implementation by States, and Congressional Issues," CRS Report for Congress, RL 30058, November 5, 1999 [cited October 17, 2002], available from www.cnie.org/NLE/CRSreports/agriculture/ag-55.cfm.

57. Bryan Curtis, "Tangled Web: 4,000 Jews, 1 Lie—Tracking an Internet Hoax" *Slate,* October 5, 2001 [cited January 3, 2002], available from slate.msn.com/?id-116813.

10

Guarding the Border: Gaining Control over Personal Data

Gaining control over personal data means taking control of the public-private border so that the individual can determine what goes into and comes out from her personal information space. As Lawrence Lessig points out, the rules that determine this may be rules of law, custom, or computer code, but all rules are political.[1] In using legal innovations and technological fixes to make our privacy borders less leaky, we are engaging in political acts. Moreover, when businesses and governments determine the rules for us, that's politics as well: private and public governance. This chapter explores the way in which governments, technologists, firms, and individuals act to secure personal information and to limit the trespasses and sequestrations described in Chapter 9. I begin by looking at the power of norms in getting others to respect our right to control the privacy boundary. I then look at actions we take to prevent violations of our privacy boundary by keeping personal data out of sight of others and by making sure we know the identity of those to whom we entrust our data.

■ Norms Obligating Others to Respect Our Privacy

An important way to protect individual privacy is to maintain rules that protect everyone's privacy. Some of these rules are social mores and carry social stigmas only for their violation. Other rules are written into civil or criminal laws and can be enforced by authorities. In this

217

section, I turn to some examples of social rules that help us maintain control over personal information.

Rules Regulating Gossip

Gossip can be a transgression of the public-private boundary in which personal information is extracted from the private sphere and released into the public against the will of the individual. Social rules, from religious commands to everyday etiquette, are responses to the problem of how to stop people from blabbing. Buddhism, for example, lists a prohibition against gossip as one of the central tenets of the faith. The teachings of Right Speech, which is part of the Noble Eightfold Path, mandate that people should "[refrain] from falsehood, slandering, harsh words, and frivolous talk."[2] Similarly, in Islam, gossip is considered heinous and is likened to eating the flesh of a dead brother. Muslims are ordered not to engage in gossip and to either renounce an act of gossip as it is being committed or to walk away from the gossipers. The Quran's Surat al-Isra', Ayah 36, proclaims that "one is responsible for what he hears, sees, and believes."[3]

Christian theologians have also argued that gossip is prohibited by their faith. For example, John Wesley, the founder of Methodism, reminded Christians to "remember, meanwhile, that all evil-speaking is, in its own nature, deadly poison." Wesley speaks of the case where one must "accuse the guilty, though absent, in order to preserve the innocent." Even in this extreme case where one must report something bad about someone, it is still incumbent upon the person speak "as little [evil] . . . as is possible; only so much as is necessary for the end proposed. At all other times, 'go and tell him of his fault between thee and him alone.'"[4]

Judaism has a significant body of religious law to regulate the dissemination of personal information. From the rabbinic period to the present, scholars have pointed to *lashon hara'* (literally, the "evil tongue") and *rechilut* (talebearing) as particularly damaging sins that are, unfortunately, extremely common. *Lashon hara'* refers to true but negative information. Any derogatory or damaging (physically, financially, socially, or stress-inducing) words that a person speaks are considered *lashon hara'*. *Rechilut* includes any speech that will result in animosity between people.

What is so bad about a little harmless gossip? The answer links the Jewish view of basic human nature with the Jewish approach to personal information. All people, Judaism holds, have both an evil tendency and a good tendency. No one can possibly be good all the time. So all people are flawed. But all people are also created in the image of God, which means that we all have something divine in us and that we must respect each other's dignity. Therefore, Judaism does not require that people confess their sins or other failings in public. That information remains private.[5] Since revealing a person's flaws is an assault on dignity, only an overwhelming necessity to provide information (e.g., pointing out to your friend that her business partner-to-be is a known con artist) can overcome the prohibition. But like other faiths, Judaism places strict limits on the conditions under which negative, though true, information may be communicated.

Etiquette also comprises rules, albeit secular ones, regulating the dissemination of information. According to the rules of etiquette a person who accidentally overhears a private conversation is supposed to act as if he had not. Social rules like this help us maintain the fiction that the public-private boundary has not been breached. Of course, the hearer cannot unlearn the information, but by not spreading it she does not actively trespass on the speakers' privacy. But when the information is communicated to others, privacy has been breached. Only serious circumstances (e.g., overhearing, "I swear I'm going to kill him") outweigh simple etiquette.

Thus etiquette and religious rules protect against the illegitimate flow of personal information into the public domain. Together, these rules can be thought of as part of a *manners regime,* though regrettably this regime is rather weak. Failure to comply seems common, and the resulting sanctions seem minimal. The manners regime relies on inculcating courtesy and religious requirements through the difficult process of raising one's children and socializing them to prevailing norms. Violate the norm and one might face the opprobrium of one's fellows—but probably not. Nevertheless, despite lack of enforcement, codes of etiquette and religious requirements codify the individual's right not to have personal information disclosed without consent. Though such rules are more often honored in the breach than adhered to, formal rules about the protection of privacy depend on society's recognition that the public does not have a right to know everything that can be discovered about everyone.

The Role of Law

Like religious requirements and manners, laws can be used to empower people to control the boundary between the public and the private.

Though laws may lack the enforcement capacity of God's wrath or social stigma, they have the benefit of legitimate governmental enforcement mechanisms behind them. Three examples are provided below, though there are many others.

Enabling individuals. Laws enable individuals to mitigate harm that has been or may be done to them. In the case of a mistakenly bad credit report, one might add more information to offset the bad. Laws, like the U.S. Fair Credit Reporting Act, which went into effect in 1997, can help people counter such information. This law requires an employer to inform a job applicant if the firm is conducting a credit or investigative report; and if the employer decides not to hire the applicant on the basis of the report, the employer must provide the applicant with a copy of the report and information from the Federal Trade Commission on rights under the Fair Credit Reporting Act.[6] What is particularly notable in this legal protection, though, is the vigilance required of people. Various governmental and consumer groups recommend that people check their credit reports at Equifax, Experian, and TransUnion, the three major credit bureaus, as well as follow up on other sources of information. In other words, it is up to individual consumers to make sure that information flowing across the public-private boundary is accurate. Though the individual has little ability to limit the flow of information, she can put information that corrects errors into the public domain.

To stave off potential harm, individuals can use laws that allow them to opt-out of a relationship. For example, the Financial modernization Act of 1999, also known as the Gramm-Leach-Bliley Act, requires that U.S. financial institutions provide customers notice of the institution's privacy policy and the opportunity to opt out of allowing the institution to disclose information to third parties.[7] To opt out, an individual must specifically request to be excluded. For financial institutions, the benefit of an opt-out mechanism is that many people will not bother.

A similar opt-out approach has been promoted for telemarketing, junk mail, and spam. In the United States, the recently passed Do-Not-Call Implementation Act and the CAN-SPAM Act create opt-out provisions for telephone solicitation and spam.[8] The opt-out approach assumes that people are interested in and welcome unsolicited information. Individuals need to take positive action to opt out of having their privacy invaded by unwanted messages.

Obligating others. Europeans take the approach that the onus is on the sender. EU rules favor an opt-in approach, reflected by the EU directives on data and on privacy and electronic communications. The EU data directive requires all companies or other entities holding personal information to ask permission before transmitting any information to another entity. Moreover, they must make sure the subject of the information knows that the data are being held and provide a way for subjects to examine the data and correct any errors.[9] Similarly, the EU directive on privacy and electronic communications requires spammers to get permission—explicit consent—from the potential recipient before sending the message.[10] Both directives draw on the "guarantee of confidentiality of communications" that are components of "the international instruments relating to human rights, in particular the European Convention for the Protection of Human Rights and Fundamental Freedoms, and the constitutions of the Member States."[11]

The data directive, which went into effect in 1998, is notable for its extraterritorial reach. The EU requires that *all* recipients of personal data about EU citizens adhere to the guidelines. This means that if a company in the EU wants to transmit information about EU citizens anywhere else in the world, the government of the recipient company must enforce the same high standards of personal data privacy as the EU. The approach in the United States (minimizing governmental interference in companies' privacy policies) clashes directly with the EU directive. U.S. law creates a regulatory environment that puts the economic interests of firms over the convenience of citizens. (One could say that the United States places profits above privacy.)

When the EU directive was first announced, the concern among U.S. policymakers and the business community was that it would disrupt the ability of U.S. firms to engage in global trade. The insurance sector has had global reach since the earliest days,[12] and many U.S. firms operate in Europe.[13] A measure preventing the transfer of personal data from EU countries to a corporation's data center in the United States could place firms at a significant disadvantage.[14]

After difficult negotiations, the United States and the EU agreed to a system in which firms voluntarily commit to being safe harbors for data on EU citizens. The program went into effect on January 4, 2001. By February 2002, 152 companies had been certified by the U.S. Department of Commerce as safe harbors.[15] And though no U.S.

law forces a firm to become a safe harbor, once a firm takes on that obligation it becomes subject to laws on false claims and misrepresentation.[16] In short, if a company demonstrates persistent failure to comply, the Department of Commerce will issue a noncompliance letter and record the problem on its website.

To be a safe harbor, an organization must agree to several provisions. First, it must pledge to notify data subjects (people whose personal information has been collected) of the data collected, its use, how the subject can make inquiries or complaints, the third parties that receive the data, and the ways the subject can opt out. Second, it must guarantee that individuals are able to opt out of having data shared with a third party. If the information is considered sensitive, the individual must opt in before the information is disclosed to a third party.[17] Third, any transfer must be contingent on the third parties also adhering to safe harbor principles, either by being certified as a safe harbor or by written agreement. Fourth, data subjects must be allowed to see the data and to correct, amend, or delete inaccurate information, unless doing so would be disproportionately costly or potentially harmful to the rights of someone else. Fifth, the organization must take positive steps to protect the security of the data from misuse, unauthorized access, and other privacy violations. Sixth, the organization is responsible for collecting only relevant information and for taking appropriate steps to make sure that the data it has collected is accurate, complete, and current.

Finally, each organization must subject itself to enforcement, which, in my view, will determine the effectiveness of the safe harbor provisions for protecting privacy. An organization that is certified as a safe harbor must promise either to monitor its own privacy practices or to rely on monitoring by an industry association. The data subjects must be able to register complaints and have ready access to dispute resolution mechanisms. The organization must subject itself to laws or private-sector initiatives that would force it to pay damages or make amends for violations. In addition, organizations must renew their safe harbor certification each year. Organizations also must make some unspecified provision to publicize any finding of noncompliance, and the Department of Commerce website will indicate which organizations have been charged with persistent noncompliance (none to date).[18] However, there is no requirement that data subjects must be notified of a privacy breach. According to Jeffrey Rohlmeier of the Department of Commerce, "The framework does not require notice of the persistent failure to comply to individuals whose information is held by the organization."[19] The onus remains on individuals to continue monitoring companies holding personal information.

Civil enforcement. Contractual arrangements, as in the case of firms that have agreed to become safe harbors, open the way to civil penalties for misrepresentation or false claims if they violate the provisions of their agreement. Similarly, individuals and privacy advocacy organizations can use the courts to sue organizations, both public and private, that they believe have violated their privacy. In the United States, complaints can also be lodged with the Federal Trade Commission (FTC). For example, the Electronic Privacy Information Center (EPIC) complained to the FTC about DoubleClick's decision (since rescinded) to use data-mining techniques to put names to otherwise anonymous Internet activity. DoubleClick's plan had been to combine the anonymous information gleaned from cookies with specialized consumer information owned by Abacus Direct Corporation, which DoubleClick acquired in 1999. The combined database would then have enough clues to allow data-mining techniques to figure out exactly who was doing what online. As a result of complaints made through established regulatory and legal procedures, the FTC, the New York State Attorney General's Office, and the Michigan State Attorney General's Office all made inquiries. The threat of civil punishment, plus the overwhelmingly bad publicity from government and consumer groups, prompted the company to abandon its plans to use the data for targeted marketing.[20] As part of its plan to rehabilitate its image, DoubleClick has signed on to be a safe harbor.[21]

European Union human rights laws also play a role in the requirement that states enforce civil penalties. Article 8 of the European Convention on Human Rights and Article 7 of the European Union's Charter of Fundamental Rights specifically creates a right to privacy as a human right. In regard to respect for private and family life, the EU Charter states that "everyone has the right to respect for his or her private and family life, home and communications."[22]

In Britain, where the broad human rights protections of the EU rules were included in the Human Rights Act (effective October 2000), several high-profile court cases have used European norms protecting privacy in legal arguments. Celebrities such as supermodel Naomi Campbell and actors Michael Douglas and Catherine Zeta-Jones have used the provision that even the famous have a right to privacy and to avoid the camera. The Douglas and Zeta-Jones case involves the publication of unauthorized pictures from the couple's wedding in *Hello!* magazine. This case, which was decided in favor of Douglas and Zeta-Jones in April 2003, reinforces privacy protections under British law.[23]

But such an outcome is not a sure thing. The positive aspects of having civil penalties for infringement of privacy have to be balanced against the need to protect freedom of expression, which is also a human right. (*Freedom of expression,* as used in this discussion, is the ability to communicate information from the private sphere into the public.) This tension is evident in the case involving Naomi Campbell. The supermodel had claimed publicly—and falsely—that she did not have a drug problem. A tabloid newspaper, *The Mirror,* published a story exposing Campbell's lie and published a picture of her exiting a Narcotics Anonymous meeting. Campbell sued for unlawful invasion of privacy and initially prevailed. On appeal, however, the judgment favored the public's right to know and the journalist's right to freedom of expression.[24]

Still, the expansion of privacy rights has had an effect on British law enforcement. British police have needed to change their actions to be sure that they do not violate a suspect's right to privacy. For example, it was common practice for police to use subterfuge to get suspects to provide a sample of their shoeprints. The suspect would be asked to place his shoes outside the door of the cell. Then, the police officer would take an ink impression of the shoe to be used as part of the crime investigation. According to Sir David Phillips, "We now have to tell suspects we are taking prints, which makes the whole process pointless. It is the Human Rights Act which has prompted this debate and yet again the criminal justice system works to defeat crime fighting."[25] Despite the difficulties posed by this new law to the police, it provides a powerful tool for suspects who wish to release as little information about themselves as possible.

A final example of how the British Human Rights Act creates opportunities for individuals to protect privacy is its usefulness in limiting employer surveillance of employee activities. The British Trade Unions Congress anticipates using the new law to protest monitoring employees' telephone calls and e-mail and to place limits on the practice of monitoring staff with closed-circuit TV.[26]

Criminal enforcement. A powerful tool that governments provide citizens is the ability to call upon the authority of the state to bring privacy violators to justice. This is especially the case when the invasion can be construed as fraud. The complication of the Information Age is that many of the trespasses use technologies that allow the miscreant to sit comfortably in one legal jurisdiction while committing a crime in another. Even when two countries are close allies and have similar legal systems, laws that protect privacy may have the unavoidable effect of hindering investigations of invasion of privacy.

This conundrum was outlined by Hugh Stevenson, associate director for the Division of Planning and Information of the FTC's Bureau of Consumer Protection, in Senate testimony. In investigations of cross-border telemarketing and Internet fraud, U.S. and Canadian law enforcement agencies face legal limits on their ability to share information. This difficulty persists even though the United States and Canada are signatories to a bilateral mutual legal assistance treaty for cross-border information exchange. Even though the FTC is charged with investigating consumer fraud, it is not a law enforcement agency and therefore does not qualify as an agency to receive certain kinds of privileged information under the treaty. The FTC is similarly hampered in sharing information with its Canadian counterpart and other foreign governments.[27]

The Council of Europe has finalized a convention on cyberspace crime that will harmonize criminal law concerning "confidentiality, integrity and availability of computers systems, networks and computer data, as well as the misuse of [them]."[28] This treaty, which will enter into effect when five countries, at least three of which are member States of the Council of Europe, ratify it, will facilitate the investigation and prosecution of "infringements of copyright, computer-related fraud, child pornography and offences connected with network security. [The treaty] also covers a series of procedural powers such as searches of and interception of material on computer networks."[29] Under the terms of the treaty, governments will be obligated to legalize the gathering of evidence by preserving data flows. Governments would then be required to aid the law enforcement authorities of another signatory country by disclosing the captured information. It also would allow a law enforcement agency in one country to obligate an ISP in another to release subscriber information and other data. In addition, the treaty requires the signatories to be able to respond around the clock (the 24/7 Network) to respond to inquiries and requests from other countries' law enforcement agencies to facilitate rapid response to crime.

However, the serious problem with moving to strengthen criminal penalties for cybercrime—including invasion of privacy—is that the rules themselves may do more to erode privacy than protect it Many privacy advocacy groups, including the American Civil Liberties Union, the Electronic Privacy Information Center, and Privacy International, oppose the Convention on Cybercrime because of the surveillance powers it confers on police and the risks that it poses to civil liberties.[30]

■ Actions Individuals Take to Protect Their Privacy

Obligating others to respect privacy is not enough. History is replete with examples of stratagems people have used to protect privacy, and current public attention has focused on technological fixes. There are additional actions we can take to protect privacy.

Secret Codes and Encryption

How do we keep secrets? This question is of concern to many. As David Banisar points out, even otherwise democratic countries conduct surveillance on dissident groups.[31] As a result, individuals may also resort to technical fixes to protect privacy. And this is not a new thing: consider secret codes and encryption. Although the calculation of encryption algorithms has become more sophisticated since the advent of computer technology, the use of secret codes has a long history. Governments have used codes to protect official secrets, merchants have used secret writing to protect theirs, and other people have encoded communications for all sorts of personal reasons. For example, a fourth-century founder of monasticism, Pachomius, is known to have used a secret alphabet in his letters.[32] And one of the more interesting footnotes of literary history is Edgar Allan Poe's affinity for cryptograms and the use of secret codes.[33]

Computer technology has, paradoxically, made encryption more difficult to crack and made cracking encryption possible. Computers generate more complex mathematical algorithms with which to encrypt material. Indeed, the U.S. government has traditionally labeled encryption programs as a munition under the Arms Export Control Act and the International Traffic in Arms Regulations, and U.S. developers of encryption software face controls on exports.[34] This restriction did not slow the development or global availability of strong encryption. Rather, it opened the way for other countries to develop encryption technology for domestic use and export. Innovative firms in Europe and Israel took the lead in the development of this technology.

The strength of encryption has improved. Earlier forms could be cracked by using computers to run routines repeatedly to find the right key; newer forms of encryption will be much more difficult if not impossible to break. By the 1990s, computers had become fast enough to decode messages using the older Data Encryption Standard (DES) in a few hours. According to the U.S. National Institute of Standards and Technology website, the new Advanced Encryption Standard (AES) is much stronger:

> Assuming that one could build a machine that could recover a DES key in a second (i.e., try 255 keys per second), then it would take that machine approximately 149 thousand-billion (149 trillion) years to crack a 128-bit AES key. To put that into perspective, the universe is believed to be less than 20 billion years old.[35]

Encryption technology increases the security of information, thereby enabling confidential communications for e-commerce and other purposes. Such protections are what makes consumers willing to buy goods and services online. Encryption is also a powerful tool for human rights activists living under repressive regimes. Pretty Good Privacy (PGP), according to David Banisar, is often used by human rights groups.

PGP uses public key encryption. Each user of PGP creates two keys—a public key and a secret key. The user then gives the public key to whomever she wishes to correspond with and can even publish it publicly like a phone number. The secret key is kept in a safe place—usually with the PGP program—and is protected by a password. The public key is used by other people to encrypt messages that they send to the secret key holder, and only that person can unscramble the message. Thus public key cryptography avoids the need to meet in person or to carry codebooks to safely exchange keys and messages.[36] The sender encrypts a message by using his own private key and the intended recipient's public key. The recipient then unencrypts the message by using her private key and the sender's public key. This method ensures that only the intended recipient can unencrypt the message and that she can be sure of the sender's identity.

The problem with encryption technology, of course, is that the bad guys can use it just as easily as the good guys. News reports have stated that Osama bin Laden and Al-Qaeda operatives used strong encryption for their communications by satellite telephone.[37] The U.S. government argues that drug cartels and other organized crime groups use encryption for their communications as well.[38] For that reason, the Justice Department under the Clinton administration advocated the use of so-called Clipper Chips, which are chips placed inside digital telephones and computers to enable the government to decrypt any encrypted material on the computer or communicated via the telephone. The Clinton administration came up with the idea of requiring computer manufacturers to build a Clipper Chip into all computers. According to the plan, the key used by the government to decrypt information by using the Clipper Chip would be available only under a subpoena. The initial recommendation was that government offices would hold the keys to the encryption in escrow. Subsequent proposals called for private firms to go into the key-vault business and create a nongovernmental haven for keys entrusted to them by computer owners.

Although the Clinton administration's proposals were met with protest from the computer science community and from many computer users and never became law, the Bush administration redoubled efforts to allow government to open a backdoor into encrypted computer files. The events of September 11 caused policymakers to reconsider Clipper Chip–like means to offset the negative ramifications of encryption, but Congress has not yet enacted any restrictions on encryption technology, despite the increased surveillance provisions of the Patriot Act.[39] Still under consideration is the appropriate balance between encouraging and discouraging encryption. The public has an interest in having the government encourage the use of encryption as a means to make electronic commerce secure, allow freedom of speech, and encourage people who are repressed to sneak their words out into the public space. At the same time, the public also has an interest in preventing criminals and terrorists from using encryption to escape law enforcement.

Locks, Doors, and Gates

Encryption places a lock on data. Locks, doors, and gates, in both their physical and their virtual forms, are all ways of protecting privacy.

Door locks do much more than prevent theft or physical harm; they also regulate the flow of information in each direction. From their beginnings as intricate knots (the Gordian knot of Greek legend) and bulky wooden apparatuses, locks have created a protected space, a physical representation of the zone of privacy.[40] When prisoners are locked in cells, they suffer the unwanted constriction of their zones of privacy and the limitation of their ability to pass the information they wish to communicate into the public domain.

Ancient walled cities had gates through which all who wished to enter had to pass, and the gatekeeper's task was to decide who had a legitimate reason for entering. When we invoke the "gatekeeper" as a metaphor today, we generally are referring to the secretary or staff assistant whose job it is to prevent people from intruding on someone else. The gatekeeper's role is to prevent the transmission of unwanted information across the public-private boundary. If I have a complaint about a product or service, I must get past the gatekeeper to lodge my complaint with the president of the company.[41] The gatekeeper can prevent my information from entering the president's private domain. Another common example is the home answering machine and caller-ID, which serve as electronic gates allowing the recipient to prevent the intrusion of unwanted calls. Gatekeeping admits some information (possibly altering it in the process) while barring entry for other information.

Gatekeeping for cyberspace requires firewalls—programs that prevent computers from being invaded by other computers. If someone accesses the Internet using a cable modem, the computer is vulnerable to unauthorized entry. The firewall alerts the user when his computer tries to access the Internet and when someone else tries to access his computer. Usually, it's an ISP pinging the user's Internet address to see if he is online. In theory, if someone tries to get into his computer without permission, the firewall will prevent entry. Firewalls are also important for business applications because organizations must protect the integrity of their computer systems. Of course, the best protection against unauthorized entry via the Internet is unplugging the connection, something that is not always practical.

The metaphor of the firewall frames the problem of how to prevent unauthorized access to computers.[42] The growing acceptance of firewalls suggests that protecting the integrity of one's computer system does not fall solely on authorities, who enforce laws against unauthorized entry, or on ISPs, who promise to provide Internet connectivity.

Users have a responsibility to lock the door by taking the appropriate actions, including installing a firewall.

The question is whether a firewall can withstand the efforts of a malicious person who is trying to break in. Some organizations, including private firms and the U.S. military, hire "ethical hackers," that is, computer experts who are hired to hack into a computer network, thereby exposing the weaknesses. Security consulting has become an important service in the information technology sector, and companies such as IBM market the services of teams of ethical hackers who evaluate the security of clients' systems. However, because the first defense against invasion of privacy is individual ethics, hiring trustworthy employees and security consultants becomes crucial. Efforts to safeguard computer systems depend on the integrity of the people who work with them.[43]

Verifying Identity

Knowing whom you are dealing with and being able to trust their integrity is fundamental to protecting privacy. Passwords are the simplest form of verifying identity. Since ancient times, people have used passwords the verify the identity of individuals who should be allowed to enter. The shibboleth of the Bible verified the identity of the Jepthah's own men, distinguishing them from the enemy.[44] Entry into speakeasies during Prohibition also required a password or secret knock. Now, of course, ATM cards, e-mail accounts, secure websites, and so on require users to enters passwords. And passwords are vulnerable to theft and hacking. A hacker can write a program that tries multiple passwords until it finds the right one.

We also verify identity with other forms of identification—a signature, a picture ID.[45] But because signatures and IDs can be forged, governments use other means, including fingerprints, face recognition, and iris recognition. These biometrics have been touted as tools for catching terrorists and other criminals, but privacy advocates point to the problems that arise from increased surveillance of the public.[46]

Despite concerns about invasion of privacy, it is likely that biometrics will be used increasingly for identification in cyberspace. Although a major attraction of the Internet is anonymity, proper identification of the parties is essential to e-commerce and e-government. If voting is online, the technology must be able to verify that the person sitting at the keyboard is the registered voter he claims to be.[47] Although password-protected access is one option, the possibility that passwords can be stolen or hacked has led technologists to create supplementary forms of ID.

Digital signatures are one solution. A digital signature is essentially an encrypted number attached to a message. Here's how it works: I want to buy something from my favorite online company. When I receive a message from the company ("Please enter credit card number here"), my browser checks to see if there is a digital signature—a string of numbers encrypted with the company's private key—that can be verified by using the company's public key. Hypertext markup language for secure sites (indicated by the "https://") automatically checks for this, as do e-mail programs. Such systems underlie the digital signature provisions of the Uniform Electronic Transaction Act being adopted by states in the United States and in the E-sign provisions of U.S. federal law.[48]

So Company sends Customer a digitally signed message; Customer uses Company's public key to make sure that the signature was created by using Company's private key. But what if Badguy impersonates Company and sets up a public key as if it were Company? Customer has no way of knowing that Company is *really* Company. Badguy might have set up a ruse. It would be easy to accomplish. Consequently digital signatures, in their simple form, are not perfect ways to verify identity. This is the case because "a public and private key pair has no intrinsic association with any person; it is simply a pair of numbers."[49]

Creating the digital equivalent of a notary to attest to a link between the keys and the person (or firm) helps mitigate this problem. Utah pioneered the licensing of digital certification authorities, private firms whose business it is to determine that the individual claiming to be Company really is Company (and not Badguy). The certification authority plays the role of notary in cyberspace by being the trusted third party who verifies the identity of the signer of a digital signature. By establishing a certification authority, Utah is able to create a reasonably secure way to determine the legitimacy of digital signatures.[50] Digital signatures that are certified by a third party have been adopted for applications that go beyond legal paperwork and into such applications as e-commerce, student loan forms, National Science Foundation grant submissions, and medical records.[51] Though the system cannot stop a determined miscreant, it goes a long way toward verifying identity so that consumers know to whom they are disclosing personal information.[52]

■ A Partial Victory or a Partial Failure?

Despite the assaults on the private sphere, people have found ways to regain some control over the boundary between public and private. Throughout history, individuals, like governments, have used secret codes and other means to encrypt sensitive information. People have put up barriers (walls, locks, gates, windows) to prevent unwanted information from coming in and personal information from going out. They have used stealth to gain information denied to them, and they have pushed information about themselves out into the public domain. They have prevented the disclosure of information to those who ought not to have it by verifying identity.

The proliferation of ways to protect privacy is a positive outcome that gives individuals greater choice and autonomy. Opportunities for creating new forms of privacy protection encourage innovation. Yet this also poses a challenge to those who wish to harmonize commercial law across borders to facilitate the growth of e-commerce and other exchanges in cyberspace. Questions remain. Should local governments be responsible for creating the legal structures supporting privacy protections? Should such a governance function fall to national governments or to international organizations instead? What privacy protections ought to be required, recommended, or prohibited by law? As with rule making for intellectual property and information property, making rules that protect privacy by limiting trespasses and sequestrations of private data is, by definition, a political process in which power is wielded to achieve a desired end.

■ Notes

1. Lawrence Lessig, *Code and Other Laws of Cyberspace* (New York: Basic Books, 1999).

2. Mathathera Narada, *The Buddha and His Teachings* (Kandy, Sri Lanka: Buddhist Publication Society, 1973), pp. 183–184.

3. Association of Islamic Charitable Projects, *Gossip (Ghibah) and Tale-Bearing (Namimah)* [cited January 30, 2002], available from www.aicp.org/IslamicInformation/GossipGhibahAndTale-BearingNamimah.htm.

4. John Wesley, "The Cure of Evil Speaking (Sermon XLIX)," *The Complete Works of John Wesley* (Albany, OR: Books for the Ages, Ages Software, Version 2.0 [1872] 1996 [cited October 18, 2002]).

5. Jewish prayers that involve public confession of sins use the first person plural and enumerate a laundry list of just about every imaginable sin so that no one is singled out for having committed a particular offense.

6. Susan J. Wells, "No, Not That John Gotti: Errors in Web Background Checks Can Derail Job Seekers," *New York Times*, October 22, 1998.

7. U.S. Federal Trade Commission, Privacy of Financial Information, Final Rule, 16 CFR Part 313, 65 No. 101, May 24, 2000, 33646.

8. *Do-Not-Call Implementation Act, Public Law 108-10, U.S. Statutes at Large* 117 (2003): 557; *Do-Not-Call Registry Implementation Authority,* Public Law 108-82, *U.S. Statutes at Large* 117 (2003): 1006; *Controlling the Assault of Non-Solicited Pornography and Marketing Act of 2003 (CAN-SPAM),* Public Law 108-187, *U.S. Statutes at Large* 117 (2003): 2699. Prior to the passage of the CAN-SPAM Act, some states had begun to attempt regulation. See, for example, SBC Pacific Bell, "California's Spam Laws" [cited August 21, 2003], available from public.pacbell.net/faq/caspam.html.

9. European Parliament and European Council, Directive 95/46/EC of the European Parliament and of the Council of October 24, 1995 on the Protection of Individuals with Regard to the Processing of Personal Data and on the Free Movement of Such Data, L 281, November 23, 1995, *Official Journal of the European Communities* 31–50 [cited November 22, 2002], available from europa.eu.int/smartapi/cgi/sga_doc?smartapi!celexapi!prod!CELEXnumdoc&lg=EN&numdoc=31995L0046&model=guichett.

10. European Parliament and European Council, Directive 2002/58/EC of the European Parliament and of the Council of July 12, 2002 Concerning the Processing of Personal Data and the Protection of Privacy in the Electronic Communications Sector (Directive on Privacy and Electronic Communications), L201/37, July 31, 2002, *Official Journal of the European Communities* 37–47 [cited January 9, 2003], available from europa.eu.int/eur-lex/pri/en/oj/dat/2002/l_201/l_20120020731en00370047.pdf.

11. Ibid.

12. Virginia Haufler, *Dangerous Commerce: Insurance and the Management of International Risk* (Ithaca, NY: Cornell University Press, 1997). See also Lloyd's of London, *Historical Overview* [cited November 22, 2002], available from www.lloyds.com/index.asp?ItemId=2622.

13. On the U.S. insurance industry's concerns regarding the European Data Directive, see, for example, Steven Brostoff, "U.S. Insurers, Brokers Look to Clear EU Privacy Hurdle," *National Underwriter,* May 17, 1999, pp. 4 and 50.

14. Steven Brostoff, "U.S. Insurance Groups Hold Their Breath as Global Privacy Talks Move," *National Underwriter,* July 5, 1999, 10ff.

15. Jeff Rohlmeier, International Trade Specialist, U.S. Department of Commerce, International Trade Administration, Office of Electronic Commerce, personal communication via e-mail, February 8, 2002.

16. U.S. Department of Commerce, Bureau of Industry and Security, "Safe Harbor Overview" [cited February 8, 2002], available from www. export.gov/safeharbor/sh_overview.html. See also Stephen J. Kobrin, "Safe Harbours Are Hard to Find: The Trans-Atlantic Data Privacy Dispute, Territorial Jurisdiction and Global Governance," *Review of International Studies* 30 (2004): 111–131.

17. The requirement specifies:

> Organizations must give individuals the opportunity to choose (opt out) whether their personal information will be disclosed to a third party or used for a purpose incompatible with the purpose for which it was originally collected or subsequently authorized by the individual. For sensitive information, affirmative or explicit (opt in) choice must be given if the information is to be disclosed to a third party or used for a purpose other than its original purpose or the purpose authorized subsequently by the individual.

U.S. Department of Commerce, Bureau of Industry and Security, "Safe Harbor Overview."

18. Rohlmeier, personal communication, February 8, 2002. More recently, Rohlmeier reports that the U.S. Department of Commerce has not received any "notifications of an organization's 'persistent failure to comply,'" and he is not "aware of any such findings having been made by a self-regulatory program, the Federal Trade Commission, or the European Union Data Protection Authorities." He notes, however, that individual complaints have been received by self-regulatory programs and by the companies themselves. Apparently the problems have been resolved. Jeffrey Rohlmeier, personal communication via e-mail, March 1, 2004.

19. Ibid.

20. Pamela Parker, "Doubleclick Drops Controversial Plan," *Internet News,* March 2, 2000 [cited February 10, 2002], available from www.inter netnews.com/bus-news/article/0,,3_314401,00.htm.

21. "Doubleclick Signs to Safe Harbor to Repair Reputation," *New Media Age,* August 30, 2001, p. 14.

22. Council of the European Union, Charter of Fundamental Rights of the European Union, 2000/C 364/01, December 18, 2000, *Official Journal of the European Communities* [cited January 10, 2003], available from ue.eu.int/df/default.asp?lang=en. The EU Charter is a joint proclamation of the EU Council, the European Parliament, and the Commission of the European Union, issued in December 2000. It brings together the various conventions and treaties regarding basic human rights and civil, social, and political rights enjoyed by citizens of the EU. See European Union, "Information on the Charter of Fundamental Human Rights of the European Union" [cited January 10, 2003], available from europa.eu.int/abc/cit1_en.htm. According to the explanatory notes to the EU Charter, Article 7 updates Article 8 of the European Convention on Human Rights by substituting the word *communications* for the original *correspondence.* The new

terminology provides an explicit reference to all forms of communication, including e-mail and other digital forms. Council of Europe, Convention for the Protection of Human Rights and Fundamental Freedoms as Amended by Protocol No. 11 with Protocol Nos. 1, 4, 6 and 7, November 1998, Registry of the European Court of Human Rights [cited January 10, 2003], available from www.echr.coe.int/Convention/webConvenENG.pdf.

23. Although an initial injunction preventing the publication of the unauthorized pictures was overturned on appeal, Douglas, Zeta-Jones, and the publishers of *OK!* did win the case in 2003. Nic Hopkins, "Downmarket Rivals Turn Heat on Hello! And OK!," *The Times* (London), August 15, 2003. However, since the ruling did not rely on the law protecting the right to privacy, this case may not, after all, do much to promote privacy rights. See also "International Developments," *Entertainment Law Reporter* 24, no. 12 (2003); "Timeline: Hollywood Couple v. *Hello!*" *BBC News Online* [cited December 12, 2003], available from news.bbc.co.uk/1/hi/entertainment/showbiz/2933541.stm. Earlier coverage can be found in "International Developments," *Entertainment Law Reporter,* March 2001. The case of the Douglas and Zeta-Jones wedding was particularly interesting because they managed to commercialize their own personal information by selling exclusive rights to photograph some parts of the wedding to *OK!* magazine. *Hello!* apparently used subterfuge and tricks to get around the physical privacy barriers that had been installed. The magazine then published their wedding pictures three days before the authorized version appeared.

24. Robert Verkaik, "Celebrities Try to Use New Law to Stop Invasion of Their Privacy," *The Independent* (London), February 11, 2002; Stuart Wavell, "Naomi Opens a Door to the Private Lives' Club," *Sunday Times* (London), February 10, 2002; and "UK Appeals Court Reverses Naomi Campbell's Landmark Privacy Victory," *AdLaw by Request,* October 28, 2002 [cited January 10, 2003], available from www.adlawbyrequest.com/international/campbell102802.shtml.

25. Philips is a chief constable and the vice president of the Association of Chief Police Officers. He is quoted in Sophie Goodchild, "Human Rights Act—Warning: Citizen Britain on the Rise; Six Months on, an Act That Enshrines the Loftiest Ideals Is Proving Handy in Plenty of Mundane Causes," *Independent on Sunday,* April 1, 2001.

26. Alan Travis and Clare Dyer, "Rights of the Citizen: Ministers Face Policy Challenges: From Postcode Rationing and School Exclusions to Privacy and Free Speech, the Government May Face Legal Confrontations across a Broad Front," *The Guardian* (London), September 11, 2000.

27. Hugh Stevenson, Federal Trade Commission, Bureau of Consumer Protection, Statement Before the Senate, Subcommittee on Investigations of the Committee on Governmental Affairs, 1st sess., June 15, 2001 [cited December 18, 2001], available from www.ftc.gov/os/2001/06/cbftest.htm.

28. Council of Europe, "30 States Sign the Convention on Cybercrime at the Opening Ceremony," press release, November 23, 2001 [cited January 11, 2003], available from press.coe.int/cp/2001/875a(2001).htm.

29. Ibid.

30. American Civil Liberties Union, "Eight Reasons the U.S. Should Reject the International Cybercrime Treaty," March 17, 2002 [cited January 11, 2003], available from www.aclu.org/news/NewsPrint.cfm?ID=9996&c =16; and American Civil Liberties Union et. al, "Comments of the American Civil Liberties Union, the Electronic Privacy Information Center and Privacy International on Draft 27 of the Proposed COE Convention on Cybercrime," June 7, 2001 [cited January 11, 2003], available from www.privacy.org/pi/issues/cybercrime/coe/ngo_letter_601.htm.

31. David Banisar [Privacy International], *Bug Off! A Primer for Human Rights Groups on Wiretapping* (October 1995 [cited February 19 2002]), available from www.privacy.org/pi/reports/bug_off.html.

32. James E Goehring, "Monastic Diversity and Ideological Boundaries in Fourth-Century Christian Egypt," *Journal of Early Christian Studies* 5, no. 1 (1977); and James E. Goehring, personal communication via e-mail, January 28, 2002.

33. Terence Whalen, "The Code for Gold: Edgar Allan Poe and Cryptography," *Representations* 46 (1994).

34. Jeanne J. Grimmett, "Encryption Export Controls," Report for Congress, Rl30273, Congressional Research Service, Library of Congress, January 11, 2001 [cited January 13, 2003], available from www.fas.org/irp/crs/RL30273.pdf.

35. U.S. National Institute of Standards and Technology, Advanced Encryption Standard (AES), "Questions and Answers," October 2, 2000 [cited January 14, 2003], available from www.nist.gov/public_affairs/releases/aesq&a.htm. It is notable that the program selected to be the AES, Rijndael, was developed by two Belgian cryptographers, Joan Daemen and Vincent Rijmen.

36. Banisar, *Bug Off!*

37. Jack Kelley, "Terror Groups Hide Behind Web Encryption," *USA Today,* February 5, 2001 [cited January 20, 2003], available from www.usatoday.com/life/cyber/tech/2001-02-05-binladen.htm; and Steven Levy, "Did Encryption Empower These Terrorists?" *Newsweek Web Exclusive, MSNBC,* September 11, 2001 [cited January 20, 2003], available from www.msnbc.com/news/627390.asp?0si=-&cpl1=1.

38. James S. Milford, Statement Regarding Anti-Narcotics Cooperation with the Government of Mexico, Senate Foreign Relations Committee and Senate Drug Caucus, 105th Cong., 1st sess., October 29, 1997 [cited January 20, 2003], available from www.usdoj.gov/dea/pubs/cngrtest/ct971029.htm.

39. Uniting and Strengthening America by Providing Appropriate Tools Required to Intercept and Obstruct Terrorism (USA PATRIOT) Act, U.S. Public Law 107-56, 1st sess., October 26, 2001.

40. The Schlage Company, which is a major manufacturer of locks, has placed a history of locks online at Schlage Company, "History" [cited August 20, 2003], available from www.schlage.com/history/history.htm. See also John H. Lienhard, "Locks, the Engines of Our Ingenuity, Episode 864" [radio broadcast] (KUHF-FM Houston), n.d. [cited January 2003], available from www.uh.edu/engines/epi864.htm.

41. Another way of looking at this scenario is that the gatekeeper prevents the uninvited from using up the company president's *time,* a scarce but intangible resource. Both interpretations are, of course, valid and are complementary. The gatekeeper protects the president's time by limiting the information that she must take in.

42. George Lakoff and Mark Johnson, *Metaphors We Live By* (Chicago: University of Chicago Press, 1980).

43. Charles Palmer, "Ethical Hacking," *IBM Systems Journal* 40, no. 3 (2001). Palmer, manager of the Network and Security and Cryptography Department at the IBM Thomas J. Watson Research Center and cofounder of the Global Security Analysis Lab (GSAL), notes that GSAL has chosen not to hire anyone who has infiltrated computer systems for fun or for malicious purposes (a former hacker or a "cracker," respectively). Instead, the company hires skilled computer experts, the kind of people who have "published research papers or released popular open-source security software."

44. Shibboleth is "the Hebrew word used by Jephthah as a test-word by which to distinguish the fleeing Ephraimites (who could not pronounce the *sh*) from his own men the Gileadites (Judges xii. 4–6)," *Oxford English Dictionary Online* [cited November 24, 2003], available from http://dictionary. oed.com.proxyau.wrlc.org/cgi/entry/00222736?query_type=word&query word=SHIBBOLETH&edition=2e&first=1&max_to_show=10&single=1& sort_type=alpha&case_id=pbFC-gOmlpX-4009&p=1&d=1&sp=1&qt=1& ct=0&ad=1&print=1.

45. When someone is hired for a job in the United States, the new employee must verify his identity and eligibility for employment. U.S. Department of Homeland Security, Bureau of Citizenship and Immigration Services, Employment Eligibility Verification, Form I-9, 2003 [cited August 20, 2003], available from www.bcis.gov/graphics/formsfee/forms/i-9.htm.

46. Information on the Bush administration's policy on biometrics can be found on U.S. Department of Homeland Security [cited January 18, 2003], available from www.whitehouse.gov/homeland. An example of recent EU policy on biometrics can be found in European Union, Laying Down a Uniform Format for Residence Permits for Third-Country Nationals, Council Regulation (EC) No. 1030/2002, L 157, June 13, 2002, *Official Journal* 1–7 [cited January 18, 2003], available from europa.eu.int/smartapi/cgi/ sga_doc?smartapi!celexapi!prod!CELEXnumdoc&lg=EN&numdoc= 32002R1030&model=guichett.

47. Elections for the at-large members of the Internet Corporation for Assigned Names and Numbers (ICANN) took place online, in an election monitored by the Carter Center and operated by a private firm (Election. com). The elections were not without their problems, some of which had to do with knowing who was a legitimate voter. Renée Marlin-Bennett, "ICANN and Democracy: Contradictions and Possibilities," *Info—The Journal of Policy, Regulation, and Strategy for Telecommunications* 3, no. 4 (2001).

48. The key national legislation is the *Electronic Signatures in Global and National Commerce Act,* Public Law 106-229, U.S. Statutes at Large 114 (2000): 464. The Utah Digital Signature Act, Utah Code, Title 46, Chapter

03, August 9, 2002 [cited November 24, 2003], available from www.le.
state.ut.us/~code/TITLE46/46_02.htm, provides the model law for several
other U.S. states. See also the results of the Internet Law and Policy Forum's
commissioned survey of other countries' digital signature policies. Chris
Kuner et. al, *An Analysis of International Electronic and Digital Signature
Implementation Initiatives—A Study* (Internet Law and Policy Forum, September 2000 [cited January 20, 2003]), available from www.ilpf.org/groups/
analysis_IEDSII.htm.

49. Utah Department of Commerce, "Digital Signature Tutorial" [cited
August 20, 2003], available from www.commerce.state.ut.us/digsig/tutorl.htm.

50. Why Utah? one might ask. According to Lee Hollaar, a computer
science professor at the University of Utah and a technical adviser to state
and national governments, the motivation driving the legislation to create a
legally recognized digital signature was the effort to enforce drug laws.
Most of Utah is sparsely populated, and in some regions of the state judges
actually ride the circuit, arriving in a particular area only on certain days. To
arrest a suspected criminal, a police officer needs to swear an affidavit,
which then must be conveyed to the judge who issues an arrest warrant.
Police officers tracking down drug runners cruising up Utah highways
would like to receive the arrest warrant expeditiously, preferably before the
alleged villain has made it across the state line. Unfortunately, the sparsely
populated expanse of the state makes it time-consuming for the required
papers to be brought to the judge. Sending the paperwork electronically
would speed up the process. And so, with a grant from the U.S. Drug
Enforcement Agency, a pilot program was launched with the Utah Administrative Office of the Courts serving as the certifying agent. When that proved
successful, digital signature advocates worked with the state legislature to
create a model law for certifying digital signatures. Utah adopted the world's
first Digital Signature Act in 1995. For the first time, digital signatures, certified by a trusted third party, were legally defined as true signatures. Lee
Hollaar, University of Utah, interview with the author, March 11, 2002.

51. Ibid.

52. A dissenting opinion on the value of digital signatures can be found
in Carl Ellison and Bruce Schneier, "Ten Risks of PKI: What You're Not
Being Told About Public Key Infrastructure," *Computer Security Journal*
16, no. 1 (2000).

11

Conclusion

In this book I have explored the political economy of intellectual property, proprietary information, and privacy. I focused on the social construction of these legal categories and on the way new technologies present challenges to the balance between public and private interests. To recap:

- Intellectual property represents the commodification of creativity or innovation.
- Compilations of facts are increasingly recognized as proprietary information or information property.
- Privacy can be conceptualized as an information space attached to an individual. The content of this space is personal information.
- Privacy rights can be understood as rights to control the flow of information into and out of this private zone.

Information, and who controls its flow from one person, group, or institution to another, is the theme that unites these three concepts. Intellectual property is information in the form of creative and innovative ideas; proprietary information is factual information that is owned; and questions of privacy concern how the individual can determine what information she has and who else is allowed to have it.

The rules (national laws, international treaties, and social conventions) for intellectual property, information, and privacy affect each of us every day in multiple ways; yet these rules are usually in the background of our lives. We know about inappropriate copying of

239

music, counterfeit products, invasions of privacy, and the like, but these generally do not grab our attention the way war and taxes do. Nevertheless, rules for intellectual property, information, and privacy set limits and create opportunities, directly and indirectly. Earnings made possible because of property rights serve as incentives, encouraging creativity, innovation, and the gathering of information. From gadgets and gizmos that make life easier, to lifesaving drugs, to databases that track local supermarkets' inventory, to *Harry Potter*—much of what we do and possess is connected to intellectual property and proprietary information. Our lives are different and, I believe, poorer when property rights for products of the mind are not respected. But our lives are also poorer when these rights are too strong. Intellectual property and proprietary information rights that are too strong stifle creativity, innovation, access to information, and the spread of knowledge.

Privacy can either be a good thing or a bad thing. The right of an individual to protect her privacy has to be weighed against the rights of other individuals and of society to control the flow of personal information. Personal information gathered by firms may increase productivity, thereby adding to the overall health of the economy, as well as to profits. Yet gathering and owning such information can violate privacy. Government practices of surveillance and information-gathering may increase national security, allowing the discovery of malefactors, but they also challenge civil liberties and may have a chilling effect on citizens' political expression.

The right balance promises increased productivity and creativity, as well as security and privacy. The wrong balance promises to enrich and empower a few at the expense of the many. In democracies, citizens participate in setting that balance, one way or the other—by voicing political opinions on these issues, by taking an active role in electing representatives, or by simply choosing not to pay attention. Passivity is the wrong answer. Finding optimal policies that balance the interests of all parties requires more people around the world who are willing to engage in informed, democratic deliberation.

▪ Key Points

The message of this book can be boiled down to four key points:

- The rules that we have today are neither natural nor inevitable; they are socially constructed.

- The history of rule making sheds light on the probable (but not inevitable) future trajectory of rule making. In other words, history matters.
- Western rules have become global rules. Globalization matters.
- Being able to control information flows and to influence or determine rule making, rule implementation, and rule enforcement is a form of power. In short, rulers and gatekeepers have power.

The Rules Are Socially Constructed

First, there is nothing natural or inevitable about intellectual property rights, protections for proprietary information, and rules governing privacy. The rules, codified in treaties and laws, as well as in social conventions, were put into place by people. Of course, we cannot always identify who the rule makers were, but we can infer something about how the rules were made and how they came to be accepted.

New rules are often adaptations of existing rules. This is clear in the expansion of intellectual property rules to new forms of communication and production. Rules for protecting broadcasts are similar to rules for copyright; they are *neighboring rights* in legal terminology. Even the notion of intellectual property is, itself, an adaptation of existing rules for tangible goods. And metaphors influence the way we understand concepts and therefore the kinds of rules that we are willing to accept.[1] For any given problem, the metaphors that people invoke may differ, but generally there is coherence within society about what makes sense and what is nonsense.[2] Unless someone comes up with a captivating, compelling new metaphor, policy options will be constrained by a limited range of plausible metaphors.

Consider alternatives to property rights for innovation, creativity, and information. The ironic neologism *copyleft* has been used by programmers who place their code in the public domain.[3] Copyleft is a license that allows others free access to a software product as long as all derivative products can also be freely accessed. In other words, copyleft, like *shareware* (another metaphor), assumes the existence of a community (of programmers, in this case) who share with each other. This metaphor works, and people are willing to write code and place it in the public domain because sharing is an underlying value of our society, just like respect for private property. The irony, of course, is the use of *copyleft,* which alludes to a communal or socialist alternative to a capitalist *copyright*.[4] Both of these metaphors coexist today. They work as alternate conceptualizations of how to treat products of the mind.

But contrast the fit of both copyright and copyleft to values that resonate with contemporary society versus the notion of copy privileges. Historically, the monopoly on copying or using an invention was a privilege conferred by the governing authority. One solution to the problem of excessive profits from copyrights and patents could be to redefine the temporary monopoly as a privilege. But "privilege" sounds wrong. "Rights" are equitable: everyone in theory has equal rights. One copyright is no stronger than another copyright. Privileges, in contrast, connote favoritism and unfairness. Citizens of today could not easily be convinced that companies had no rights whatsoever to their inventions, only privileges. The notion of rights to intellectual and information property is generally accepted by the public in Western societies and increasingly by other societies; consequently these rights are real.

History Matters

The history of intellectual property and proprietary information reveals the general trend toward expanded property rights. Once something becomes property in the minds of people, it is difficult to take away its propertyness. Optimally, however, policymakers and citizens who wish to influence policymakers would examine the history of intellectual property and related forms to determine how well the existing policies work. A critical analysis of existing policies can identify who benefits, who is excluded from receiving benefit, and who is harmed. Most often, the winners in the property game are people and firms who fit the Western liberal model of *homo economicus,* the selfish, wealth-seeking individual who resolutely makes choices maximizing his own utility, regardless of the effect on others. Furthermore, the historical evolution of rules for intellectual property leads to the development of policies favoring entrenched interests—people in countries that industrialized first—at the expense of late industrializing societies.

Globalization Matters

Under conditions of globalization, the policy decisions made in economically powerful countries have direct and indirect effects on the rest of the world. Consequently, rational rule making requires careful attention to the impact of policies at domestic and international levels. I believe that avoiding policies that cause harm on a domestic or global scale is a moral obligation as well as a political and economic imperative. Morally, we must weigh questions of fairness. Rights to own information and intellectual property do not fall into the category of natural rights; nor are they socially constructed to be held in perpetuity. Rather they represent a social compromise between the rights of the individual (a person or a firm) and the rights of the public. Although people and firms have a right to benefit from their efforts, that right must be understood in the context of the rights others have to the results. The world has a moral claim on knowledge and art as the cultural heritage of humanity simply because no one creates something wholly new. Imagine a highly creative and original artist. She cannot cut herself off from the intellectual and creative contributions of untold people who have created art before her. She has seen other works of art; she uses a brush and watercolors developed by others; she creates her painting in a spirit of appreciation for, rejection of, or perhaps irony toward others' works. Likewise, the inventor has examined previous inventions and learned the principles of basic science and engineering from some teacher or book. When Isaac Newton wrote "if I have seen further [than certain other men] it is by standing upon the shoulders of giants," he was saying that he could not have made his discoveries without having learned from Galileo's and Kepler's prior discoveries in astronomy and physics.[5]

Indeed, new inventions and creations are possible because of the inventions and creations of the past. Aspirin would not have been invented without the chemists' knowledge of folklore about willow bark. Synthetic interferons would not have been invented without the biologists' knowledge of the human immune system. So if we say that knowledge in the public domain is a necessary, though not sufficient, component of new inventions, how much does the inventor owe the public? Where is the just balance between his right to profit and our right to have access to what could not have been invented without humanity's common heritage—the existing knowledge in the public domain? This is what is at stake in the debates over the affordability of patented medications; who has precedence for getting desirable Internet domain names; access to the information contained in the human genome or to an individual's genetic information; and the like. Global society must address the question of what reasonable incentives and rewards would be, in balance with the legitimate claims of others and the rights that all of humanity have to knowledge in the public domain.

Global society must also face the moral question of whether existing rules for intellectual property, information, and privacy reinforce or worsen existing economic inequalities in the world. It seems that the current rules are more likely to provide property rights for *scientific* knowledge than for *traditional* knowledge. Moreover, innovators and creators in the developing world are less likely than their counterparts in advanced industrial countries to have the means to acquire and enforce property rights. If developing-country innovators and creators manage to secure property rights, they face yet another disadvantage. When DVDs of films made by U.S. companies are pirated, the United States can use its substantial economic leverage to punish the country that is failing to enforce intellectual property rights. This was why, in August 2001, the United States revoked Ukraine's benefits under the Generalized System of Preferences and, in January 2002, imposed trade sanctions amounting to $75 million.[6] This big stick contrasts sharply with the power that Nigeria and its film industry might have to punish countries where piracy of "Nollywood" DVDs goes practically unnoticed and unpunished.[7]

A just balance between property rights and public access is also a political and economic imperative. Put simply, policies that protect the intellectual property and related rights of the wealthy at the expense of the poor may look good in the short run, but in the long run this will not be in the national interest. Slow growth, due in part to an unfairly formulated set of global rights, to intellectual property and information will lead to a sense of relative deprivation.[8] This disgruntlement with the pace of economic development and improvements in material well-being will contribute to domestic and international unrest. The rich countries will not make friends by exploiting the poor.

Moreover, it is not good economic policy to make the poor any poorer. Poor people represent potential demand. Though they cannot afford what the rich are selling, they would buy products if they could. Many people who need medications for AIDS and other illnesses are simply not buying them because of cost. The pharmaceutical companies claim that they cannot cover their costs if they lose revenues due to relaxation of patent protections. Is that really true? Would additional sales fail to provide sufficient profit to cover costs? I suspect not, since pharmaceutical costs include marketing expenditures and executive compensation, as well as the risky business of drug research and development. Fair rules, though, would provide incentives for companies while enabling competitors and new innovators to succeed as well. Fair and balanced rules would create a more level playing field, thereby helping new entrants compete in the global marketplace. The end result, I expect, would be consumers who have more money to spend, as well as higher levels of production and innovation.

Rulers and Gatekeepers

Power is the ability to determine or influence outcomes, a quality possessed by human beings and social aggregates of human beings, including states and firms. Those who rule—who identify the problem, make the rule, implement it, and enforce it—have power. The rules define who has the legal right to control the flow of data—to be a gatekeeper—and the limits of that right. Gatekeepers exercise the power granted to them by these rules. They may also use extralegal means to exert power in ways that get around or even violate the rules. A calculus of relative power among states, individuals, firms, and other groups shows that control of knowledge power is not uniform. The power of a nation-state is usually broader than the power of a firm.[9] Large firms and states have large amounts of power, while the individual's power is limited to a micro-quantum of power. It is power, nonetheless.

Rulers are powerful because they create the structure in which they and others can legitimately control information flows. Gatekeepers are powerful because they are able to control the flow of information, including personal information, intellectual property, and proprietary information.[10] When rulers—policymakers—devise, implement, and enforce fair rules, there is a potential to benefit to all members of society. Unfair rules benefit some at the expense of others.

With the implementation of the Trade Related Intellectual Property Provisions (TRIPS) agreement under GATT, the World Trade Organization has become the primary venue for formulation and enforcement of global rules protecting intellectual property. The WTO's involvement in intellectual property and related matters is important because the WTO provides global governance consistent with the liberal trade principles of the United States and other major economic powers. Although current discussions on a database treaty are going on under the auspices of the World Intellectual Property Organization (WIPO), if and when such a treaty takes effect the WTO will probably play a substantial role in its enforcement. Under WTO rules, when a country is found to be harmed by a violation of an intellectual property rule, the WTO enforces the rule by allowing the country suffering the harm to impose countervailing tariffs. Nigeria and its film industry, which are harmed by unchecked piracy of DVDs, are stuck. They have no practical means to force other countries to enforce their rights, while firms in the economically powerful countries benefit from the ability of their countries to levy meaningful sanctions.

▪ A Dangerous Historical Juncture?
Creeping Commodification and Privacy Violations

Today's global political economy is marked by the creeping commodification of new forms of property and by private and governmental assaults on privacy. The material resources needed to control the flow of information and its use is easily available to firms and governments, less so to individuals. One result seems to be the fulfillment of the private sector's interests over those of the public—especially when the private sector has a strong lobby. Another result seems to be an increased tendency for governments to surveil more and divulge less.

Fencing the Global Knowledge Commons

Are we witnessing a fencing-in of the global information commons? I think the historical trajectory of increasing property rights in products of the mind suggests this to be so. A complex web of ownership rights is being crafted for global markets, primarily under the aegis of WTO, WIPO, and unilateral initiatives in the United States and the European Union. The evolution of university research activities into profit centers is, perhaps, the most worrisome aspect of this trend.[11]

If this is indeed a real trend, then what comes next? Although it seems farfetched, a world in which basic scientific truths can be owned by their discoverers is not impossible. Already we may be seeing a glimmer of that world as scientists in genetics and other fields increasingly turn to the patent system to safeguard the products of their research. The collegiality of scholarly, scientific, and artistic communities suffers when everyone is counting dollar signs. Possibilities for profits limit what people will disclose to each other, thereby closing off opportunities for cross-fertilization of ideas and greater productivity. Similarly, the traditional relationship between professor and student is warped by excessive commodification. When laboratory notebooks, including work a student has done for her dissertation or postdoctoral fellowship, are the professor's property,[12] the traditional mentoring relationship between professor and student is broken. Marxist terms fit the scenario: the knowledge worker—the graduate student—has been alienated from the production of her intellectual labor. Taking a liberal, market-oriented view, it is fair to say that excessive commodification is inefficient. The former student no longer shares her expertise with the professor's research group; nor can she continue from where she left off on her project when she joins another research group. This is not an efficient use of intellectual capital.

This trend toward increased—and perhaps excessive—commodification could contribute to the breakdown of the norms of the scholarly and scientific communities, thereby distorting friendships and human connections. I am not claiming that everyone in academia is nice. Of course, there's always someone who dines on sour grapes, and everyone knows of the uncollegial person who gloats over the missteps of others. Still, by and large the norms of scholarship have promoted the values of sharing knowledge. Though scientists have always competed to be first to make the important discovery, and writers might want to beat their colleagues by publishing a blockbuster, the competition rarely slides into the unpleasantness of actual conflict. Will colleagues stop sharing knowledge with each other, pointing each other toward helpful references, and offering helpful criticism on papers? With excessive commodification, people would have a profit motive to prevent others from knowing what they know, and brilliant students might be seen as threats rather than as worthy intellectual heirs. I find this possible outcome sad.

I am not, however, taking an extreme anti–intellectual property, anti–proprietary information position. *Excessive* commodification is a problem. However, the economic evidence and my own personal experiences convince me that reasonable degrees of commodification do indeed contribute to productivity by providing incentives for engaging in innovative or creative work and for expending resources to gather information.

Privacy Violations

The related danger is to privacy. Citizens' power to act as gatekeepers of personal information seem to be waning as governments and firms collect more information. Furthermore, citizens' inability to access information when they want and need it is troubling. Firms restrict access to information by commodifying it and asserting property rights over it. One repercussion has been a failure to disclose information that ought to be made public. The failures of transparency in accounting practices that led to the scandals of Enron, Worldcom, and other financial misdealings represent privacy violations in the sense that people have been prevented from getting the information that would have allowed them to make efficient choices. Governments similarly restrict access to information and limit the transparency of decisionmaking. For a government to deny access to information is simple: it need only declare the information secret. Alternatively, it can substitute false information to displace the desired information. Although the failure of firms to disclose information has undoubtedly caused social harm, I find the threat to civil liberties and democracy caused by governmental failures even more damaging to society.

In a democracy, government operations and officials' actions must be transparent for the governments and its officials to be accountable to the people. Information must flow out from the government and be accessible to citizens. This information must be correct and not tainted with deliberately misleading interpretations. Consider the Bush administration's use of intelligence on weapons of mass destruction prior to the March 2003 Iraq War. Was it appropriate, a mistake, or an intentional deception?

Democracy also requires that the government's intrusion into citizens' lives to conduct surveillance be restricted. The need to know information about an individual must always be balanced against the individual's right to keep that information private. Are we so at risk that the government ought to be collecting information on where we go and what we do by recording our image on surveillance cameras in public places? How much personal information must people be required to disclose before they are allowed to travel on an airplane or other public conveyance? For foreign students in the United States, new visa regulations require that universities keep tabs on them. This may seem unwelcoming at best, intrusive at worst.

Lawrence Lessig predicts that "we are entering an age when privacy will be fundamentally altered—an age when the extent of the monitored, and the searchable, is far greater than anything we have known thus far."[13] Though engineering advances seem to run ahead of society's ability to develop policies to rein in the use of new technologies, citizens need not give up on changing the rules. If citizens find this alteration in privacy to be unwarranted or wrongheaded, it is up to them to take political action to stop or at least to deflect the trend.

■ Questions Remain

Intellectual property, information, and privacy are vitally important in the global political economy of the Information Age. Who is making the rules about property rights? How are the rules being made? Are protections for rights holders strong enough? Do we need more rights and better-enforced rights? How is the public interest protected? Are we preserving a global knowledge commons? Are we allowing people to control the flow of information in ways consistent with their own needs and those of the public?

These questions remain central to what should be an ongoing global debate. The complex web of rules about intellectual property, information, and privacy determines how knowledge will flow around the globe, both across societies and within them. The tensions between market interests and privacy, and between commodification and the commons, transcend national boundaries. As a global society, we must ask: Who benefits?

■ Notes

1. Joseph R. Gusfield, *The Culture of Public Problems: Drinking-Driving and the Symbolic Order* (Chicago: University of Chicago Press, 1981); and George Lakoff and Mark Johnson, *Metaphors We Live By* (Chicago: University of Chicago Press, 1980).

2. Mark Schlesinger and Richard R Lau, "The Meaning and Measure of Policy Metaphors," *American Political Science Review* 94, no. 3 (2000): 611–626.

3. The term *copyleft* seems to have been coined by Richard Stallman, who is the founder of the Free Software Foundation. Richard Stallman, *Copyleft: Pragmatic Idealism* (February 8, 2002 [cited August 26, 2003]), available from www.gnu.org/philosophy/pragmatic.html.

4. Johan Soderberg, "Copyleft Vs. Copyright: A Marxist Critique," *First Monday* (peer-reviewed electronic journal) 7, no. 3 (2002).

5. The Columbia World of Quotations (1996 [cited November 24, 2003], available from www.bartleby.com/66/18/41418.html.

6. United States Trade Representative, "Special 301 Report," May 1, 2003, p. 10 [cited November 8, 2003], available from www.ustr.gov/reports/2003/fullreport.pdf.

7. Steven Gray, "Nigeria on Screen; 'Nollywood' Films' Popularity Rising Among Emigres," *Washington Post,* November 8, 2003. The reporter notes:

> Intellectual property law experts noted that the pirating of Nigerian films will probably continue, in part because the filmmakers can't afford the high legal costs of fighting it.
>
> Pedro Agbonifo Obaseki, a Nigerian filmmaker who is president of the Filmmakers Consortium of Nigeria, expressed outrage at the pirating. 'For all the films sold in the Bronx or Washington, not a dime comes to the Nigerian filmmaker, not a dime,' he said from Lagos, during a break from rehearsals for his latest movie.

8. The connection between expectations of improved economic well-being and actual improvements to conflict was introduced by Ted Robert Gurr, *Why Men Rebel* (Princeton, NJ: Center of International Studies, Princeton University, by Princeton University Press, 1970).

9. See, for example, Gregory P. Nowell, *Mercantile States and the World Oil Cartel, 1900–1939,* Cornell Studies in Political Economy (Ithaca, NY: Cornell University Press, 1994).

10. This control may be both legitimate and in accordance with appropriate laws, or illegitimate, as in the case of identity theft.

11. Derek Curtis Bok, *Universities in the Marketplace: The Commercialization of Higher Education* (Princeton, NJ: Princeton University Press, 2003).

12. An article in the *New York Times* science section described such as case, which Michael Kalichman, professor of a course on ethics in science, places before his students. The case was apparently drawn from an actual event. In the interview, Kalichman notes that many universities now have explicit guidelines about the ownership of laboratory notebooks. Gina Kolata, "Ethics 101: A Course About Pitfalls," *New York Times*, October 21, 2003.

13. Lawrence Lessig, "The Architecture of Privacy," *Vanderbilt Journal of Entertainment Law & Practice* 1 (1999): 57. Lessig's attention to the monitored and the searchable concentrates on wresting information out from the private sphere. His definition of privacy is more narrow than mine, and he does not consider any of the other aspects of what I define as privacy.

Selected Bibliography

Abbott, Frederick M. "TRIPS in Seattle: The Not-So-Surprising Failure and the Future of the TRIPS Agenda." *Berkeley Journal of International Law* 18 (2000): 165ff.

Alford, William P. *To Steal a Book Is an Elegant Offense: Intellectual Property Law in Chinese Civilization.* Stanford, CA: Stanford University Press, 1995.

Andermann, Anne A. J. "Physicians, Fads, and Pharmaceuticals: A History of Aspirin." *McGill Journal of Medicine* 2 (1996): 115–120.

Ang, Peng Hwa, and Berlinda Nadarajan. "Censorship and the Internet: A Singapore Perspective." *Communications of the ACM* 36, no. 9 (1996): 72–78.

Arden, Thomas P. "The Conflicting Treatments of Compilations of Facts Under the United States and British Copyright Laws." *American Intellectual Property Law Association Quarterly Journal* 19, no. 4 (1991): 268–281.

Bates, Charles C., and John F. Fuller. *America's Weather Warriors, 1814–1985.* College Station: Texas A&M University Press, 1986.

Bleek, Wolf. "Witchcraft, Gossip, and Death: A Social Drama." *Man* [New Series] 11, no. 4 (1976): 526–541.

Boas, Taylor C. "The Dictator's Dilemma? The Internet and U.S. Policy Toward Cuba." *Washington Quarterly* 23, no. 3 (2002): 57–67.

Bok, Derek Curtis. *Universities in the Marketplace: The Commercialization of Higher Education.* Princeton, NJ: Princeton University Press, 2003.

Boling, Patricia. "Privacy as Autonomy vs. Privacy as Familial Attachment." *Policy Studies Review* 13, no. 1/2 (1994): 91–111.

Borgmann, Albert. *Holding on to Reality: The Nature of Information at the Turn of the Millennium.* Chicago: University of Chicago Press, 1999.

Boyle, James. *Shamans, Software, and Spleens: Law and the Construction of the Information Society.* Cambridge, MA: Harvard University Press, 1996.

251

Braithwaite, Dorothea. "The Economic Effects of Advertisement." *Economic Journal* 38, no. 149 (1928): 16–37.

Branscomb, Anne Wells. *Who Owns Information? From Privacy to Public Access.* New York: Basic Books, 1994.

Burch, R. Kurt. *"Property" and the Making of the International System.* Boulder, CO: Lynne Rienner, 1998.

Burgiel, Stanley. "Negotiating the Trade-Environment Frontier: Biosafety and Intellectual Property Rights in International Policy-Making." Doctoral diss., American University, 2002.

Cho, Hyunyi, and Robert LaRose. "Privacy Issues in Internet Surveys." *Social Science Computer Review* 14, no. 4 (1999): 420–434.

Chopoorian, John A., et. al. "Mind Your Business by Minding Your Data." *S.A.M. Advanced Management Journal* 66, no. 2 (2001): 45–51.

Comor, Edward A. "Governance and the 'Commoditization' of Information." *Global Governance* 4 (1988): 217–233.

Crawford, Sue E. S., and Elinor Ostrom. "A Grammar of Institutions." *American Political Science Review* 89, no. 3 (1995): 582–600.

Damasio, Antonio R. *The Feeling of What Happens: Body and Emotion in the Making of Consciousness.* 1st ed. New York: Harcourt Brace, 1999.

Dehqanzada, Yahya A., and Ann M. Florini. *Secrets for Sale: How Commercial Satellite Imagery Will Change the World.* Washington, DC: Carnegie Endowment for International Peace, 2000.

Denning, Dorothy E. "Who's Stealing Your Information." *Information Security* (April 1999 [cited August 16, 2003]). Available from infosecurity-mag.techtarget.com/articles/1999/aprilcover.shtm.

de Sola Pool, Ithiel. *Technologies of Freedom.* Cambridge, MA: Harvard University Press, 1983.

Donahue, Charles Jr. "Symposium: Relationships Among Roman Law, Common Law, and Modern Civil Law: Ius Commune, Canon Law, and Common Law in England." *Tulane Law Review* 66 (1992): 1760ff.

Downes, David. "How Intellectual Property Could Be a Tool to Protect Traditional Knowledge." *Columbia Journal of Environmental Law* 25 (2000): 253–282.

Drucker, Peter F. "Beyond the Information Revolution." *Atlantic Monthly,* October 1999, pp. 47–57.

———. *Landmarks of Tomorrow.* 1st ed. New York: Harper, 1959.

Dutfield, Graham. "The Public and Private Domains: Intellectual Property Rights in Traditional Knowledge." *Science Communication* 21, no. 3 (2000): 274–295.

Eagleman, Joe R. *Meteorology: The Atmosphere in Action.* 2nd ed. Belmont: Wadsworth, 1985.

Eisenbeis, Kathleen M. *Privatizing Government Information: The Effects of Policy on Access to Landsat Satellite Data.* Metuchen, NJ: Scarecrow, 1995.

Ellison, Carl, and Bruce Schneier. "Ten Risks of PKI: What You're Not Being Told About Public Key Infrastructure." *Computer Security Journal* 16, no. 1 (2000): 1–8. www.counterpane.com/pki-risks.pdf.

Etzioni, Amitai. *The Limits of Privacy.* New York: Basic Books, 1999.

Fischelis, Robert P. "What Is a Patent or Proprietary Medicine?" *Scientific Monthly* 46, no. 1 (1938): 25–31.

Fischer, Horst. "Basic Principles of International Space Law and Civilian Use of Outer Space." In *Outer Space: A Source of Conflict or Co-Operation,* edited by Bhupendra Jasani, pp. 251–252. Tokyo: United Nations University Press, in cooperation with the Stockholm International Peace Research Institute, 1991.

Fleming, James R. *Meteorology in America, 1800–1870.* Baltimore: Johns Hopkins University Press, 1990.

Foucault, Michel. *The Birth of the Clinic: An Archaeology of Medical Perception.* 1st American ed. Translated by A. M. Sheridan Smith. New York: Pantheon, 1973.

Franda, Marcus F. *Launching into Cyberspace: Internet Development and Politics in Five World Regions.* Boulder, CO: Lynne Rienner, 2002.

Fraser, Stephen. "The Conflict Between the First Amendment and Copyright Law and Its Impact on the Internet." *Cardozo Arts & Entertainment Law Journal* 16 (1998): 1ff.

Friedman, Robert Marc. *Appropriating the Weather: Vilhelm Bjerknes and the Construction of a Modern Meteorology.* Ithaca, NY: Cornell University Press, 1989.

Gardner, William, and Joseph Rosenbaum. "Database Protection and Access to Information." *Science,* August 7, 1998, pp. 786–787.

Gellman, Robert. "Twin Evils: Government Copyright and Copyright-Like Controls over Government Information." *Syracuse Law Review* 45 (1995): 999ff.

Giddens, Anthony. *The Constitution of Society.* Berkeley: University of California Press, 1984.

Glennerster, Rachel, and Michael Kremer. "A Better Way to Spur Medical Research and Development." *Regulation* 23, no. 2 (2000): 34–39.

Global Internet Liberty Campaign [website, cited October 6 2002]. Available from www.gilc.org.

Goehring, James E. "Monastic Diversity and Ideological Boundaries in Fourth-Century Christian Egypt." *Journal of Early Christian Studies* 5, no. 1 (1977): 61–84.

Goldfinch, Shaun. *Remaking New Zealand and Australian Economic Policy: Ideas, Institutions, and Policy Communities.* Washington, DC: Georgetown University Press, 2000.

Greely, Henry T. "The Revolution in Human Genetics: Implications for Human Societies." *South Carolina Law Review* 42 (2001): 377–390.

Griffin, Keith, and John Gurley. "Radical Analyses of Imperialism, the Third World, and the Transition to Socialism: A Survey." *Journal of Economic Literature* 23, no. 3 (1985): 1089–1143.

Gurr, Ted Robert. *Why Men Rebel.* Princeton, NJ: Center of International Studies, Princeton University, by Princeton University Press, 1970.

Gusfield, Joseph R. *The Culture of Public Problems: Drinking-Driving and the Symbolic Order.* Chicago: University of Chicago Press, 1981.

Haas, Peter. "Introduction: Epistemic Communities and International Policy Coordination." *International Organization* 46, no. 1 (1992): 1–35.

Hafner, Katie, and Matthew Lyon. *Where Wizards Stay up Late: The Origins of the Internet.* New York: Simon and Schuster, 1996.

Han, Jiawei. "Data Mining" [online article], 1999 [cited August 17, 2003]. Available from ftp.fas.sfu.ca/pub/cs/han/pdf/ency99.pdf.

Haufler, Virginia. *Dangerous Commerce: Insurance and the Management of International Risk.* Ithaca, NY: Cornell University Press, 1997.

Hertz, Allen Z. "Proceedings of the Canada–United States Law Institute Conference, NAFTA Revisited; Shaping the Trident: Intellectual Property Under NAFTA, Investment Protection Agreements, and the World Trade Organization." *Canada–United States Law Journal* 23 (1997): 261–325.

Holland, Suzanne. "Contested Commodities at Both Ends of Life: Buying and Selling Gametes, Embryos, and Body Tissues." *Kennedy Institute of Ethics Journal* 11, no. 3 (2001): 263–284.

Hollander, John. "The Language of Privacy." *Social Resarch* 68, no. 1 (2001): 9–28.

Hugenholtz, P. Brent. "Chronicle of the Netherlands, Dutch Copyright Law, 1995–2000." Revue Internationale du Droit d'Auteur, 2001 [cited August 18, 2003]). Available from www.ivir.nl/publications/hugenholtz/PBH-RIDA2000.doc.

Jonatansson, Hrobajartur. "Iceland's Health Sector Database: A Significant Head Start in the Search for Biological Grail or an Irreversible Error." *American Journal of Law and Medicine* 26, no. 1 (2000): 31–67.

Jones, Daniel M., Stuart A. Bremer, and J. David Singer. "Militarized Interstate Disputes, 1816–1992: Rationale, Coding Rules, and Empirical Patterns." *Conflict Management and Peace Science* 15, no. 2 (1996): 163–213.

Jonietz, Erika. "Personal Genomes: Individual Sequencing Could Be Around the Corner." *Technology Review,* October 2001, p. 30.

Jurin, Jacob. "Invitatio Ad Observationes Meteorologicas Communi Consilio Instituendas." In *Royal Society of London Philosophical Transactions,* 1723, pp. 422–427. Translated by H. E. Landsberg. Available from Historical Manuscripts and Archives Department, University of Maryland, College Park Libraries.

Kampelman, Max M. "The United States and International Copyright." *American Journal of International Law* 41, no. 2 (1947): 406–429.

Kaplan, Benjamin, and Ralph S. Browne Jr. *Cases on Copyright, Unfair Competition, and Other Topics Bearing on the Protection of Literary, Musical, and Artistic Works.* 3rd ed. Minneola, NY: Foundation, 1978.

Kelin, Sabra-Anne. "State Regulation of Unsolicited Commercial E-Mail." *Berkeley Technology Law Journal* 16 (2001): 435ff.

Keohane, Robert O. *After Hegemony: Cooperation and Discord in the World Political Economy.* Princeton, NJ: Princeton University Press, 1984.

Kobrin, Stephen J. "Safe Harbours Are Hard to Find: the Trans-Atlantic Data Privacy Dispute, Territorial Jurisdiction, and Global Governance." *Review of International Studies* 30 (2004): 113–131.

Kocken, Joris, and Gerda van Roozendall. "The Neem Tree Debate." *Biotechnology and Development Monitor*, 1997, 8–11.

Krasner, Stephen D., ed. *International Regimes*. Cornell Studies in Political Economy. Ithaca, NY: Cornell University Press, 1983.

Kratochwil, Fredrich, and John G. Ruggie. "International Organization: A State of the Art on an Art of the State." *International Organization* 40, no. 4 (1986): 753–775.

Lakoff, George, and Mark Johnson. *Metaphors We Live By*. Chicago: University of Chicago Press, 1980.

Landsberg, Helmut. "Historic Weather Data and Early Meteorological Observations." In *Paleoclimate Analysis and Modeling*, edited by Alan D. Hecht, pp. 27–70. Somerset, NJ: John Wiley and Sons, 1985.

Lang, Josephine Chinying. "Management of Intellectual Property Rights: Strategic Patenting." *Journal of Intellectual Capital* 2, no. 1 (2001): 8–26.

Leeson, Robert. *The Eclipse of Keynesianism: The Political Economy of the Chicago Counter-Revolution*. New York: Palgrave, 2000.

Le Menestrel, Marc, Mark Hunter, and Henri-Claude de Bettignies. "Internet E-Ethics in Confrontation with an Activist's Agenda: Yahoo! On Trial." *Journal of Business Ethics* 39, no. 1–2 (2002): 135–144.

Lessig, Lawrence. "The Architecture of Privacy." *Vanderbilt Journal of Entertainment Law & Practice* 1 (1999): 56ff.

———. *Code and Other Laws of Cyberspace*. New York: Basic, 1999.

Locke, John. *Two Treatises of Government*, 1690. Locke's 1690 text taken from 1980 edition edited by C. B. MacPherson (Indianapolis and Cambridge: Hackett). Posted by Dave Gowan [accessed November 1, 2003]. Official release date: 2005. Available from www.ibiblio.org/gutenberg/etext05/trgov10.txt.

Long, Pamela O. *Openness, Secrecy, Authorship: Technical Arts and the Culture of Knowledge from Antiquity to the Renaissance*. Baltimore: Johns Hopkins University Press, 2001.

Lubonja, Fatos. "Privacy in a Totalitarian Regime." *Social Research* 68, no. 1 (2001): 237–254.

Mann, Charles C., and Mark L. Plummer. *The Aspirin Wars: Money, Medicine, and 100 Years of Rampant Competition*. New York: Knopf, 1991.

Marden, Emily. "The Neem Tree Patent: International Conflict over the Commodification of Life." *Boston College International and Comparative Law Review* 22 (1999): 279–295.

Margalit, Avishai. "Privacy in Decent Society." *Social Research* 68, no. 1 (2001): 255–268.

Margolis, Howard. "Equilibrium Norms." *Ethics* 100, no. 4 (1990): 821–837.

Marlin-Bennett, Renée. *Food Fights: International Regimes and the Politics of Agricultural Trade Disputes*. Langhorne, PA: Gordon and Breach, 1993.

———. "ICANN and Democracy: Contradictions and Possibilities." *Info—The Journal of Policy, Regulation, and Strategy for Telecommunications* 3, no. 4 (2001): 299–311.

Marx, Karl. "Value, Price and Profit." In *The Portable Karl Marx,* edited by Eugene Kamenka, pp. 391–432. New York: Penguin, 1983 [1865].

Matthews, Brander. "The Evolution of Copyright." *Political Science Quarterly* 5, no. 4 (1890): 583–602.

Maurer, Stephen M., P. Bernt Hugenholtz, and Harlan J. Onsrud. "Europe's Database Experiment." *Science,* October 26, 2001, 789–790.

May, Christopher. *A Global Political Economy of Intellectual Property Rights: The New Enclosures?* Routledge/RIPE Studies in Global Political Economy. London and New York: Routledge, 2000.

McEwen, Jean. "DNA Data Banks." In *Genetic Secrets: Protecting Privacy and Confidentiality in the Genetic Era,* edited by Mark A. Rothstein, pp. 231–251. New Haven, CT: Yale University Press, 1997.

Metzl, Jamie F. "Information Technology and Human Rigths." *Human Rights Quarterly* 18, no. 4 (1996): 705–746.

Murphy, Craig. *The Emergence of the NIEO Ideology.* Westview Special Studies in Social, Political, and Economic Development. Boulder, CO: Westview, 1984.

Murphy, Richard S. "Property Rights in Personal Information: An Economic Defense of Privacy." *Georgetown Law Journal* 84 (1996): 2381ff.

Nadelmann, Ethan A. "Global Prohibition Regimes: The Evolution of Norms in International Society." *International Organization* 44, no. 4 (1990): 479–526.

Narada, Mathathera. *The Buddha and His Teachings.* Kandy, Sri Lanka: Buddhist Publication Society, 1973.

Neumann, Peter J., and Eileen A. Sandberg. "Trends in Health Care R&D and Technology Innovation: The Pace of Innovation Shows No Sign of Slowing, but More Funding Is Now Drawn from Private-Sector Sources." *Health Affairs* (1998): 111–119.

Nowell, Gregory P. *Mercantile States and the World Oil Cartel, 1900–1939.* Cornell Studies in Political Economy. Ithaca, NY: Cornell University Press, 1994.

Obomsawin, Raymond. "Indigenous Knowledge and Sustainable Development." *Development Express* [Canadian International Development Agency—Policy Branch] 3 (2000–2001).

O'Brien, Rita Cruise, and G. K. Helleiner. "The Political Economy of Information in a Changing International Economic Order." *International Organization* 34, no. 4 (1980): 445–470.

Oddi, A. Samuel. "Un-Unified Economic Theories of Patents—the-Not-Quite-Holy-Grail." *Notre Dame Law Review* 71 (1996): 267ff.

Onuf, Nicholas Greenwood. *World of Our Making: Rules and Rule in Social Theory and International Relations.* Columbia: University of South Carolina Press, 1989.

Orwell, George. *1984.* New York: Harcourt Brace, 1949.

Ostrom, Elinor. *Governing the Commons: The Evolution of Institutions for Collective Action.* Political Economy of Institutions and Decisions. Cambridge, UK, and New York: Cambridge University Press, 1990.

Palmer, Charles. "Ethical Hacking." *IBM Systems Journal* 40, no. 3 (2001): 769–780.

Penrose, Edith Tilton. *The Economics of the International Patent System.* Baltimore: Johns Hopkins University Press, 1951.

Petuchowski, Samuel J. "Toward a Conceptual Basis for the Protection of Literary Product in a Post-Printing Era: Precedents in Jewish Law." *University of Baltimore Intellectual Property Law Journal* 3 (1994): 47ff.

Polanyi, Karl. *The Great Transformation.* 1st Beacon paperback ed. Boston: Beacon, 1957.

Poovey, Mary. "The Twenty-First-Century University and the Market: What Price Economic Viability?" *Differences* 12, no. 1 (2001): 1–16.

Raymond, Gregory A. "Problems and Prospects in the Study of International Norms." *Mershon International Studies Review* 41, no. 2 (1997): 205–245.

Rhodes, Carolyn. "Reciprocity in Trade: The Utility of a Bargaining Strategy." *International Organization* 43, no. 2 (1989): 273–99.

Richelson, Jeffrey. "Desperately Seeking Signals." *Bulletin of the Atomic Scientists* 56, no. 2 (2000): 47–51. www.bullatomsci.org/issues/2000/ma00/ma00richelson.html.

Ricketson, Sam. *The Berne Convention for the Protection of Literary and Artistic Works: 1886–1986.* London: Centre for Commercial Law Studies, Kluwer, 1987.

Rittberger, Volker, ed., with Peter Mayer. *Regime Theory and International Relations.* Oxford: Clarendon, 1993.

Rosen, Jeffrey. "Out of Context: The Purposes of Privacy." *Social Research* 68, no. 1 (2001): 209–232.

———. *The Unwanted Gaze: The Destruction of Privacy in America.* New York: Random House, 2000.

Ruggie, John Gerard. "Collective Goods and Future International Collaboration." *American Political Science Review* 66, no. 3 (1972): 874–893.

Ryan, Michael P. *Knowledge Diplomacy: Global Competition and the Politics of Intellectual Property.* Washington, DC: Brookings Institution, 1998.

Salmon, Marylynn. "Women and Property in South Carolina: The Evidence from Marriage Settlements, 1730 to 1830." *William and Mary Quarterly* [3rd ser.] 39, no. 4 (1982): 655–685.

Samuel, Tony. "Sports Rights Are Valuable Too." *Managing Intellectual Property,* May 2001, p. 45.

Samuelson, Pamela. "A New Kind of Privacy? Regulating Uses of Personal Data in the Global Information Economy." *California Law Review* 87 (1999): 751–778.

Samuelson, Paul A., and Peter Temin. *Economics.* 10th ed. New York: McGraw-Hill, 1976.

Sauvant, Karl P. "Transborder Data Flows and the Developing Countries." *International Organization* 37, no. 2 (1983): 359–371.

Scherer, F. M. "Pricing, Profits, and Technological Progress in the Pharmaceutical Industry." *Journal of Economic Perspectives* 7, no. 3 (1993): 97–115.

Schlesinger, Mark, and Richard R Lau. "The Meaning and Measure of Policy Metaphors." *American Political Science Review* 94, no. 3 (2000): 611–626.

Sell, Susan K. *Power and Ideas: North-South Politics of Intellectual Property and Antitrust.* SUNY Series in Global Politics. Albany: State University of New York Press, 1998.

Sell, Susan K., and Christopher May. "Moments in Law: Contestation and Settlement in the History of Intellectual Property." *Review of International Political Economy* 8, no. 3 (2001): 467–500.

Shannon, C. E. "A Mathematical Theory of Communication." *Bell System Technical Journal* 27 (1948): 379–423, 623–656. Version with corrections [cited September 13, 2002] available from cm.bell-labs.com/cm/ms/what/shannonday/shannon1948.pdf.

Shelley, Louise I. "Crime and Corruption in the Digital Age." *Journal of International Affairs* 51, no. 2 (1998): 605–620.

Shenk, David. *Data Smog: Surviving the Information Glut.* San Francisco: Harper'sEdge, 1997.

Skolnikoff, Eugene. "Science and Technology: The Implications of International Institutions." *International Organization* 25, no. 4 (1971): 759–775.

Smith, Anthony. *The Geopolitics of Information: How Western Culture Dominates the World.* New York: Oxford University Press, 1980.

Soderberg, Johan. "Copyleft vs. Copyright: A Marxist Critique." *First Monday* 7, no. 3 (2002). www.firstmonday.dk/issues/issue7_3/soderberg/index.html

Soghlan, Andy. "Selling the Family Secrets." *New Scientist,* December 5, 1998, p. 20.

Sokol, Alan. "Transgressing Boundaries: Towards a Transformative Hermeneutics of Quantum Gravity." *Social Text* 46 (1996): 217–225.

Spinello, R. A. "Ethical Reflections on the Problem of Spam." *Ethics and Information Technology* 1, no. 3 (1999): 185–191.

Sprout, Harold. "Geopolitical Hypotheses in Technological Perspective." *World Politics* 15, no. 2 (1963): 187–212.

Stecklein, Linda, and George Stone. "An NIH Perspective on the Bayh-Dole Act and Invention Reporting Responsibilities." *SRA Journal* 31, no. 2 (1999): 21–24.

Stienstra, Deborah. "Disabling Globalization: Rethinking Global Political Economy with a Disability Lens." *Global Society* 16, no. 2 (2002): 109–121.

Tamari, Meir. *With All Your Possessions: Jewish Ethics and Economic Life.* New York: Free Press, 1987.

Tan, Zixiang (Alex), William Foster, and Seymour Goodman. "China's State-Coordinated Internet Infrastructure." *Communications of the ACM* 42, no. 6 (1999): 44–52.

Taubenfeld, Rita F., and Howard J. Taubenfeld. "Some International Implications of Weather Modification Activities." *International Organization* 23, no. 4 (1969): 808–833.

Warren, Samuel, and Louis D. Brandeis. "The Right to Privacy." *Harvard Law Review* 4 (1890). Available from www.louisville.edu/library/law/brandeis/privacy.html.

Weiss, Edith Brown. "International Responses to Weather Modification." *International Organization* 29, no. 3 (1975): 805–826.

Westin, Alan. *Privacy and Freedom.* New York: Atheneum, 1967.

———. "Social and Political Dimensions of Privacy." *Journal of Social Issues* 59, no. 2 (2003): 421–453.

Whalen, Terence. "The Code for Gold: Edgar Allan Poe and Cryptography." *Representations* 46 (1994): 35–57.

White, Robert. "A Cloud over Weather Cooperation." *Technology Review,* May/June, 1994, p. 64.

Woodmansee, Martha, and Peter Jaszi, eds. *The Construction of Authorship: Textual Appropriation in Law and Literature.* Durham, NC, and London: Duke University Press, 1994.

Young, Oran. *Resource Regimes: Natural Resources and Social Institutions.* Berkeley: University of California Press, 1982.

Zimmerman, Diane. "Requiem for a Heavyweight: A Farewell to Warren and Brandeis's Privacy Tort." *Cornell Law Review* 68 (1983): 291ff.

Index

Global Change Research Program,
138
Global information commons:
category of, 103–104; and EU
database directive, 114; and
obligation to share information,
109–110; and scientific
knowledge, 104–105
Global intellectual property policy,
242–244; and biotechnology,
76–84; and computer technologies, 84–91; legal framework for,
47–64; and pharmaceutical
patents, 71–76; and public versus
private good, 71–76. *See also*
Treaty(ies)
Global Positioning System (GPS),
140–143; armed forces and, 142;
civilian applications of, 141, 142;
economic benefits from, 142; and
signal degradation, 141–142
Global protection system treaties,
56–58
Global public good, 4; constructing
weather data as, 129, 130, 132–
134; domain-name system for,
89
Global trade: copyrights/patent
agreements on, 26; and intellectual property rights protection,
49, 61; piracy and, 26; and safe
harbor program, 221–223; and
trademark infringement, 33. See
also World Trade Organization
Gossip, religious prohibitions on,
218–219
Government censorship, of Internet
websites, 205–206
Government information/data:
commodification of, 154; ease of
access to, 108–109; and export
prohibitions, 107; and intelligence
analysis, 107; legal guarantees of
free access to, 108; legitimate
privacy intrusions of, 179–180;
proprietary, 105–106; and sexual
behavior regulation, 180; user

fees for, 108. *See also* Public
information
Government intelligence gathering:
and Carnivore electronic surveillance system, 156–157; civil
rights issues in, 155–156;
electronic system for, 156–160;
and eminent domain, 160; international collaboration in, 156–
160; and national security, 155–
156; safeguards and limits on,
155, 156; secret, 106–107, 157–
160; and surveillance of groups,
181
Gramm-Leach-Bliley Act, 220
Green Revolution, 38, 80
Griswold v. Connecticut, 180
Gulf War, and GPS navigation, 142
Gutenberg, Johannes, 24

Hallgren, Richard, 133
Hate speech, 206
Health information. *See* Medical
information
Hemmer, Johann Jacob, 127
Homeland Security Department,
Operation TIPS of, 182
Homosexuality, disclosure of,
183–184
Hugo, Victor, 53
Human genome project, 82, 83
Human rights: and civil rights and
liberties, 155–156, 159, 160;
encryption as tool for, 227;
European laws on, 221–224;
and government monitoring of
individuals, 155–156, 159;
privacy as, 173, 221, 223–224;
and right of eminent domain, 160

Iceland, genetic research project in,
160
Identity cards: national, proposal
for, 155; social security cards as,
181
Identity theft: and accidental
breaches of privacy, 193; and

135–144; commercialization potential of, 139; defined, 134, 147*n43;* espionage and, 134; government oversight and responsibility for, 138–140; and international obligations, 139–140; and LANDSAT data, 136–138; mapping and, 152–153; as private good, 136, 138; and privatization, 135–138; as public good, 135, 138, 143; and satellite navigation systems, 140–144

Scholarly writing, obfuscation in, 111–112

Scientific discoveries: and commercialization of research, 104–105; commodification of, 2; evolution of ownership of, 12; versus invention, 34–35, 83–84; meteorological, 128; obligation to disseminate, 104; as unowned knowledge, 104

Secret intelligence-collection system: accountability and oversight of, 159; overview of, 157–160

Securities industry, oversight technology for, 164–165

Seeds, saving and exchanging of, 38, 60

September 11 terrorist attacks: and citizens' right to privacy, 14–16; and encryption technology, 228; false information on, 209; and increased government surveillance, 155–156, 182

Service marks. *See* Trademarks

Services, commodification of, 21*n34*

Sexual behavior, government regulation of, 180

Shannon, Claude, 97

Signals intelligence (SIGINT), 158

Singapore, restricted Internet access in, 205–206, 208

Social good, and pharmaceutical patents, 73–76

Social security numbers, illegitimate use of, 181

Software companies, licensing of, 87–88

Sokal, Alan, 111

Sonny Bono Copyright Term Extension Act, 36

Spam, opt-out/opt-in provisions for, 220–221

Sports information, free versus restricted access to, 7–10

Statute of Anne (1709), 25

Stockholm Act, 50

Stores Protective Association (SPA), 193

Surveillance, employer, 224. *See also* Electronic surveillance; Government intelligence gathering

Sustainable development, and technology transfer, 153

Technology(ies): and breaches of individual privacy, 192, 194, 196; dual-use, export restrictions on, 108; and economic espionage, 107; encryption, 226–228; and information collection, 100–101; oversight, 165; social effects of, 56; transfer, 62–63, 110

Telemarketing: cross-boarder, 225; opt-out provisions for, 220

Terrorism: alerts, as privacy violations, 200; and Internet websites, 206; and surveillance of groups, 182. *See also* September 11 terrorist attacks

Test data, protection of, 63

Thatcher, Margaret, 108

Tobacco Institute, propaganda use of, 208–209

Trade. *See* Global trade

Trademark Law Treaty, 55, 66*nn19–20*

Trademarks: and common usage of brand names, 31; and counterfeit products, 31; and geographic

About the Book

Knowledge Power introduces the interconnected roles of intellectual property, information, and privacy and explores the evolution of the domestic and international rules that govern them.

What roles are played by governments, individuals, firms, and others in shaping our knowledge world? How will the rules that we create—or unquestioningly accept—affect the contours of global society and of our own lives? Marlin-Bennett's provocative exposition highlights the tensions between market interests and privacy, and between property rights and obligations, that have been exacerbated by the new digital technologies. It is an impressively clear introduction to an exceedingly difficult subject.

Renée Marlin-Bennett is associate professor of international relations and chair of the Global Intellectual Property Project at American University.